Beata Springer

THE VICIOUS CIRCLE OF CHANGE

The Political and Legal Conditions of the Establishment of the Civil Service in Poland after 1996

Franz Steiner Verlag

The printing of this book was made possible with support provided
by University of Zielona Góra.

Bibliographic information published by the German National Library:
The German National Library lists this publication in the Deutsche Nationalbibliografie;
detailed bibliographic information is available at dnb.d-nb.de.

www.steiner-verlag.de
Layout and production by Franz Steiner Verlag
Typesetting: DTP + TEXT Eva Burri, Stuttgart
Print: Beltz Grafische Betriebe, Bad Langensalza
Printed on acid-free and age-resistant paper.
Printed in Germany.
ISBN 978-3-515-13811-6 (Print)
ISBN 978-3-515-13814-7 (E-Book)
DOI 10.25162/9783515138147

Table of Contents

Magistratum legem esse
loquentem, legem autem
mutum magistratum
(The official is the speaker of law, and the law
a silent official)

Introduction

The functioning of the state is not possible without a well-organised clerical structure. In the first state structures we had to deal with officials performing specific functions that could not be fulfilled by the ruler. Of course, as territorial expansion took place, as a result of social and political processes, the number of officials steadily increased, but care was also taken to ensure that their functioning was organised. Thus, the scope of duties was defined, and very often the qualities of character that allowed one to hold a particular office or function were also enumerated. In the genetic phase of state development, it was usually the case that a single official had a wide range of powers and performed a variety of functions. As the state developed, the number of cases increased and thus the duties of officials became more specialised, which naturally increased their number and role. This process has varied from country to country, and so today we have, for example in Europe, many models of public administration, and thus the public service or civil service corps has been shaped in different ways. The main dividing line is between closed systems (French, German) and open systems (English). Nowadays, however, it is inappropriate to speak of model solutions on the example of specific countries, most of them accumulating features of both systems (often with a clear predominance of one of them), hence more and more often in the literature on the subject we find – a mixed – hybrid model. In addition, the 'national' models developed are overlaid by a variety of historical, geographical, cultural and social conditions. The civil service is a special type of structure, functioning in the state in order to perform its tasks. It belongs to the executive sphere of the state and is organisationally subordinate to the executive. The special legal status of persons employed in the civil service (public service) corps should allow for relative independence and isolation from the vested interests of political parties, which does not imply complete separation of the two spheres. The creation of appropriate conditions for the functioning of the service should ensure the professional performance of state tasks. The Polish Civil Service Corps is still in a permanent phase of creation and transformation. There are many reasons for this state of affairs, ranging from the legacy of the previous system, through the lack of political will (or to be more precise, political will does exist, but in terms of subordinating the corps to those currently in power), to the uneducated political culture of the organisation, which young democracies also need to build. Building an efficiently functioning corps is a long-term process, and results should not be expected within 5 years, but rather – 50 years. The process of creating the Polish Civil Service and its permanent transformation is inextricably linked to the alternation of power in successive parliamentary elections. This is undoubtedly related to the inclinations of the political sphere to influence the civil service sphere, attempts at appropriating areas of administrative authority, and a misunderstanding of the role and significance of a politically neutral civil service corps.

At the same time, a thesis should be put forward that the term "process" in the case of the creation of the civil service in Poland is, in the author's opinion, an abuse. Understood by the term "process" – a course of consecutive and causally linked specific changes[1], it should be noted that in the case of changes in the civil service corps they were undoubtedly not causally linked. Rather, they should be described as chaotic and ad hoc, pursuing current political priorities. Resulting from a concern for the lack of subordination of officials to those currently in power. The key to categorising the changes, apart from timing, is the subsequent parliamentary elections.

It should be remembered that all the transforming countries of Central and Eastern Europe struggled with problems during the establishment of the civil service corps. It is rightly argued in the literature that weak institutional structures and their development problems are dominant features of post-socialist countries (Chrabąszcz at al. 2003: 9–20). The legacy of communist policies, centralisation are the main obstacles standing in the way of civil service reforms in countries such as Poland, the Czech Republic or Slovakia. However, as some researchers note in the case of Poland, these difficulties have been exacerbated by traditionally negative attitudes towards public administration dating back to the period of Poland's partitions 1795–1918 (Majcherkiewicz 2008: 140).

The aim of the monograph is to answer the question of how the Civil Service Corps in Poland evolved after 1996, and in what conditions, political and organisational problems, this evolution took place. The timeframe was set by normative acts and their amendments. Starting with the first Civil Service Act of 1996, through the subsequent ones of 1998, 2006, 2008 and the most recent amendment of the Act of 2015, which

1 The term "process" https://sjp.pwn.pl/sjp/proces;2508456.html (accessed 2017/10/18).

came into force at the beginning of 2016. In 1996, the first Civil Service Act was passed and thus began the process of building a civil service corps in Poland after the 1989 breakthrough. During the communist period, the corps did not function and the administration, called state administration, was a uniform system subordinated to the political will of those in power. The premise of the publication and, at the same time, the hypothesis of the research was that, for almost 30 years after the change of the political system, no efficiently functioning civil service corps had been created. The evolution of the civil service was thus going nowhere, becoming hostage to the ongoing political and organisational problems of the Polish state. In fact, attempts at building it came to nothing, due to political infighting and the desire to subordinate civil servants to successive ruling teams. This assertion is undoubtedly demonstrated by successive normative acts, which only changed the principles of functioning of the service. I am not saying that a fully formed corpus can be built in a period of 30 years, however, the foundations can be laid. The first stage in which the corps began to be consistently built was during the 1998 Act (until October 2006). The change of service philosophy in the 2006 normative acts, together with the simultaneous abolition of corps structures, nullified the previous achievements. The normative acts of 1996 and 2006 were in force for too short a time to speak of the existence of a civil service concept on their basis. In 2008, the legislator largely returned to the 1998 solutions and, as a result, between 2008 and 2015 we have another period in which attempts were made to build the corps. The parliamentary elections in 2015 and the alternation of power brought about further conceptual changes in the functioning of the service.

Building the corps will undoubtedly be arduous. It will not be so much the process of setting up the structures that will take a long time, as the process of shaping the principles and instilling behaviours that reflect the idea of service to the state. It can be said with certainty that at this stage no efficiently functioning civil service corps has been developed in Poland. Despite its formal establishment (this is only a preliminary element), there is still a need to shape the standards that apply in the Corps, to develop mechanisms for its effective operation, to ensure political neutrality, observance of the rules of a democratic state under the rule of law, and respect for the principles of official ethics. These elements will not function properly only with precisely constructed legal norms, for which there is also a need for mutual respect of the legal status (differences) of the political and official spheres. There is a need for mutual relations to be established on a partnership basis (with the rules defining administration as an executive sphere being respected) and for mechanisms to be worked out which, on the one hand, inhibit the desire of politicians to exert influence on the civil service sector (politicisation of administration) and, on the other hand, eliminate the bureaucratisation of politics.

I have used a variety of research methods in the book. In the part devoted to the problems of the evolution of the functioning of the administration, I applied a chronological approach to the presented process. In the chapters dealing with the historical outline of the civil service, I applied a historical approach showing the genesis of phenomena and processes. The method of comparative analysis was also helpful, which I used in the development of the chapter on model solutions in the corps. In the main part of the monograph, I used the institutional-legal analysis method, the comparative method and the content analysis method, which served to establish similarities and differences between the analysed normative solutions. A systemic analysis of the administration subsystem as a whole was also applied. Using quantitative analysis, selected aspects of the functioning of the civil service corps after 1996 were presented. The technique I used in the course of research was the analysis of documents, mainly normative acts, but also statements, reports, political and legal opinions, press articles, scientific articles, book publications and websites. The book is therefore interdisciplinary in nature, presenting the issue of the civil service from various perspectives (mainly political and legal) and at many levels.

The issue of the Civil Service in Poland has been the subject of many publications and studies. Already in the inter-war period, monographs on this topic were published, e.g. (Hekajłło 1924). Two years after the end of the war, a commentary to the Act of 1922 on the State Civil Service was published by (Kościołek 1947). From the 1950s onwards, for obvious reasons, there was no publication on this subject. In the years 1989–1996 justifications for successive drafts of civil service acts were published, as well as materials on the reform of public administration, such as a study by Government Plenipotentiary for Reform of Public Administration (Zonn – Pasternak 1993). Researchers analysing the functioning of the civil service include: prof. E. Ura, prof. T. Liszcz, prof. T. Rabska, prof. R. Herbut, prof. H. Izdebski, prof. M. Kulesza, prof. G. Rydlewski, prof. J. Hausner, prof. W. Sanetra, prof. J. Jagielski, prof. Z. Cieślak, prof. K. Rączka, prof. B. Kudrycka, prof. J. Itrich-Drabarek, prof. T. Górzyńska, prof. S. Mazur, prof. J. Czaputowicz, dr hab. H. Szewczyk, dr hab. K. Gadowska, dr hab. K. Mroczka, dr A. Ferens, dr I. Macek,

After the Act was passed in 1996, few monographs and commentaries on the Act appeared (Cieślak at al. 1998). Publications on the 1996 solutions often appeared when the subsequent Act on the service was in force. The short duration of the legislation eliminated some of the publications as the doctrine began to deal with the new legislation. Most publications were produced between 1999 and 2006, the period during which the 1998 Act was in force. The most well-known ones include the commentary by authors: (Jagielski&Rączka, 2001; Rydlewski 2001; Sinkowska 2002). Subsequent monographs started to appear only after the enactment of the 2008 Act, for example (Szewczyk 2010; Itrich-Drabarek 2010; Drobny at al. 2010; Pryciak 2011; Przywora 2012). At the same time, in the literature we can find publications about the service in a broader context, analysing the corpus in the world, e.g. (Kudrycka 1998; Rydlewski 2007; Śledzińska – Simon 2010). The problem of civil service, both in Poland and internationally, has been repeatedly addressed in collective publications, e.g. (Zuba 2007; Kudrycka 2003; Sanetra 2001; Gadowska 2015; Itrich-Drabarek 2012, 2013; Pastwa 2016).

The Polish civil service was also addressed by researchers from the European Institute of Public Administration (EIPA) in Maastricht, the Netherlands (Bossaert&Demmke 2003; Demmke 2004, 2006; Demmke&Moilanen 2010; Peters&Pierre 2006; Raadschelders at al. 2007). In addition, between 1996 and 2016, a number of continuous publications were published on both Polish regulations and systems in Europe and the world. Numerous publications were published in: *Studia Prawnicze, Pracy i Zabezpieczenia Społecznego* or *Samorząd Terytorialny*. Beginning in 1997, the Civil Service Office began to publish a biannual magazine devoted to the functioning and development of the civil service at home and abroad. Initially it was: *Biuletyn Służby Cywilnej* and then a biannual entitled *Służba Cywilna*. It also published on the functioning of public administration in the broadest sense. When the Office was liquidated, the magazine ceased publication. At the turn of July/August 2009 the Civil Service Department of the Chancellery of the Prime Minister started to publish *Przegląd Służby Cywilnej*, an electronic periodical devoted to the service, which is primarily a collection of information on the functioning of the civil service corps. A number of political and legal opinions on successive laws and the jurisprudence of the Constitutional Tribunal and the Supreme Court are also a source of knowledge.

In general, the state of scientific research on the civil service in Poland is satisfactory, but it is a pity that it does not reflect the actual state of the Polish civil service. Among the works devoted to Polish systemic solutions we will find few cross-sectional and comparative publications, covering the entire period of the corps' functioning.

The publication consists of four chapters devoted to the civil service corps in Poland and around the world. The first chapter discusses the evolution of the role of the state in the context of the functioning of public administration. It characterises the changes taking place in state structures, various concepts of management in public administration, from the Max Weber model to the goodgovernance model and neo-Weberism. The chapter will also include the genesis of the formation of the civil service corps. An analysis of the interrelationship between the civil service corps and the political sphere (administration versus politics) is made.

The second chapter contains a discussion of the development of the Polish civil service in the interwar period, as well as in the period of the People's Republic of Poland. Chapter Three, in turn, analyses the issues surrounding attempts to build a modern corps after the 1989 breakthrough. The premises and conditions are characterised. In the fourth chapter, I made a comparison of normative solutions after 1996, i. e. after the enactment of the first Civil Service Act after the breakthrough of 1989. I characterised the systemic position of members of the civil service corps under the four Acts of 1996, 1998, 2006 and 2008. (together with the 2015 amendment). I analysed areas related to the functioning of the corps: the legal nature of the employment relationship, the analysis and description of organisational structures, the scope of rights, duties and disciplinary responsibility to which members of the civil service corps are subject. I showed the problems and doubts related to the construction of a modern corps and the concepts of the authorities of the time as regards systemic solutions. The chapter is enriched with statistical analyses of the functioning of the corps after 1996.

Chapter 1
The changing role of the state and the mechanism of public administration

1.1 The evolving role of the state. From the pre-modern state to the post-modern state

Administration has been an integral part of the functioning of the state, from the ancient state to the post-modern state, in various forms, with different tasks, competences and capacities. Being an essential element of the state, it has not withstood doctrinal disputes as to how to define it and explain its principles of operation. It is impossible to point to a single universal definition of administration, since, being a subject of research with a very complex structure, it is of interest to many scientific disciplines. Since ancient times, its task has been to perform tasks imposed by the sovereign. In modern democracies, it is the servant of the law, but also serves the public. Depending on the orientation, doctrine distinguishes between legal approaches, theories specific to the fields of organisation and management, sociological and political science (Ferens 1999: 16). Administration is analysed from different points of view, using a variety of research methods depending on the scientific discipline. Among the oldest approaches are legalistic, analysing administration in normative-institutional categories. H. Izdebski and M. Kulesza construct a mixed subject-object definition of administration of legal provenance. Taking into account the realisation of the public interest, they state that it is (...) a set of activities, actions and organisational and executive undertakings, conducted for the realisation of the public interest by various entities, bodies and institutions, on the basis of a law and in the forms specified by law (2004: 93).

From the point of view of this dissertation, the most relevant definitions will be those with a political science orientation – e. g. R. Herbut defines administration: "(...) as a mechanism, as well as a system of institutions, by means of which the assumptions and canons of state public policy are put into practice (implemented)" (1999: 30). On the one hand, it should be treated as a static element, while on the other hand as a dynamic element of social, political life, which interpenetrate, serving the realisation of state tasks. At this point, it is also necessary to cite the definition of administration in the terms of B. G. Peters, who treats it in two parts. In terms of its functions, it is "the process of applying specific rules, i. e. transforming general rules into concrete decisions concerning individual cases" and in terms of its object, it is "the structures of political power whose primary task is to fulfil the above-mentioned functions" (1999: 16).

As can be seen, definitions with a political science orientation pay attention both to the structures of administration and, above all, to the relations, the interrelationships between political power and executive structures. They do not confine themselves to treating administration as a set of institutions serving only administration, but see a broader aspect of its functioning in contrast to legal orientations, which place the primary emphasis on normative issues. At the same time, it should be borne in mind that the political science approach is not homogeneous; many research concepts and methods can be found. The former include the traditional (1980s and 1990s) methods based on formal-legal and historical aspects of political life, while the latter include the contemporary ones that emphasise decision-making processes and behavioural elements (Ferens 1999: 22). Economic approaches, on the other hand, oscillate around financial aspects, the budget and the impact on the economy. Public administration, in terms of organisational and management theory, is a discipline that describes and explains the process of satisfying collective needs and organisational and management dilemmas, particularly in terms of human resource preparation. This approach differs in the way in which it looks at aspects of management, especially human resource management, supervision, control or accountability. The concepts of New Public Management were built on this approach. In sociological terms, on the other hand, public administration is a formalised social group linked by a system of structures and institutions and the internal relations between them. Characteristic of this approach is the concept of the German sociologist Max Weber's model of ideal bureaucracy, in which he treated administration as an organised bureaucratic machine (Ferens 1999: 20). From the above review of different types of approaches to defining public administration, it is apparent that it is a complex subject of research in various scientific disciplines, which pay attention to different aspects of its functioning. It is a multidimensional phenomenon and can therefore be analysed in terms of its subject, object and, most importantly, as a process serving the realisation of specific citizen concerns. Due to the complexity and interdisciplinary nature of the matter, a number of definitions have been proposed depending on the context and scientific discipline. In conclusion, it must be said that multidimensionality leaves researchers with a wide room for discussion, without limiting the tools or the area of analysis. Following A. Ferens, it can be pointed out that administration is:

> (…) a subsystem of the political system, the boundaries of which are difficult to define precisely, comprising entities with a legal-political status, locating them in the area of political executive power. It is characterised by a relative level of autonomy, conditioned by

> the nature of the political system. It performs significant functions derived from those of the political system, ensuring its permanence, stability and continuity, while the content of its activity is to take decisions aimed at authoritative distribution of public goods and services (1999: 23).

With the evolution of the role and tasks of the state, the institutionalisation of various types of administrative structures, the desire to ensure the protection of democracy, guarantee respect for the rule of law and, above all, to protect public sector employees from political influence and pressure, the construction of a civil service corps was created. It is treated as a professional, independent and specialised group of persons employed in the clerical apparatus (Rexed 2004–2005: 48–49). In order to be able to move freely in the complexities of the legal and organisational nature of the Civil Service, it seems necessary at this point to clarify the terminological differences and the conceptual scopes of the terms used to designate this part of the administration. Generally speaking, under the term civil service we shall understand a permanent, professional corps of civil servants, hierarchical, divided internally into grades, categories, classes and corps, in which people with a variety of training and skills find work. The very term service falls within the colloquial meaning of the word, denoting subordination, carrying out not only the orders of those currently in power, but above all serving the interests of the state, performing public tasks with respect for the values accepted in a democratic state of law, reflected in the constitutional provisions and legal order (Grosse 2000: 34). In different countries, the conceptual scope of the term civil service includes various categories of persons employed in public administration. Thus, the term used in France is *la Fonction Publique* – the public service, in the United Kingdom – *Civil Service*, and in Germany the term used is *Beamtendienst*, in the United States – *Federal Employee*. The scope of the subject matter is also different, in France it covers not only government administration, but also local government, the hospital service, while in England it applies only to government officials (as in Poland). In Germany, only about 40 % of civil servants belong to the civil service corps – officials of the federal and state governments and university professors on special terms.

By contrast, a broader term will be the public service, as we will understand all those employed in the public sector, regardless of the employment relationship between the person and the employer. It will be of secondary importance whether we are talking about government administration, local government administration or a yet another distinct part of administration. The conceptual scope of the civil service falls within the term public service, which means that members of the civil service are one element of the public service corps. However, not all members of the public service will be included in the category of members of the civil service corps. The Recommendation of the Committee of Ministers of the Council of Europe of 24 February 2000 on the status of public servants in Europe refers to the institutional and functional meaning of the term public service. The institutional meaning is defined through the prism of the state structure/institution as the determinant that defines the service, while the functional meaning is the definition of the service through tasks of a public nature, whether performed by the public or private sector (Śledzińska-Simon 2010: 16). Civil (public) service systems have also been structured in various ways. In other words, the institutional forms within which the service has been set up vary. Different types of terminology are used to describe those employed in the public sector, e. g. civil servant, officer. Forms of creation, in different systems, are specific, depending on political, social, economic and historical circumstances. The construction of the civil service corps is a consequence of the adopted concept of the structure of public administration, the construction of which results from the perception of the role of the state. The organisation of the administration in a particular, typical way is the result of the needs and preferences of the state at a particular time, which change as the conception of the role and functions of the state evolves (Herbut 1999: 42).

The organisation of public administration structures, their scope, degree of decentralisation, freedom of action, accountability, functions, as well as the scope of action, are in each case strongly influenced by the system of a particular state and it is impossible to separate these elements connected to each other by a kind of feedback (Rydlewski 2007: 17). Ancient states were characterised by different needs and functions, the functions of absolute monarchy were understood differently and the role of the state was presented even differently during the development of liberal doctrines. The tasks of administration in democratic and non-democratic states are perceived and performed differently. The effect of the change in the role of the state over the centuries was an evolution in the structures and functions of administration, a change in its scope of action, mode and organisational forms. What has remained unchanged, however, is its character – servile (executive) towards the sovereign, regardless of how it was conceived. The way in which the administrative system is constructed, the model of its functioning, and the directions of evolution depend on many factors, among which are tradition, culture, historical fate or the nature of production relations.

In ancient states, the functioning of the official apparatus was fully subordinated to the will of the ruler – the sovereign on the basis of absolute subordination and obedience. Ancient administration was characterised in its initial phase by a high degree of centralisation, concentration of power in the hands of the ruler, execution of his orders. As territory expanded, decentralisation became necessary. In the Middle Ages in Western Europe, the magnates were of great importance, and they created their own offices in independence from the ruler. In addition, there was also a royal administration as an expression of the king's will. The creation of absolute monarchies in the 16th century was aimed at centralising state power in the hands of the monarch, eliminating the influence of the magnates and initiating the process of nation-state building. A manifestation of the change in the role of the state was the creation of hierarchical administrative structures subordinated to the unlimited will of the king, who had absolute power without any control (Mazur 2005: 41–51). In the later period of absolute monarchy, it is possible to speak of the emergence of a police state, with the possibility of interfering in all areas of subjects' lives, whose existence was justified by the administrative theorists of the time – *the policyists* – on the grounds of caring for the state (Boć 2004: 26–32). The administration was based on the principle of centralisation and bureaucratism, and the state, almost exemplary, was *Bourbon* France (this system was called the 'see-saw'). There was no relationship between administration and law that was relevant from the point of view of the rules of the democratic state. The dominant mode of employment was the purchase of offices with widespread patronage and nepotism. However, this period must be characterised as a time when the foundations of the structures of modern administration were formed (Mazur 2002: 17; 2005: 48). The development of liberal doctrines contributed to the change from an absolute state to a constitutional monarchy and then to a republic. As a result, the monarch's administration also had to be transformed. Through the introduction of the principle of the tri-partite division of power, a new quality of state functioning was created. The Legislature began to create legal norms that defined the tasks and forms of action of the administration. The administration was subordinated to the executive, and local self-government was singled out, so that we can begin to speak of a dualism of public administration. One of the assumptions of the liberal doctrine was to limit state interference in the affairs of citizens, which inevitably involved limiting the influence of administration on public life (Mazur 2005: 52).

The effect of the postulates of the new ideology was, among other things, to create a neutral, substantively prepared, professional corps of civil servants. The image of the civil servant was changed, and he became a servant of the state, performing public tasks on the basis and within the limits of the law. The Northcote – Trevelyan report of 1845, which will be discussed in detail in the next chapter, should be regarded as the beginning of the changes in Great Britain. In the United States, the foundations were laid by The Pendelton Act of 1883 (Civil Service Act) and the theoretical basis was formulated by political scientist and President Woodrow Wilson. The author who had a very important influence on the construction of the administration was the German sociologist Max Weber. His theory of the ideal bureaucracy assumed that a bureaucracy was the permanent and law-bound execution of tasks by skilled workers organised in a hierarchical way (Weber 2002: 161). This way of organising it was to guarantee that it would be efficient and rational and, most importantly, it was to become depersonalised, impersonal, guided only by legal norms and confining administrative discretion to a minimum. The term bureaucracy[1] is associated with a number of meanings and ways of interpretation depending on the scientific discipline. One can analyse the phenomenon of bureaucracy or the process – bureaucratisation or a mutation of the political system – bureaucratism (Rubisz, 2007: 85). From the point of view of my

1 The term was first coined by the physiocrat Jean Claude Marie Vincent de Gournay in 1747.

interest, comparative political science, bureaucracy is the administrative machinery of the state, in which bureaucrats are unelected state functionaries or civil servants (Heywood 2009: 441). The common denominator, however, remains the context of performing, organising, managing public affairs. Today, bureaucracy, especially in the colloquial sense, is perceived negatively – as an inefficient, laborious and overly formalised structure.

The rapid development, economic growth (on the assumptions of Keynesianism) of many countries after 1945 meant that Max Weber's doctrine was for many years regarded as an effective way of organising and operating executive state structures (Jabłoński 1999: 82–84). The rule of the welfare state evident in *New Deal* policies in the United States and in the British and Swedish reforms of social democratic governments did not break with the doctrine of liberalism, but shifted state activities (in many areas of social life) into the sphere of regulation and intervention (Rubisz, 2007: 95–96). For the liberal democratic state, a well-organised Weberian public administration became a tool for distributing national income and an instrument for embodying the idea of democracy. The result, of course, was an excessive expansion of the administration's competences, with particular emphasis on social affairs. Administration in *welfare state* countries pretended to be a 'super-institution' solving citizens' problems, ensuring material well-being and socio-cultural development (Jabłoński 1999: 83). At this point, it is impossible not to mention the communist doctrine of the state – the dictatorship of the proletariat – which, over a period of some fifty years, laid the foundations for an extensive system of state administration. Due to the totalitarian nature of the state, the activities of the administration were to serve the purpose of total control over all spheres of citizens' lives. The legacy of the post-communist states is also an overly developed and complicated administrative system with centralising tendencies and often 'diluted' responsibility for state affairs. The implication of both systems became extensive administrative structures, constantly 'budding' and appropriating further spheres of social life.

In the 1930s, criticism of Weber's theory began. The American functionalists accused Weber of failing to take into account the 'human factor', which generates various types of informal relationships influencing the shape and functioning of the administration. In general, the American functionalists disagreed with the vision of a rigid, uninfluenced clerical apparatus. Criticism of the Weberian model of administration, which appeared in various countries, was the impetus for the creation of a new concept of bureaucracy, the so-called theory of rational choice or public choice, also called the 'New Right model'. According to A. Heywood "(…) in the 1970s a set of more radical beliefs developed within conservatism that directly challenged Keynesian welfare orthodoxy" – the New Right model (2007: 105). The model combined the economic demands of neo-liberalism and social conservatism, emphasising the provision of free choice to the citizen, which is preferable to bureaucratic management. Providing the citizen with more choice is linked to individual freedom, but it also increases efficiency. The second half of the 20th century is associated with processes that change the organisation and functioning of the state, the economy and society, i. e. processes that introduce a new social order. These have resulted in a change both in organisational structures and in the way the state functions, which is transforming from a centralised organisation into a decentralised organisation in a slow process. The state model formed in the late 19th and early 20th centuries is accused of being 'ungovernable' related, firstly, to the legitimacy of power and, secondly, to the problems of implementing public policies. This is the first of the factors in the administration's environment that has influenced change. Further ones include: the exhaustion of the welfare state formula, the change in the previous type of sovereignty of the state apparatus due to changes in international and domestic relations (Jabłoński 1999: 84). J. Hausner distinguishes the following factors having a significant impact on the evolution of public administration: decentralisation of the state and development of territorial self-government, moving away from the isolation of the state, economy and society to their mutual interaction, internationalisation and globalisation of economic, social and political organisations, change in the central level of state organisation manifested, inter alia, in the independence of central banks (2007: 46–47).

In Western Europe in the 1970s and 1980s, in the wake of the crisis of the welfare state formula, authorities began to reform their administrative structures, accusing them of organisational weakness and an outdated model of economic governance. The traditional administration was unable to cope with the financial burden of ever-increasing social expenditure. It was alleged that the sluggish Weberian administration was inefficient, ineffective and generated excessive costs. In addition, attention was drawn to the considerable overgrowth of civil servants, excessive interference in the spheres of citizens' lives and inefficiency in carrying out tasks due to the overly broad range of state functions that could be carried out by the private sector. A reform of the administration through the introduction of market mechanisms was postulated, which consequently entailed changes in state structures. Since the functions of the state were changing (there was a visible change in the role of government, its relations with society), as the welfare state formula was being abandoned, administrative structures had to be restructured and adapted to the new conditions. The concepts of New Public Management grew out of the ideological assumptions of European liberalism and American conservatism pursued by Margaret Thatcher and Ronald Reagan. The flagship slogans of their policies were the processes of deregulation, minimisation and marketisation of the administrative system (Izdebski 2007:13). New trends in the functioning of the administration were, among other things, the result of the economic stagnation of the 1970s. Critics of the traditional model of administration postulated an increase in the quality of services provided with a reduction in expenditure on their delivery. It was suggested that market mechanisms could be used to meet the needs of citizens more efficiently. In addition, the traditional administration was made up of institutions with very low efficiency, and control over them was illusory.

In the wake of the wave of criticism that swept through not only Western Europe, but also the United States, New Zealand and Australia, economically-oriented administrative reforms began in some countries. Particularly in the Anglo-Saxon countries: United Kingdom, United States, New Zealand, Australia, Canada, but also Norway. In the case of France, Germany, Japan or Third World countries, new ideas were not so readily introduced (Izdebski 2007:14). In the doctrine of the subject, they are called New Public Management[2]. It is a collective term for various types of reforms characterised by a common denominator – the introduction of market-oriented reforms, management techniques used in the private sector. The aim of the reforms is to reduce the costs of the clerical apparatus, to reduce the interference of the public sector in the affairs of citizens, to improve the quality of services provided and to change the style of administration management. New Public Management was an emanation of the criticism of the traditional Weberian model of administration functioning, its ossified structures, inefficiency, sprawl and domination, as well as archaic management methods ill-suited to a changing environment. There is no single creator of this trend; rather, the doctrine points to the common features (instruments) of the various concepts distinguished by researchers within New Public Management. Three features: deregulation, privatisation and marketisation – are key elements of NPM. New Public Management should be seen not as a specific model ready to be applied, but as a set of means of action, structures, certain techniques that can be used in a variety of formulas (Rexed 2004–2005: 47). According to S. Mazur, a number of concepts have taken shape within the framework of New Public Management, among which we can distinguish: managerialism, market-oriented public administration, entrepreneurial government, business management (2005: 58).

Regardless of the assessment of the reforms associated with NPM concepts, the important fact is that public administration opened up to change. State structures in many countries ceased to be centralised, so this affected the design and functioning of the state itself. The reduction of state interference in some areas of social life, the introduction of market-based methods, as well as the transfer of some matters into the hands of non-governmental organisations reduced the operating costs of the public sector in some countries. The introduction of new solutions in public administration resulted in changes, in terms of human resource management, in the civil service corps. New Public Management changes the relationship between civil servants and their political superiors, undermining the traditional model of responsibility of the former through the creation of autonomous structures – agencies (Mazur 2005: 62). At the same time, the negative impact of the new management methods is pointed out, e.g. in Australia, as a result of deregulatory techniques, attention is drawn to the

---

2 The term *New Public Management* was first used in 1991 by Ch. Hood in the article: *A Public Management for All Seasons* (1991). In the same year, the book by D. Osborne and T. Gaebler, *Governing differently*, was published.

under-representation of the Ministry of Finance, while in the UK, in turn, there is talk of a significant deterioration in the quality of rail infrastructure services as a result of their privatization (Matheson 2003–2004: 32–33).

It has also been alleged that New Public Management concepts unreflectively transfer models used in the private sector without regard to the specifics of the public sector. A focus on economics can, in the long term, overshadow the idea of public service. The private sector is, by definition, profit-oriented, while the administration largely performs tasks that cannot generate revenue and even generate losses. The private sector has the possibility to exclude a certain group of recipients, while in the public sector there is no such possibility. The citizen is more important than the customer, as he or she has a shared responsibility for governance. Cost reduction must not obscure the broader vision – to act for society, to implement social policy (Dębicki 2002–2003: 112). An imbalance is also pointed out by focusing too much on the results achieved by the administration, with insufficient recognition of the importance of procedures (Supernat 2003: 28–46). Despite the many criticisms levelled at the New Public Management, it is undeniable that these concepts contributed to a certain rationalisation of the functioning of administrative structures and triggered a kind of mechanism in the form of attempts to improve existing concepts and solutions. The New Public Management policy, initiated in the 1980s in Anglo-Saxon countries, began to give way in the early 1990s to the so-called Good Governance concept. While New Public Management was based on the implementation of management methods used in the private sector into the public sector, Good Governance focuses more broadly on the social context. Good Governance is based on professionalism, openness, participation, accountability, efficiency and cooperation to avoid conflicts of interest[3]. Good Governance is a process/phenomenon defined in many different ways in contemporary science. Among the dominant ones are: network governance – meaning co-management by autonomous actors outside the control of state institutions, network society or multilevel governance – in which actors make decisions in a decentralised decision-making process, seeking to aggregate societal interests. Good Governance encompasses a whole system of values, based as much on the formal aspect (adherence to legal norms) as on the maintenance of ethical rules, transparency, personal integrity, openness, efficiency, solidarity with citizens. M. Dębicki, describing Good Governance stated that: "It is both an ethical principle and the result of a rational choice. Without Good Governance, democracy is an empty slogan and confines itself to certain procedures and conventions" (2002–2003: 104). The emphasis in Good Governance is not on structures, but on the functions they perform in an appropriate way. When we think of *Good Governance*, we think of its quality and the socially desirable effects it produces. Attention is focused on the highest pos-

---

3 The White Paper lists five principles of good governance: oppeness, participation, accountability, effectiveness, coherence (European Governance a white paper 2001: 10).

sible level of desired outcomes. It is not so much the effect produced that is important, but rather the course of action and its conduct. Citizens are treated as stakeholders. This term is broader than the term customer/consumer and refers to any person who has a connection with the decisions of an authority (Izdebski 2007: 16).

Good governance, as R. Herbut calls it, is a project in which the state and society interact. It represents a new style of governance and management of society, which automatically implies a change in the nature of the governance process and, above all, a changed role of government in the whole process. The inclusion of the state in Good Governance processes is linked to a change in the traditional functions of the state, a redefinition of its role in the modern world, due to widespread globalisation, which has undoubtedly contributed to the erosion of the traditional functions of the state and the need to redefine its role. Among the factors having a significant impact on changing the way the state functions are: external factors (globalisation and Europeanisation) and internal factors (decentralisation, fragmentation of decision-making, bridging the gap between the public and private sectors, the functioning of independent agencies) (2008: 26–29). The new trends associated with the introduction of Good Governance do not prove the necessity of replacing and completely eliminating the *New Public Management* policy. Both concepts can coexist and work together, as they are not mutually exclusive. They should complement each other. There are claims in doctrine that the ideal solution would be to combine the best features of both principles (Dębicki 2001: 48–51; Czaputowicz 2005: 30–31). The economic calculation, which is important from the point of view of the citizen and the state, is only one level of the performance of public tasks. The doctrine emphasises that the idea of Governance creates a new quality for the development of democracy, as it stops seeing citizens as voters, volunteers and consumers and starts treating them as co-decision makers creating reality, co-responsible for the tasks performed (Izdebski, 2007: 15). A second, contemporary theoretical approach to public management is the concepts of New Public Governance and neo-Weberian administration, which is a conglomerate of classic Weberian bureaucracy with the ideas of new public management (Mazur 2016: 15). New Public Governance places significant emphasis on the relationship between citizens and government, interaction, co-management, citizen participation in co-governance. Neo-Weberism, on the other hand, as a model of public management is a combination of two theoretically contradictory currents: classical bureaucracy and New Public Management (Sześciło 2014: 652).

To recapitulate, towards the end of the last century, the optics of perceiving the principles of functioning, structures, methods of operation in public administration, including of course the civil service, underwent a kind of evolution. Starting with a rational Weberian approach, through an orientation towards market principles, and ending with a network model expressed in the principles of Good Governance and the ideas of neo-Weberian administration. Let us remember that each successive one drew some patterns from the previous one. The introduction of new ideas does not mean a complete rejection of the previous acquis. To quote H. Izdebski: "One must speak of a peculiarly cumulative evolution of administrative thought – from the simple patterns of Rechtsstaat or Fayol's thought to the complex, in its own way postmodern, view of administration in the concepts of Good Governance" (2007: 18).

From the 18th century onwards, public administration changed as the state model changed (from a police state to a constitutional democracy), resulting in a stabilisation of the relationship between administration and politics. The administration ceased to be a tool for the mere consolidation of political power and began to function on the basis of a legal framework established through procedures (Rydlewski 2006: 26). The introduction of performance standards and a control system reduced political influence to a certain extent, leaving the administration with more freedom of action. Administration had to change because, as Ch. Demmke rightly states, "(...) the classical model of administration was created in a world that no longer exists" (2004: 11). The reshaping of the role of the state was influenced by economic changes, i. e. the crisis in the 1930s resulting in increased state interventionism, followed by the questioning of the provider state in the 1980s (Hausner 2007: 48). In contemporary doctrine we find a number of proposals to redefine the role and tasks of the state and to create a new state model. Bresser Pereira, for example, assumes that we are moving towards a social-liberal model of the state, with the need to define more precisely the limits of state action, to minimise the extent of state regulation of the private sector, to strengthen the functions of government and the capacity to govern. These factors condition institutional change, mainly in public administration (Hausner 2007: 49). Changes in the way the administration functions are also related to its assumption of new tasks and functions (it implements state government policy, but also deals with insurance, employment, health care). In addition, modern administration is made up of a variety of structures of diverse nature and intricate internal construction. The privatisation of some public tasks has greatly complicated the system by introducing elements of the private sector. There is no single ideal model of administration, which, for a variety of reasons, will never and nowhere emerge. Each country, due to its specifics, should work out its own way, using, however (especially the former Eastern Bloc countries), for example, the proven solutions of Western countries.

To recapitulate, it is possible to identify, over the course of the twentieth century, a number of theoretical concepts describing the functioning and structures of public administration. Historically, the first is the *classical* concept, operating at the beginning of the twentieth century, which emphasised structured organs of state power, elaborate forms of bureaucracy. Another is the behavioural theory (1930s), focusing attention on the role of the human factor in structures (communication, motivation, participation in organisations, leadership). The 1940s bring the quantitative concept, based on the implementation of methods used in the sciences, e. g. mathematics, management to improve administrative functioning. The next, in the mid-1960s, is the contingency concept – the concept of open systems, which sees administration as part of a larger whole operating in a social, political and economic environment, linked to that environment, which is, as a result, reflected in the way it functions. The next concept – politicisation – emerges in the late 1960s and early 1970s, subordinating decision-making processes to political will while limiting the independence of public institutions. The second half of the 1970s brings us the qualitative concept based on the use of qualitative methods to develop administration. The next decade (second half of the 1980s) saw the slow implementation of the managerial concept, i. e., the market/economic principles hitherto used in the private sector (e. g. the principles of New Public Management) (Wiszniowski 2005: 9–11). The most recent is the multi-faceted phenomenon of New Public Governance and the concept of neo-Weber administration.

A determinant of the formation and functioning of administration, as pointed out by contemporary researchers (e. g. G. B. Peters), is tradition, and above all the attitude to the state and its scope of action. Accordingly, four models of public administration can be distinguished in Europe: Anglo-Saxon (Great Britain and Ireland), Germanic (Germany, Austria, the Netherlands, Spain, Belgium, Hungary), Napoleonic (France, Poland) and Scandinavian (Sweden, Norway, Denmark, Estonia). In all models, except the Anglo-Saxon model, the state is important for the functioning of the administration. The state-society relationship is different in the various models (e. g. pluralistic in the Anglo-Saxon model, while antagonistic in the Napoleonic model), the form of political organisation is different – from limited federalism in the Anglo-Saxon model, through integral federalism in the Germanic model; concentrated unitarism in the Napoleonic model, to decentralised unitarism in the Scandinavian model. Differentiation also occurs at the level of the form of decentralisation: local authority – Anglo-Saxon model; cooperative federalism – Germanic; regionalised unitary state – Napoleonic; local autonomy – Scandinavian. Also in all models, with the exception of the Anglo-Saxon one, public law remains the dominant instrument of regulation. In the Scandinavian model, it is reinforced by organisational and management science, and in the Anglo-Saxon model by political science and sociology (Wiszniowski 2005: 11–13). In general, newer and newer conceptions of the functioning of the administration, usually originating from criticism of previous theories, have forced reforms with an already irreversible effect (a return to classical Weberian administration is not possible). One very important effect is the increased importance of the role of managers and their political involvement, which automatically implies questions about the interrelationship between politicians and civil servants (Mazur 2002: 26–27). The change in the role of the organisational manager, his politicisation, 'being a bureaucratic politician' makes it plausible to argue that the administration has become one of the more important political players, involved in decision-making processes. The distinction between the political and administrative spheres, the links between politicians and civil servants, the interrelationship, the way they communicate, the obligation to cooperate, and finally the desire to influence (evident in both spheres) have been a problem and at the same time an object of scientific research for more than a century.

1.2 The interplay between the political and administrative spheres

In the European tradition, the science of administration was the domain of lawyers and was, and still is, placed among the legal sciences, whereas in the United States it is treated as a branch of political sciences, despite the theory put forward by Woodrow Wilson back in the 19th century. He claimed that:

> Administration is not within the realm of politics. Administrative problems are not political problems. Politics does define tasks for administration, but it should not influence individual offices. Administration is first and foremost the calm, unhurried and conflict-free handling of various matters (…) (Peters 1999: 18).

For a long time, this statement became a canonical view of the interaction between administration and politics. As J. Boć states:

> (…) the American developers of the theory of the separation of politics and administration showed historical abnegation by not drawing on the earlier models of European researchers dealing with the problem. Europe had much earlier bent on this problem (2004: 308–313).

Today, this thesis is not substantiated and the perception of mutual relations is quite different (Demmke&Moilanen 2010: 36–39). The Weberian model of administrative organisation has consolidated the above idea. Consequently, some researchers assume that public administration must be politically neutral, understanding it, on the one hand, as loyalty to any new superior (government/cabinet) and, on the other hand, as equal treatment of citizens, free of any discrimination (Kudrycka 1998: 25). The theory concerning the separation of the two spheres finds in doctrine many supporters as well as a considerable number of opponents. From today's perspective, it seems to be fraught with error, or at least with a kind of unfortunate connection with the English term politics. This requires clarification. In English, we can distinguish between the term politics (pol. polityka), meaning a planned and organised effort to gain or maintain power, and the term policy (pol. polityka), meaning the practical aspects of governing, the systematic management of state affairs (e.g. polityka transportowa – transport policy – policy making, policy implementation). Polish, French or Italian do not have such a distinction (Rydlewski 2006: 20–21). In summary, while the separation of administration from politics is correct and justified, the attempt to separate administration and policy is unjustified, because the essence of policy is precisely administration.

Opponents of the theory of the separation of politics and administration argue that it is impossible to separate these planes, as they are internally linked and integrated processes with feedback between them (Herbut 1999: 370. As one Spanish (L. Lopez Rodo) expert on the subject argued:

> There is no divorce between administration and politics. Administration is an instrument in the hands of government to concretise political ideals and programmes in action. Politics requires a harmonious combination of lofty ideals and a healthy sense of reality. Administration without politics would have no direction. Politics without administration, on the other hand, bears another name – utopia (Izdebski 1993: 58).

In the same vein, E. Łętowska and J. Łętowski also expressed themselves, stating that there is no neutral administration, free of value judgements, as administration has the task of reconciling interests that are, as a rule, irreconcilable, so every action takes on a political tinge, as: "(…) administration acts, as a rule, in someone's interests and, at the same time, also against someone's interests (…)" (1995: 146–147). E. Zieliński also stated that administration is always political in nature, acting in each case on the account of a specific government, pursuing specific political objectives formulated by the government. According to the author: "It is not met that the government is a neutral body. (…) The whole action of the administration is permeated by politics" (2001: 19). The theory of the separation of politics and administration, does not aim at a real separation of the two spheres, but firstly, at extending the freedom of officials to interfere in politics without political responsibility, secondly, at preserving discretionary influence by officials, thirdly, at increasing the freedom of politicians by ceding socially sensitive decisions to officials, for which they will not have to explain themselves to the electorate (Peters 1995: 153).

Theories characterising the relationship between the political and administrative spheres have been formulated in doctrine, which can be organised in a continuum. Starting with the mutual separation of politics and administration (e.g. Max Weber's conception), in which civil servants are strictly subordinated to political decision-makers, through theories adopting the interaction of the two spheres – the 'village idyll' (village life) model, which assumes horizontal integration of politicians and civil servants and generates in practice rules for the employment of civil servants in political positions and the filling of political supporters in civil service positions; the modified 'village idyll' model (functional village life), which considers the above issue not at the scale of government as a whole, but of the individual office, ending with the administrative state model, in which bureaucrats dominate due to their substantive preparation. The last theory, which should be placed (within this continuum) just before the administrative state model, is the 'adversarial' theory, which, apart from defining a rather significant separation between the two spheres, lacks a dominant player (Bach-Golecka 2008: 332–333). For many years, a process has been noticeable in which administration is being ennobled. The political-administrative system is changing (or, in fact, the change has already taken place) into an administrative-political one due to the increasing scale of social problems, the change in the quality of public affairs, the inefficiency of the parliament and the executive in solving social problems and the problems of public administration (Peters 1999: 46).

Paradoxically, the modern administration, which is a creation of the democratic system, poses a dilemma for it, which was aptly illustrated by K. Zuba, writing: "The bureaucracy, which was supposed to be the main tool for the realisation of the ideals of the modern democratic state, turned out to be a 'genie let out of the bottle', which was less and less a servant and became the master of the situation" (2007: 108). The dilemma relates to mutual relations. The cause of the problems is the excessive 'appropriation' by the administration of the powers of the democratic state, without, however, the encumbrance of political accountability. The rise of the 'administrative state' must cause a change in the relationship with the democratic state (Mazur 2007: 99). The reasons for this are to be found in the weakness of parliaments and the delegation of legislative powers to the administration.

Analysing the interrelationship between the political and administrative spheres, the questions immediately arise: is it possible to 'peacefully' coexist and reconcile them? What should be the way to act together if mutual dependence is essential? The political sphere would not be able to function without officials, and the actions of the latter are very often at odds with the democratic order. However, it is impossible not to notice that the scales of victory are tipping towards the bureaucracy, reinforcing already existing structures. Modern states are faced with the demand to "de-bureaucratise" administration, or to democratise it, which consists of: a democratic culture as a constitutive element of administration, ensuring representation of the entire community in which it operates, openness and transparency of administration structures (including the obligation to provide full, exhaustive information – as one of the basic civil rights), participation of citizens in carrying out the administration's tasks, as well as in defining its objectives (Zuba 2007: 119–122). It can be concluded that current development trends in the form of the introduction of Good Governance rules are aimed precisely at democratising and de-bureaucratising administration. One of the most important factors is public participation, in which the state (its structures) interacts with citizens, who must want and be aware of their role and the possibility of co-deciding their own affairs.

In most countries, we encounter the phenomenon of the politicisation of administration, whereby high-ranking state positions are filled by members or supporters of the winning party who are not professionally trained civil servants but politicians (Antoszewski 1999: 56–57). The phenomenon of politicisation results from the fear of the administration's capabilities and "power", which politicians fear and results in attempts to exercise political control over the administration. In many countries, with a strongly established civil servants' position, they are not subject to replacement with a changing Cabinet, hence they constantly increase their influence on politicians' decisions. Their position is linked to the information they possess and their access to it, as well as their analytical skills in processing information. Thus, on the one hand, they pose a threat to politicians by taking over the sphere of political decision-making, while on the other, they become an indispensable element in the operation of politicians, without which the latter, subject to permanent exchange, are unable to govern.

In most countries in the world, the civil service is, in the words of H. Izdebski: "(...) an important part of the issue of the relationship between administration and politics" (2007: 11). The phenomenon of the politicisation of administration was evident in the UK, France, as well as in the Scandinavian countries. In the United States in the 1980s, during the administration of President Ronald Reagan, under the slogan of "restoring accountability of bureaucratic staff to politicians", a large proportion of officials were replaced using non-substantive (political) criteria in their hiring. The opposite phenomenon, found in modern democracies, is the bureaucratisation of politics – meaning the increased influence of the administration on policy-making through a series of informal links (Herbut 1999: 37). It is clear that politicians cannot function without administration, as it is officials who maintain direct contact with the public. The determinants of cooperation between politicians and officials are diverse. These include: the extent of cooperation conditioned by political priorities and the capacity to implement them; the level of trust and mutual understanding; the relationship between officials and citizens (the better the better the implementation of political objectives) (Bach-Golecka 2008: 329).

The administration is a subsystem of the political system, so the analysis of this system should be carried out in two ways, paying attention, on the one hand, to the relations of the administration with other political subsystems, which determines the type of political regime, the nature of the spatial distribution of power and the type of party system (A. Antoszewski defines this after J. Gaus as the "ecology of public administration"). On the other hand, it is necessary to analyse the administration subsystem from the inside, examining the complex relations between the political and professional parts (Antoszewski 1999: 57–59). It must be remembered that administration is a formed, formalised system, built by means of the right type of procedures, norms, rules and values. It remains an open question for researchers whether this system is mainly shaped by political mechanisms, i. e. external institutions influencing its construction, or whether there is self-creation, based on internal factors. The most pertinent question still remains whether and possibly how to draw a 'demarcation line' between politics and administration. It can also be questioned whether there is a need to separate the two spheres. Is this desirable from the point of view of the functioning of the state?

Undoubtedly, each system (within democratic states), due to different types of factors such as history, tradition, economics will carry out this line in a different place. This arrangement is also evolving, changing, especially in democratising states. However, creating a stable interface between politics and administration in post-communist countries still remains a major problem (Verheijen&Rabrenovic 2001: 423–424; Ban 2014). D. Osborne and T. Gaebler, in their book "To govern differently' citing the well-known American professor-economist E. S. Savas, argue that it is the government's task to steer (create strategy), while rowing is to be handled by the administration, as the latter is about providing services and is not one of the government's strengths. One of the most important elements of effective governance is to separate, as so vividly put, steering from rowing (2010: 53). Seeing administrative structures merely as servile executors seems to be fraught with error, as the administration undoubtedly creates policy to a large extent and bureaucrats make political decisions – if only because of their substantive training, which often places them in a superior position over politicians. The danger arises from the lack of public scrutiny of bureaucrats, unlike politicians, who are subject to a vetting process during cyclical elections. Politicians, having no other choice, agree to informally surrender part of their powers (in terms of political decision-making) to the administration, as knowledge, competence, access to information create opportunities for officials to manage more effectively. Bearing in mind that modern governance is not possible without access to a range of information and the specialised skills to analyse it, which are the domain of civil servants, the special role of administration in the political system emerges. After all, the 'political' power of administration entails a fairly significant degree of discretion in the execution of decisions and a significant number of people employed in it (Peters 1999: 250–262).

Despite significant differences in perception (politicians see bureaucrats as holding back change, while bureaucrats see politicians as a short-term obstacle to a stable, routinised world), the most desirable pattern of behaviour is cooperation, collaboration and complementarity. However, if we divide the administration into "tasks of governance" and "tasks of the core of the state", the latter are of a strictly control and inspection nature hence the services performing them should remain non-party and apolitical. On the other hand, the administration performing tasks of governance, which relate to decision-making in the regulatory sphere, cannot by its very nature be apolitical, but should nevertheless be non-party (Peters 1999: 222–223).

It should be borne in mind that the administration has in principle no social legitimacy to exercise power. Informal delegation by politicians of some of their tasks to the administration does not find any normative justification. It is necessitated by many of the factors mentioned above and is a manifestation of the administration's inclusion in the decision-making process, but as an entity not subject to social control. Although politics and administration should be placed within the same process, but as two separate elements of it. The limited role of politicians in the substantive preparation of decisions is undoubtedly the reason why they cede part of the decision-making process to administration. They accept this reluctantly because of their power to govern, hence the creation of their own sources of information, teams of analysts and advisors. However, this does not imply a diminution of the administration's advantage in collecting and disseminating information on the state of public affairs. Politicians, in order to dominate the administration, use the instrument of the budget both by defining it, but above all by controlling it. The predominance of the administration is linked to the fact that it sits on advisory bodies that allow it to control the course of public affairs. Moreover, it is a simple consequence of the number of people employed in the administration. Politicians, unlike civil servants, do not have the skills to manage large structures and therefore prefer to place this in the hands of professionals, such as civil servants (Peters 1999: 262–295). Another way of 'involving' the administration in the decision-making process will be for officials to hijack functions assigned to politicians due to the latter's incompetence (Zuba 2007: 108–113). In theory, the interests of government and society should determine the scope and functioning of the administration, but it turns out that it can (and often does) behave according to its own particular interests. It should be borne in mind that it is a very heterogeneous structure, hence its interests will remain diverse. This does not mean, of course, that they cannot be aggregated at a higher level (Zuba 2007: 112). It can be hypothesised that bureaucrats have all the predispositions to compete for power with politicians, with the appropriate instruments and tools at their disposal, among others: the ability to control information, professional preparation, access to information and, above all, the ability to analyse and provide this information to politicians (Peters 1999: 56).

In a democratic system of government, certain standards of state governance are observed (e.g. cyclical competitive political elections). One of the principles is the principle of representation, according to which democratically elected authorities represent citizens with social legitimacy. The administration, by participating in the decision-making process (especially those related to discretionary power), encroaches on the powers of the people's representative and does so without social legitimacy, while being politically unaccountable. In view of the above, some researchers put forward the thesis that "(…) the discretionary power [of public administration] remains in opposition to the canons of operation of a democratic state under the rule of law". However, the need for limited discretionary power is recognized (Mazur 2007: 103). At the same time, the strengthening of the administrative state results in the growth of discretionary power and vice versa, which can be described as a self-perpetuating force. In theory, and also in practice, it is the government that is called upon to control the administration. When analysing the issue of control, it must be noted that the possibility to do so is hampered by the considerable autonomy of the administrative structures and thus the impossibility of determining what elements are malfunctioning and who should be held responsible. In addition, the imbalance in the availability of information limits the ability of the auditor, as he or she does not have the detailed knowledge and therefore the possibility to make a sound inspection and thorough analysis. Information provided by officials may be biased and subject to manipulation. The apolitical nature of the administration, in the literature on the subject, is a contentious issue and causes polemics. According to Ch. Demmke, civil servants cannot remain politically indifferent in the performance of their duties, as they bring with them social backgrounds, attitudes and behaviours, professional and life experience, and carry over certain elements from the socialisation process. The only extent of neutrality we can require is the absence of political indoctrination and corrupt behaviour (2004: 82).

In summary, in modern democracies, politicians have to share (informally) power with civil servants, even though the latter have no democratic legitimacy to make decisions. Despite its lack of formal authority, the administration possesses a number of qualities that predestine it to fulfil such a role. These include access to resources, information, analytical analytical skills, stability and continuity in office, a decision-making capacity learned over the years, political backing in the form of interest groups, lack of political accountability to the electorate, and a formal 'neutrality' that allows it to maintain the fiction that all decisions taken are free from political pressure and based on merit alone. This raises several questions. Who decides, and to what extent, to meet the needs of society? Which interests and which social groups should be satisfied first? The answer will not be clear-cut, but from the analysis carried out, it can be concluded that, to a large extent, the decision-maker will be the public administration. Taking this a step further, the question is whether officials can and should be neutral? If so, towards whom and what is the key to depoliticisation?

1.3 Models of the civil service

Civil service corps around the world are structured, as I have already suggested, in a variety of ways. They constitute internally complex structures both horizontally and vertically. The multiplicity of solutions at the legal level is conditioned by the shape of the legal system, either the continental, legalistic civil law approach, or the less formalised, Anglo-Saxon common law system. In the literature on the subject, it is argued that nowadays the civil service is more divided than united (Kudrycka 1998: 9–10). It is difficult not to agree with this view, but it is only a one-dimensional view, from the point of view of the corps' organisational structure. What the Civil Service certainly has in common (irrespective of whether we call it a public service or a public function) are common principles, values that are binding in any democratic system. Setting the principles by which members of the civil service corps must be guided is the foundation for building a modern administration. The fundamental values on which an efficiently functioning corps should be based include: legality of action (on the basis of the law and within its limits), responsibility, loyalty to the state and democratic authority, honesty, rationality of action, apoliticality, impartiality, efficiency (Gintowt-Jankowicz 2000: 5). These qualities sometimes codified, sometimes not (depending on the system) are only a general framework that must be filled by human behaviour, depending on culture, history and developed and implemented rules of operation.

Building a well-functioning civil service corps is a permanent process, even spanning several hundred years. The problem, however, is that the system will always be imperfect, as it constantly has to adapt to changes in the social, economic and political environment. Among the features characterising the Civil Service (irrespective of the system in which it operates and the institutional and legal framework), we can distinguish the two most important, constitutive elements of the service, namely – the regulation by public law of the legal status of civil servants, and the executive nature of the tasks performed (in relation to the government). The reasons for the emergence of

Civil Service Corps in the democratic states of Western Europe and the United States can be traced to the ever-increasing influence of the state administration on the lives of citizens. The constant encroachment of the administration into new areas of citizens' (society's) lives has forced the state authorities to create professionally trained officials. The expansion of state functions, new trends, technologies, changing economic, political conditions have necessitated the creation of an administrative apparatus that provides a guarantee of impartial, professional, apolitical performance of state tasks. Tasks should not be performed in the particular interest of the political party currently in power, but in the interest of citizens, society as a whole.

The evolution of the civil service is certainly rooted in the quest for an ideal state in which public officials, when performing tasks on behalf of the state, act in accordance with the values outlined above. Looking for the genesis of the civil service corps (in historical terms), it can be assumed that it originally constituted the closest environment for monarchs. Over the years, the corps began to function as a separate social caste. Civil service systems around the world are structured in a variety of ways. Individual countries often use historically shaped models when creating their own regulations, and sometimes adopt them from other countries. A civil service system (model) is a set of legal and organisational solutions concerning personnel management in administration. We can distinguish between two civil service models: the positional model, known also as the open model, and the career model, known as the promotion or closed model. Both solutions do not exist in a pure form, although we can point to countries where the shaped system comes close to the ideal (e. g. the position model in the UK or the career model in France). The formation of traditional civil service systems is related to historical processes and the organisational development of states, the institutionalisation of the political regime. Weak countries with a high level of internal instability and a need for institutional strengthening generally opted for the career model. On the other hand, where the political system functioned without major disturbances, they tended towards the positional model (Rydlewski 2001: 17). Nowadays, we can also speak of the so-called mixed, hybrid model, i. e. a combination of features of both systems. This is probably due to the constant search for new ways of managing human resources in the administration, which is expected to result in an increase in the quality of its tasks.

The career system is a hierarchical, centralised model, involving a gradual progression up the career ladder, culminating in occupation of the highest positions in the administration. It reflects the Weberian concept of viewing public administration as a rigid, bureaucratic, bony structure. As J. Czaputowicz notes, this system fully illustrates the continental approach to administration – i. e. attachment to administrative procedures and hierarchy (2001: 2). The structure of the career system assumes an internal division into grades, categories, corps and levels. Employment in the form of an act of appointment is in the name of the state, not to a specific office, not to a specific post, but to a corps (or the relevant level found in the state). The formal-legal status,

i. e. rules of employment, promotion, remuneration, pension rights, is regulated by public law (special pragmatics issued for this purpose). The career system, known as a closed system, does not allow employees too much mobility, either in terms of changing job positions or fast-tracking their careers past certain levels. Promotion follows strictly defined criteria and is preceded by the acquisition of experience at each level of the hierarchy. At the heart of this model is the assumption that it is only by gaining experience in the various positions (starting with the lowest) that one is qualified for the top positions. Frequent, mandatory training, both internal and external, is an essential element. Particular emphasis is placed on further training and the acquisition of knowledge. The system of salaries, allowances, bonuses is rigid, depending on the seniority system rather than on the results achieved at work. Specific pragmatics are applied, separately regulating all issues related to the situation of officials. The obligation to publicly announce vacancies creates a special kind of administrative transparency, showing the mechanisms for hiring and filling vacancies in the administration, as well as allowing equal access to positions for citizens. This system, not in its pure form of course, but with various solutions, is prevalent in countries such as: France, Germany, Spain, Belgium, Greece, Portugal, Austria, Ireland, Luxembourg.

The second system is the positional model, known as the open model. It is characterised by a different approach, a different philosophy of employment, as well as the performance of tasks by the public administration. The goal of the administration's activities remains of course the same, the efficiency of the tasks performed, while the means leading to this goal are quite different, based on other criteria. The system bases part of its assumptions on models taken from the private sector, using methods and techniques proven there. The openness of the model is based on the possibility of employing people who do not necessarily have degrees from specific universities or certificates, but above all experience, practical knowledge confirmed by experience. This is related to the need to recruit an employee who can perform tasks at a high level without unnecessary preparation, and therefore there is no need to create a preparatory period for the employee, an internship that is decisive for employment. Contracts, modelled on the private sector, are the predominant form and employment is not of a "lifetime" nature, i. e. until pension rights are obtained. What is taken into account here is the creative, imaginative capacity of the employee, which, after many years of working in the same position, may disappear and be replaced by routine. The system therefore tends to be extremely mobile, which means frequent job changes. The flow of workers is not only within the public sector, but also from the private to the public sector and vice versa, with the experience gained being recognised and even desired. In general, this model is characterised in all its aspects by a lack of formalisation. There are no formal recruitment methods, no rigid promotion system, no compulsory training system, there is no obligation to publicise vacancies, salaries depend on the results of the work done and are negotiable with the employer. Employment is made on behalf of a specific office at each of the levels available in the hierarchy, is often not regulated

Table 1 Features of the career model and the positional model

	Career model	Positional model
Employability	Employment at entry level	Employment at almost any level
	Education attested by a diploma or certificate	Not necessary diplomas but practical skills
	Specific age limit	No specific age limit
	Preparation period (internship, training, probationary period) often a condition for employment	No preparation period
Recruitment	Using formal recruitment methods, often provided for in legislative acts	No formal recruitment methods, methods used modelled on private sector
Access for EU nationals	Entry-level, sometimes mid-level positions	Entry-level and mid-level positions
	Professional experience (especially from the private sector) not recognised	Professional experience (from the private sector) has a strong influence on employment and salary
Career path	Promotion system – rigid, often standardised	No rigid promotion system
	Promotion and salary changes do not take into account work experience outside the public sector	Experience outside the public sector has a huge impact on promotion and raises
	Opportunities for frequent changes in position, responsibilities, remuneration are limited	Frequent changes in employee's (civil servant) situation
Further training	Training and development systems in each unit – mandatory	No mandatory training and development systems
Administrative transparency	Normative obligation to publicly communicate existing vacancies	No normative obligation to communicate vacancies
Rights and obligations	Employment until pension entitlement	Employment in the form of temporary contract
Remuneration	Regulated by law	Individual negotiation
	Seniority-related increases in the public sector	Individual negotiation
	Seniority system – more seniority equals higher pay	No seniority system
	Salary independent of performance	Salary directly linked to performance

	Career model	Positional model
Pension entitlements	Regulated by law	Collective agreement
	Company pragmatics	Pension contributions
Disciplinary legislation	Normative acts	No normative acts
Staff legislation	Pragmatics – special legal acts regulating the formal legal status of employees	Formal legal status regulated through union negotiations

Source: Table by author. Based on Auer at al. (1996) and Mróz (2000).

by public law, there are no specific pragmatics, and the formal-legal status is regulated through collective union bargaining. Among the countries that use this system are: UK, Sweden, Denmark, the Netherlands, Finland and Italy. In extreme cases (New Zealand), the legitimacy of a separate civil service status is questioned at all, believing that the market (managerial) model will bring the best solutions (Rydlewski 2001: 18; Izdebski&Kulesza 2004: 267; Czaputowicz 2001: 25–26). Table 1 provides a comparison of the models: career and positional.

Both systems presented should be regarded, as I have already mentioned, as model proposals, which therefore do not exist in their pure form. Certainly, the career system creates a kind of closed, rigid structure which, together with sluggish procedures, can be administratively inefficient, generating enormous financial costs. Long-term employment in one position can in turn lead to a fall into routine, mechanical execution of activities, lack of creativity and commitment. A rigid promotion and remuneration system that is not geared towards performance appraisal does not create competitiveness and at the same time does not foster motivation. The certainty and stability of the employment relationship through appointment can create a reluctance to change, learn and acquire new skills. On the other hand, this system ties the employee to the organisation in an extremely permanent way, through the stability and certainty of the employment relationship, the creation of special statutory regulations, and makes the employee independent of external pressures. The guarantee of pension rights has the effect of making the employee task-oriented. The transparency of promotion and remuneration rules makes the system clear and transparent. The positional model, as I have already mentioned, reflects the development trends of public administration. Perhaps it lacks the transparency and orderliness of a career system, but the flexibility expressed in the possibility to hire at any level of the hierarchy, the mobility of employees, the negotiation of salaries, the evaluation through results undoubtedly make this model attractive. It forces employees to be creative, it does not result in stagnation or sluggishness when performing tasks. Through contract employment, it forces creative effort, competition and the acquisition of new practical and theoretical skills. At the same time, by allowing workers to move freely between sectors – public and private – it does not create a bond with the institution. Employees do not feel that they are an integral part of the system, through the temporality of the contract. There is a fear that the temporary employee will be exposed to external factors, and that links and commitments from the private sector may interfere with the function. The instability of the employment relationship in turn becomes a positive motivator to perform more effectively. Negotiating salaries, appraisal by outcomes allows the best to be hired, not just those with many years of seniority.

From the point of view of a modern, task-oriented administration, the position system appears to be more effective in the selection of administrative personnel, performing, after all, such important state tasks. A tendency to gradually transform, or rather to take some solutions from the position system and transfer them to the career system is becoming noticeable (Kudrycka 2001: 33).

The rigid division into traditional systems is unreliable and incompatible with the contemporary face of administration. In many countries, the characteristics of the open (position) system prevail in the creation of modern public administration. Among the trends that have determined the 'popularity' of positional system solutions are: changing functions of the state, new principles of public management (New Public Management, Good Governance, Neoweberism), decentralisation of administration and flexibility in hiring. Added to this are new communication technologies, electronic media and the ecological reduction of paper consumption The positional system, already in its assumptions, is open to change, seeking these changes, hence undoubtedly its success.

Chapter 2
Civil service in Poland between 1918 and 1989 – historical background

2.1 Civil service in Poland in the interwar period

The regaining of independence by Poland in 1918 necessitated the administrative unification of the Polish lands. Unification of the three different administrative systems was necessary for the smooth functioning of the state. The young state therefore faced the problem of building an administrative apparatus, having at its disposal the remnants of the various models of administration in the partitioning states. Administrative structures in the restored Republic were quite different depending on the partition. In the Prussian partition, despite the existence of an efficient and effective administration, Poles were not allowed to hold official posts, unlike in the Austrian partition, where Polish citizens speaking German were allowed to hold office. It should be remembered that the Austrian system was inefficient and bureaucratic, functionally ineffective. It became necessary to introduce its own regulations and to create its "own" model of public administration, undoubtedly making use of certain solutions applied in the former partitioning states. According to H. Izdebski, from the Austrian model we adopted administrative procedure and administrative judiciary, from the Prussian model – the system of local self-government, while from the Russian model – the concept of the Supreme Chamber of Control and other models of financial institutions (1993: 34–35). In the literature on the subject, we can also find claims that neither valuable models nor qualified clerical cadres remained after the Russian partition (Jakubowska 1998: 26).

In the period of the Second Republic, the creation of the administrative apparatus, including a uniform civil service corps, had to start basically from scratch, as there were no previous regulations in this respect unless to include *the Civil Service Act in the Kingdom of Poland of March 1859*, which, however, was repealed in February 1879 (Smyk 2004: 77–78).

The creation of administrative structures began at the beginning of 1918, i. e. at a time when Poland had not yet formally regained its independence. The literature on the subject distinguishes three stages of building the administrative system in pre-war Poland. The first stage began when the Regency Council issued *The decree on 3 January 1918 on the temporary organisation of the Supreme Authorities in the Kingdom of Poland* and lasted until 1922. During this period, temporary service regulations for civil servants were issued, attached to *The Rescript of the Regency Council of the Kingdom of Poland of 11 June 1918*. Stage two covers the years 1922 to 1926, together with the most important regulation, i. e. the Act on the State Civil Service and other norms, which I will characterise in detail later in this chapter. The third stage, on the other hand, began in 1932, i. e. when the civil servants' law was thoroughly amended (Jakubowska 1998: 26–27). Temporary service regulations for civil servants were issued when Poland was still under partitions, but the feeling of imminent liberation forced the authorities of the Kingdom of Poland to regulate the administration of the country. These regulations, although written in archaic language, are close in concept to our contemporary solutions applied in the civil service. The regulations covered both general provisions (Title I), entry into the service (Title II), the duties of civil servants (Title III), civil servant rights (Title IV), civil servant liability (Title V), and termination of service (Title VI). In the case of the temporary provisions, we can also speak of the public-law nature of the service relationship concluded on the basis of an appointment (probationary, provisional or definitive). Both employment and "discharge from service" (as dismissal from service was defined in the provisional regulations) were left to the discretion of the superior authority, which clearly demonstrates the inequality of the parties in this relationship. Candidates for service had to hold Polish citizenship and have: "due aptitude, civic integrity and morality of character (Article 5)". Of course, an official was obliged to take an oath referring to God (the content of the rota varied according to religion). Among the duties of officials were: observance of the law, zeal, conscientiousness, devotion to duty, courtesy, impartiality, obedience to duty, prohibition of criticism of the authorities and participation in illegal associations, prohibition of additional employment, duty of secrecy, which, according to Article 16, read: "even after leaving office, he must remain silent as to what has been entrusted to him, as confidential, under the seal of official secrecy". Officials were equipped with an additional catalogue of rights, such as special legal protection, the right to leave, promotion, retirement, while being subject to increased disciplinary responsibility (Górski 2000–2001: 73–75; Stelina 2005: 17).

One of the elements of creating administrative structures in the Second Republic was the introduction of the institution of a civil service. This was, however, a preliminary element, as a greater problem turned out to be a shortage of appropriately educated human resources. The introduction of civil service rules had to entail filling those institutions with educated people prepared to administer. The shortage of human resources in inter-war Poland was enormous, and it should be remembered that Poles did not hold positions in the Prussian and Russian partitions. Officials from the former Austrian partition, where Poles were allowed to hold positions, therefore became the cradle of administrative personnel in interwar Poland (Malec 2003: 147–148).

The Act of 17 February 1922 on the State Civil Service (Journal of Laws 1922, No. 21, item 164 as amended) established the Civil Service Corps. The Act came into effect on 1 April 1922 and formally remained in force for 52 years, until 31 December 1974. This was because 1 January 1975 saw the end of the vacatio legis period for the Labour Code, which finally brought to an end the phase of the existence of clerical law (having its origins in the 2nd Republic of Poland) and the façade regulations concerning administrative employees during the PRL. The Act on the State Civil Service introduced modern solutions, used in many countries, concerning the functioning of the civil service, granting a special legal status to persons employed in administration. It introduced, inter alia, qualification assessments of civil servants, anti-corruption regulations, disciplinary responsibility, the principle of official secrecy, preparatory service and many other solutions that will be the subject of my further reflections. A phenomenon almost without precedent given that the Act was drafted three and a half years after independence was regained, in a country in which no modern principles for the functioning of the administration had been in place for over a century, and in which the partitioners had formed structures and defined the manner in which the administration operated, and in which no tradition of administrative functioning had been established. The admirable ideas contained in the Act are still largely relevant today. It clearly shows modern, enlightened and creative administrative thought, which over the course of several decades was distorted, depreciated as a result of the changed social and political conditions caused by the introduction of the socialist system. The Act covered a wide group of administrative employees as well as ministers and constitutionally responsible heads of other supreme authorities and central offices. Judges, prosecutors, court trainees, employees of state railways, employees of post offices, telegraphs, telephones, as well as teachers of all state schools were not subject to it (Article 2 in conjunction with Article 118). It should be borne in mind, however, that not all provisions were applied to each of the listed groups subject to the Act. Among other things, the regulations on categorisation related to education and the obligation to do preparatory service were not applied to ministers. The doctrine of the time rightly pointed out that "(…) the role of ministers is primarily political, and the nature of his functions and position is distinctly different from that of a professional civil servant (…)", and therefore it was postulated that ministerial positions should be excluded from the pragmatics concerning civil servants (Kościołek 1947: 15–16). In J. Bocia's opinion, none of the laws regulating this matter passed to this day had such an extensive subjective scope (2004: 225).

Article 1 of the Act prejudged the public-legal nature of the employment relationship. This meant subjecting the rules of operation of the corps to the regulations of public law, which obviously entailed a special mode of establishing, changing and terminating the employment relationship. The unequal nature of the parties to this legal relationship was evident, as I mentioned earlier. The state, as the party employing through a particular office, was the stronger party in the relationship, having authority, while the civil servant, being in a relationship of dependence on the state, was the weaker element, subordinated to the state interest (Kasznica 1946: 119–120). The service relationship established by the state with the state official meant that the official remained in service as a disposable subject and bound by an oath. In return, he or she was offered various privileges, mainly social and above all employment stability (Stelina 2005: 27). The law divided employees into two categories: civil servants and inferior state functionaries, dividing the former into three categories according to their level of education (Article 3 in conjunction with Article 11). A division into twelve official ranks was also established, which were in close correlation with positions. Category I required tertiary education confirmed by relevant examinations, category II required general or vocational secondary education, while category III required completion of general school or lower grades of secondary school. Cf. Art. 11 of the Act of 17 February 1922 on the State Civil Service (Journal of Laws 1922, No. 21, item 164 as amended).

The official's service relationship was established, in the light of section 5 of the Act, by means of a permanent appointment or until dismissal, i. e. provisionally. The nature of the appointment was determined by a letter of appointment in which, in the case of a provisional appointment, the date of expiry of the official relationship or the date of notice of dismissal could be specified. The letter of appointment had to contain information about the office, the official title, the rank of service converted into a salary group in 1933 as a result of an amendment to the Act. A permanent appointment entailed permanence of the employment relationship and non-removal from office, with exceptions provided for in the Act. An exception to the rule of appointment was the employment of employees in the form of contracts, essentially omitted by the Act. The rules of contractual employment were regulated in separate acts. In the ordinance of the President of the Republic of 16 March 1928 on the employment contract of white-collar workers (Journal of Laws No. 35, item 323) and in the ordinance of the President of the Republic of 16 March 1928 on the employment contract of labourers (Journal of Laws No. 35, item 324). During this period, there were also employed the so-called "dietarians" – i. e. contractual workers who performed work during periods of increased demand (e. g. during military conscription) and technical, auxiliary activities. It seems to me that today we could compare their employment to a contract of mandate (Kościołek 1947: 11–15).

Article 6 of the Act contained the prerequisites that candidates for appointed officials were required to meet: Polish citizenship, an impeccable past, capacity to act in law, physical and mental aptitude to perform official duties, fluency in spoken and written Polish. There was a prohibition on accepting into service persons against whom criminal or incapacitation proceedings were pending or who had been sentenced by a final judgment for offences for financial gain. The general rule was to employ persons between the ages of 18 and 40; other cases were left to the discretionary decision of superiors and required the approval of the 'competent chief authority' (Article 8). Just how highly discretionary this system was is evidenced by the fact that the Presidential Decree of 19 January 1928 on the organisation and scope of action of general administrative authorities (Journal of Laws 1928, No. 11, item 86) stipulated, prior to the establishment of an official relationship, the obligation to consult the competent voivode, as a representative of the government, who had the possibility of consulting local authorities (Korczak 2006: 292). The appointed official was obliged to take, in accordance with Article 15, the oath of office to his superiors or to the President in special cases (e. g. the President of the Supreme Chamber of Control). The text of the rota in 1922 included a declaration of service to the Polish State with reference to a god, depending on religion. The *sine qua non* for appointment was the completion of one year's preparatory service, with the possibility of its shortening or exemption by superiors. We saw the widespread use of exemptions during the period of the Sanacja government. There were exemptions from the obligation to undergo preparatory service, as well as from the obligation to have a higher education for Category I officials, which clearly indicates an attempt to politicise the administration and fill posts with trusted people. According to E. Ura, posts were very often filled by military officers, with political merit being the only consideration (1995: 17).

Chapter 2 of the Act regulated the duties of public officers. The basic duties of an official were: "(…) to serve the Republic faithfully, to observe strictly the laws and regulations, to discharge the duties of his office zealously, conscientiously and impartially, and to take care, according to his best will and knowledge, of the good of the public cause (…)" (Article 21 of the Act). The duties of civil servants, which were treated broadly, included: obeying the instructions of superiors, as well as performing such official activities which were not part of his ordinary official duties (e. g. working on public holidays and outside office hours) – Article 22 and Article 23, observing official secrecy, both during service, after retirement and on retirement (Article 24), guarding the solemnity of the post (Article 25), prohibiting entry into conspiracies and associations disrupting the course of state management. This provision was a consent to political activity by officials, membership of political parties that were not considered anti-state, and political activity could not interfere with the performance of service (Górski 2001–2002: 76).

In addition, the official was obliged to be impartial, courteous, respectful of superiors, forbidden to accept donations, use his official position to gain advantages, refrain from criticising superiors, forbidden to take up additional gainful employment without the consent of his superior, carry out tasks as quickly and purposefully as possible, inform about his current place of residence (even during the period of idleness). One of the more interesting solutions was Article 25(4) in the light of which: "in his official relations with the public, the official shall, with due solemnity, be impartial, courteous and, within permissible limits, give them advice and assistance". This provision clearly shows that the authors of the law at the time understood perfectly the ideas of a modern civil service and the fulfilment of conscientious duties by public servants.

Remaining in service, a type of subordination to state authority, involved the possibility of changing the service relationship through a unilateral decision of the authority. It was expressed in the freedom to transfer an official to work in another locality, to another post "insofar as the good of the service required it" (Article 52). Such an enigmatic-sounding provision left a great deal of discretion to superiors and could be used in a manner inconsistent with the 'good of the service'. The Act also created the institution of the "state of inactivity of an official", i. e. a situation where there was no suitable official position for an official. An official on inactive status received his or her full emoluments and could be called up to active service at any time. If the appointment did not take place within six months, the official retired (Articles 54, 55, 56). With regard to the possibility of combining a position in the service with a mandate as a parliamentarian, the law reproduced and developed the provisions of the March Constitution, exempting for the duration of the mandate from holding office with a concomitant withholding of emoluments and the obligation to ensure the official's return to service (art. 57). Article 16 of the March Constitution stated:

> State and local government employees, upon their election, shall be granted leave for the duration of their parliamentary mandate. This provision does not apply to ministers, undersecretaries of state and university professors. Years spent carrying out a parliamentary mandate count towards years of service.

The partial restriction of civil liberties in relation to civil servants and the extensive catalogue of statutory duties was the result of guaranteeing them a number of privileges that contractual employees could not enjoy during the Second Republic. The basic element was the permanence and stability of employment expressed in the establishment of an employment relationship on the basis of appointment and limited possibilities of dismissal from service. Officials were entitled to special legal protection guaranteed by the provisions of the Penal Code (Article 34), the right to a title, official position, wearing a uniform, official badges, annual leave, the length of which depended on years of service, special leave, and health leave. It was also possible to obtain leave for training purposes exceeding even 2 months (e. g. to complete studies or to prepare for and take examinations at universities), as well as leave for trade union work (Kościołek 1947: 93–94).

Officials also benefited from free medical care, various social subsidies and retirement emoluments, and were entitled to promotion, which was largely left to the discretionary power of the immediate superior. The State Civil Service Act, in its original formulation, also stipulated the obligation for civil servants to undergo qualification assessments by qualification commissions (Article 20). The Decree of the Council of Ministers of 23 July 1923 on qualification commissions established the types, composition and scope of action of the commissions, as well as the qualification procedure (Journal of Laws 1923, No. 82, item 638). Chapter V of the Act was devoted to the official liability of officials. In general, during the Second Republic officials were subject to three types of liability: official and disciplinary, criminal and civil. Attention was also drawn to moral responsibility as a fourth type, which was not, however, a legal responsibility (Kościołek 1947: 138–139).

Liability concerned 'impropriety in office or conduct and negligence in service' (Article 66). In addition, an official was liable for breach of the duties of his position and office both in and out of the service. Liability was divided into disciplinary liability, which applied to official misconduct, and orderly liability applied to official misconduct. Misconduct, according to Article 69, was defined as such a breach of official duties that caused offence to the public interest or exposed the public good to harm. It was placed higher in the hierarchy than misconduct, as an act subject to more severe sanctions. The following disciplinary penalties were envisaged: reprimand, deduction of years of service from one to three years, reduction in rank by one or two, with suspension of promotion for a period of one to three years, transfer to permanent retirement with a reduction in pensionable emoluments of up to 50 % at the most, and expulsion from the service (Article 77). On the other hand, misconduct in the service could be punished with a warning, refusal of leave or reduction of leave. This was a disciplinary penalty. The possibility of imposing punishments of order lay with superiors or disciplinary committees, while disciplinary penalties could only be imposed by disciplinary committees. A decision on a disciplinary penalty could be appealed by the civil servant within eight days, but without the possibility of challenging the decisions of the disciplinary committees and the decisions of the supreme authorities, which had the value of finality. On the same day that the Law on the State Civil Service was enacted, i. e. 17 February 1922, the Law on the Organisation of Disciplinary Authorities and Disciplinary Proceedings against State Officials (Journal of Laws 1922, No. 21, item 165) was also enacted. The full implementation of the provisions concerning disciplinary proceedings did not take place until 1932 under two regulations: President of the Republic of Poland of 7 October 1932 on the organisation of disciplinary commissions and disciplinary proceedings against state functionaries (Journal of Laws No. 87, item 738) and Regulation of the Council of Ministers of 17 October 1932 on disciplinary commissions and disciplinary proceedings against state functionaries (Journal of Laws No. 92, item 790) (Kościołek 1947: 158–159).

The commissions ruled on both civil servants and lower state functionaries. A decree of 17 October 1932 established the position of a disciplinary ombudsman and his deputies (the choice was up to the authorities of the office) and the position of defence counsel, who was chosen by the accused. Of course, the choice could only be made for both positions from among officials. The reason for guaranteeing transparency and, more interestingly, the obligation of secrecy in the proceedings was "to guard the good of the service, violated by the misconduct of official duties" (Jakubowska1998: 26–27). The importance of the issues related to the disciplinary responsibility of officials is most fully expressed in Article 87 of the S. C. S. Act, in the light of which, the prosecution of misconduct and official misconduct is not subject to the statute of limitations. A considerable part of the provisions of the Act had to be applied to the category of inferior state officials. Except that the Act in many cases understated the requirements for this group. According to Article 90, "Anyone applying for a position as a lower officer should be able to read and write in Polish". On the other hand, the provisions on disciplinary responsibility were applied in their entirety to inferior officers, as opposed to rights and duties, which were regulated separately (in the same Act).

The Act was amended several times (fourteen amendments by September 1939). The most significant amendments were made in 1932 and 1933. The amendment of 7 October 1932 eliminated the obligation of appointment. Another amendment, on 28 October 1933, separated the automatic attainment of a higher rank from promotion to a post. According to the amended provisions, the President of the Republic of Poland (on the proposal of the competent supreme authority) appointed, inter alia, persons to the posts of undersecretaries of state (Article 17). Undersecretaries were divided into political and non-political (the latter were then called 'professional ministers'). The objection of the doctrine of that time that the application of the State Civil Service Act to so-called 'political undersecretaries' was unjustified seems correct today. The same allegation can be made in relation to the positions of ministers (Kościołek 1947: 49–50). Analysing the provisions of the 1922 Act, one may come to the conclusion that it was equally unjustified for the President to make appointments of "non-political undersecretaries". Since their task was to perform the tasks of state administration in a professional and substantive manner, the rigours of the Act should have been applied to them in their employment.

The aforementioned amendment of 7 October 1932 abolished the qualification commissions issuing opinions on the personal matters of civil servants, trainees and candidates for entry into the service, replacing them with opinions of the relevant supreme authority. It also removed the provision allowing an official to see the opinions expressed by the selection committees. In addition, the amendment removed the possibility for disciplinary committees to impose disciplinary sanctions, leaving this to the superior or higher authority (Article 74). Another change contained in the amendment of 28 October 1933 was the removal of the rationale that should guide the 'superior authority' when making promotions to a higher salary group (Article 41). In the original wording of this article, the authority was required to take into account: "the aptitude, usefulness, degree of confidence and special qualification of the official", while after the amendment, the sole premise for promotion remained the discretion of the superior authority.

Most of the changes made during the Sanation government proved beneficial from the point of view of those currently in power, and did not contribute to the creation of a democratically functioning civil service corps. There was a noticeable tendency towards changes creating broad discretionary authority for "immediate superiors" or "the supreme power". The abolition of collegiate bodies and the transfer of powers to the so-called 'superior authority' proved to be a reliable way. In certain aspects, the solutions contained in the Civil Service Act of 1922 began to lose their democratic character already at the time of the changes made by the Sanacja camp, to finally take on an extreme form in the post-war period. It should be remembered that the young

Polish state after regaining independence faced serious shortages of specialised administrative staff. In 1923, the state administration employed some 120,000 people, of whom only some 15,000 had a university degree. According to A. Komar-Morawska, the 1923 census showed that 13 % of civil servants had a university degree, 40 % had a high school diploma, 30 % had completed 4–6 years of secondary school, while 17 % had an elementary or "home" education (1998: 17–18). These proportions changed positively as the Polish statehood developed. Only about 15 per cent of all employees had experience in the administration of the partitioning states (Malec 2003: 149–150).

During the Second Republic attempts were made to reform the state administration. By the outbreak of the Second World War, as many as four Administrative Reform Commissions had been set up. The first, appointed in 1920, was chaired by the future President of the Republic, Stanisław Wojciechowski. Another commission was set up in 1923 under the chairmanship of Władysław Sikorski, then Prime Minister and Minister for Military Affairs. The third commission was active in 1926, and its members included Michał Dobrzyński and Stanisław Kasznica. The last of the commissions, called the Commission for the Improvement of Public Administration, was active between 1928 and 1933, chaired by Maurycy Jaroszyński. Financial considerations made it necessary to discontinue its work, but it was never formally dissolved. None of the commissions ever achieved their objectives, i. e. worked out the full, final shape of the Polish model of public administration. However, the last of the commissions, the Jaroszyński Commission, left behind a huge body of work that was used by other countries, and which only became helpful during the systemic changes after 1989. A body of work which, for a variety of reasons, was not put to use either before the outbreak of the Second World War or immediately afterwards (Izdebski 1993: 36–40).

Despite many shortcomings and makeshift solutions, in H. Izdebski's opinion the administrative system created during the Second Republic was an original one, and not an amalgamation of the solutions of the former partitioning states. Moreover, it was shaped very quickly, at the same time allowing for rapid administrative, economic and social unification, laying the foundations for the construction of a modern state (1993: 35).

The Act was the beginning of the construction of a modern administration, which was brutally interrupted by the outbreak of war. It was also innovative in terms of the European achievements of the time. According to W. Mikułowski: "The first comparable civil service statute was not created in France until 1946, 24 years later" (2003: 76). The state civil service had a clear public law character and was understood as such by the doctrine of the time. The regulations introduced in 1922 laid a solid foundation for the formation of the modern civil service corps. Their slow depreciation, as has been mentioned, began with the Sanacja government, and continued uninterruptedly until the end of 1974.

2.2 State administration after World War II

While the Second World War was still in progress, changes were made that heralded a departure from the idea of civil service. By the decree of the PKWN of 27 December 1944 *on* the temporary standardisation of the service relationship and classification of state officers (Journal of Laws 1944, No. 16, item 89), the competent supreme authority was allowed, within one year, to change the group of emoluments and official position, retire or dismiss an officer from service (introducing a 3-month notice period), without observing the conditions and deadlines provided for in the service regulations (art. 6). On the other hand, by the Decree of the Council of Ministers of 14 May 1946 on the temporary standardisation of the service relationship of state officers, the subjective scope of the Act was amended to include judges, prosecutors, court assessors and trainees, employees of state enterprises and establishments in the group of persons subject to standardisation, if they were not subject to exclusion under specific provisions. In addition, the decree introduced the uniform term "state officer" for both civil servants and lower state officers (Article 1.1) and reproduced, following the 1944 decree, all rules concerning dismissal, transfer, change of salary group. One can clearly see here a departure from the principle of stabilisation of the service relationship. According to J. Bocia, the reason for this state of affairs was "the desire to get rid of 'sanacja' civil servants who, after the liberation, took up public service, to which they felt obliged, and in which they proved to be useless for political reasons" (2004: 226). Interestingly, the decree entered into force retroactively, from 29 December 1945, and pre-war civil servants who did not declare their readiness to take up their service within three months, counting from 22 July 1944, lost the rights deriving from their service relationship, acquired before the outbreak of war. It should be borne in mind that the mere declaration of return to service was not tantamount to it, as the authorities of the time left themselves free to carry out verifications at their own discretion. These changes clearly imply unlimited possibilities of the new authorities in the selection of administrative personnel, the application of a system based on free discretion and the absence of any obligation to justify decisions (Ura 1995: 23). J. Korczak states that an important element in the hiring of new cadres became the Instruction on the Technique of Proceedings in the Admission of Officials and Contractual Employees of the Prime Minister of 28 December 1946, together with Circular No. 8, which was not published. The instruction dealt with the authorities' conduct in the admission to the ranks of government employees. The authorities were able to use a variety of institutions to check the credibility of a candidate (including the security service) (2006: 293).

The concept of the service relationship changed. Modelled on Soviet solutions, the aim was to make the employment relationship equal for all professional groups, eliminating the special legal status of civil servants. This situation was also reflected in the doctrine of the time, which denied with great zeal the need for special features of civil servant law, based on the norms of public, administrative law. It was assumed that the assumptions of socialism contradicted the bureaucratic model of service relations, referring to the absolutist era. It was postulated that 'the antithesis of the traditional civil service, based on the old 19th-century Austro-Prussian models, is the Leninist conception of state service, according to which state employees have basically the same legal status as other people engaged in gainful activity' (Zieliński 1984: 92–93). Reference was made to 'the developmental tendency of the socialist state to unify the legal situation of all working people' (Jaśkiewicz 1969: 16–18). At the same time, every manifestation of sympathy for the new regime was ennobled. Hence, by Circular of the Prime Minister No. 33 of 10 October 1946, the institution of leave for work in political parties and organisations was introduced, not exceeding ten days at a time. Interestingly, this was a paid leave granted to attend conventions, congresses and ceremonies (Kościołek 1947: 94).

A subsequent decree of 25 October 1948 amending the State Civil Service Act (Journal of Laws 1946, No. 50, item 381) eliminated regulations reflecting modern ideas of the civil service. A division of state officers (no longer civil servants or officers) into two categories was made: general service employees and special service employees, with special theoretical and practical preparation required for the latter category. Pursuant to Article 1(3) of the same decree, the Council of Ministers could, by regulation, make admission to particular divisions of the general service or special service conditional on completion of appropriate studies, completion of preparatory service and passing the qualification and practical examination independently of or instead of completion of studies. Although formally appointment was retained as a form of employment, obviously dependent on the relevant supreme authority (mainly the Prime Minister and the President), in practice it was used sporadically, mainly in relation to higher posts in administration (e. g. employees of the President's civil chancellery, the Sejm chancellery, employees of the Supreme Chamber of Control). Article 17 of the State Civil Service Act of 1922, as amended by the above decree. The decree also introduced a number of regulations related to the so-called "participation of trade unions in the implementation of the Act" granting participation with an advisory vote in labour matters. Aiming at the elimination of differences in the formal and legal status of civil servants, subsequent circulars, decrees and regulations were used to eliminate such differences. The aim of the authorities of the time was to eliminate from Polish civil servant law the remnants inherited from the partitioners: "the monarchical version of the service relationship formed in Austria-Hungary and the German Empire" (Zieliński 1984: 99). A circular issued by the Prime Minister on 31 January 1949 ("Official Journal of the Ministry of Public Administration" No. 12, item 57) finally resolved the problem of appointments, leaving them each time to the discretion of the Prime Minister or the relevant minister, while recommending employment based on an employment contract (Jaśkiewicz 1969: 27). The practice followed since the end of the war was confirmed by a decree issued in 1955 by the Prime Minister obliging all heads of administration to apply the contractual employment formula. On the other hand, a year earlier, in the Decree of 25 June 1954 on universal pension provision for employees and their families (Journal of Laws No. 30, item 116), pension privileges for state administration employees were abolished.

Apart from changing the forms of employment, these measures were aimed at creating a new class structure of personnel, adapted to the newly introduced regime. The dismissal of pre-war civil servants was followed by the recruitment of new ones, in particular of workers' and peasants' origin, very often lacking the necessary qualifications and education, but dedicated to the new authorities and loyal to their decisions. The politicisation of personnel policy led to the replacement of personnel in the administration with people who were inexperienced and very often uneducated, but completely subordinated to their political superiors. The equalisation of the status of appointed and contract employees, meant that, in terms of duties, the authorities of the time applied the regulations on the state civil service to contract employees, contractually extending the scope of their duties. The elimination of appointments involving an obvious stabilisation of the employment relationship imposed on contractual staff the same responsibilities as for appointments (Ura 1995: 24–25).

The next stage in the liquidation of civil servant law in the People's Republic of Poland was the Act of 15 July 1968 on employees of national councils (Journal of Laws 1968, No. 25, item 164), excluding another group of administration from the subjective scope of the Act on the State Civil Service of 1922. Although the Act formally concerned employees of national councils, in accordance with Art. 1 para. 2, the Council of Ministers had the possibility to extend the Act or some of its provisions to employees of other territorial state administration bodies by way of a regulation (however, this was not done, applying to the remaining groups the amended provisions of the pre-war Act on the State Civil Service). The Act specified that the basic form of the employment relationship with employees was the employment contract, with the exception of persons in managerial positions employed on the basis of appointment. The contractual method of establishing an official relationship in administration also found wide support in the literature of the time. Opinions in this vein were expressed by M. Jaroszyński, W. Dawidowicz, E. Iserzon, F. Longchamps, among others (Zieliński 1984: 100–101).

According to J. Boć, the Act on employees of national councils constituted a kind of 'ground' for the future codification of labour law and basing all labour relations in the People's Republic of Poland (PRL) on it. Despite these socialist (modelled on USSR solutions) assumptions, the Act benefited to some extent from the norms of the 1922 Act (e.g. with regard to employee availability, transfer, suspension or disciplinary liability) (Boć 2004: 227). Moreover, the Act did justice to the socialist ideals of the state by obliging employees to guard the authority of the people's government and to avoid anything that could lower the confidence of citizens in the people's government (Article 5(2)) and by establishing selection rigours in the form of appropriate personal and professional qualifications. According to Article 11(1)(4), only a person who, due to his or her ideological and moral level, gave a guarantee that the tasks of a national council employee would be duly performed could become an employee.

As a result, according to T. Zieliński, "the cult of the clerical career based on stability and special privileges, which had been widespread before the war, began to disappear from the society", while at the same time work in managerial positions in industry began to be seen as the most prestigious profession (1984: 99). According to J. Boć, a sociological study conducted in the 1970s noted a definite decline in the attractiveness of the civil servant profession within the society (2004: 227). In justifying the removal of the norms of clerical law, it was argued (legislator, doctrine) that clerical/administrative work was no longer an elite profession, separating clerks from the rest of society (Zieliński 1984: 154–155). Of course, according to the conception of the socialist state, this was supposed to be an expression of the democratisation of employment, and the civil service began to be not an elite profession, but a democratic one with free access for all citizens. Undoubtedly involving a drastic reduction in the level of expertise of the staff employed (Zieliński 1984: 92).

The elimination of the separate formal and legal status of civil servants in Poland took place when the Labour Code Act of 26 June 1974 came into force (Journal of Laws 1974, No. 24, item 141), i.e. on 1 January 1975. The provisions introducing the Code (Journal of Laws 1974, No. 24, item 142) repealed a number of norms, including the 1922 Act on the State Civil Service. Pursuant to Article 15 § 1, the employment relationships of employees appointed under the 1922 Act were transformed into employment relationships based on a contract of employment for an indefinite period of time, while for managerial positions they were changed to employment relationships by appointment. The depreciation of civil servant law was most fully expressed in the fact that the legislator authorised the Council of Ministers to issue, on the basis of the Labour Code (Article 298), a service pragmatics concerning employees of state offices. On 20 December 1974, a decree was issued on the rights and duties of state office employees (Journal of Laws 1974, No. 49, item 300), which defined the prerequisites for employment, qualification requirements, rights, duties and even a particular type of subject scope, as the decree concerned the chief, central and territorial administrative bodies and their subordinate offices. In matters not regulated, the provisions of the Labour Code were applicable. Despite the formulation of the prerequisites of possession of appropriate professional qualifications in terms of education and length of service and, in the case of managerial positions, the possibility of examinations, these provisions remained a mere paper formula with no reflection in reality. As is well known, the decision-makers remained in the party committees.

As can be seen from the above, the evolution of labour relations in public administration went through a long and turbulent journey. Beginning with the special legal status in the interwar period and ending with the equalization of this status with other employees by bringing everyone under the regulations of the Labour Code. These changes were the result of the adoption of the doctrine of the unification of labour relations. W. Jaskiewicz described this phenomenon in this way: "from clerical law as administrative law to labour law", distinguishing four stages in the evolution of official relations in administration: the equalisation of the situation of appointed and contractual employees, the elimination of the official relationship in the form of appointment, the unification of the legal situation of employees in different groups of administration, and the application of general labour law to all employees, including employees of state offices (Jełowicki 1986: 15–28). The process of changing the pre-war idea of the civil service, deprecating the basic principles and values of civil servant law took place for almost 30 years, starting with the Polish Committee of National Liberation (PKWN) decree of 1944, and ending with the enactment of the Labour Code in 1974. After that period, little remained of the old ethos of the civil servant, although according to some authors "(...) the awareness of the need to have a professional civil servant corps", which should have appropriate competences and qualifications, was constant throughout the construction of the new regime (Mikułowski 2003a: 77). The downgrading of the rank of the clerical profession, creating a negative image of it in society, and the lack of specific regulations relating to persons performing state tasks meant that eight years after the total abolition of the special legal status of clerks, the idea of its restoration was revived. The outcome of the changes in the perception of the status of state employees turned out to be the Act of 16 September 1982 on State Office Employees (Journal of Laws 1982, No. 31, item 214, as amended, which, in a modified form, is still in force today, regulating the status of some public administration employees. The Act is described by the doctrine as a slow attempt to change the way of thinking about the formal and legal status of civil servants and the first step towards the reconstruction of civil servant law. In part of the regulations, the Act referred to its predecessor from 1922, and despite the socialist doctrine in force at the time, it was possible to restore the special legal status of civil servants in the Act without the possibility to use the pre-war terminology. According to W. Mikułowski, the very name of the 1982 Act does not change the fact that it was in fact the first Civil Service Act in the socialist bloc. It should be added that, in the author's opinion, the construction of the Act (consistency, legislative technique) stands at a much higher level than later Civil Service Acts. It was also a mistake, based on ideology, to dissociate oneself from this law as a product of the communist period, as it was in fact a good and sensible regulation (2003a: 77). In the literature, the contrary can also be found (Korczak 2006: 294).

The civil servants' pragmatics included in its regulations the establishment, modification and termination of the employment relationship, the duties and rights of civil servants, awards, distinctions and medals, liability for order and discipline, disputes over claims arising from the employment relationship, and trade union rights limited, however, to some employees of state offices. On the other hand, the law completely neglects recruitment and selection procedures for employees. Only the establishment of selection rigours in Article 3 was made in the form of having Polish citizenship, full capacity to perform legal acts, enjoyment of full public rights, appropriate education, completion of an administrative application and a state of health permitting employment. According to the doctrine of the time, the Act also required that a candidate for an official: "by his or her civic attitude give a guarantee of the proper performance of the tasks of an employee of a state office of a socialist state". With the benefit of hindsight, it is not surprising that there were no recruitment and selection procedures for employees in the Act, since, according to established practice, employment depended on membership of a party organisation and acquiescence in the functioning of the system of the time. The Act already made a distinction between civil servants and other employees in Article 1. According to the original version of the Act, officials in managerial and independent positions were employed on the basis of appointment (Article 4), while other employees performed their duties on the basis of employment contracts (Article 5). Since there is no definition in the law as to who is a civil servant, one can try to create one by interpreting the individual provisions. In the doctrine, the view has become established (Ura 1985: 45; Boć 2004: 230) that this is a special category of public servants, while the clarification (specification) of official positions took place in the ordinance of the Council of Ministers of 8 November 1982, issued to the Act, on the definition of official positions and the principles of establishing an employment relationship with public servants on the basis of appointment (Journal of Laws 1982, No. 39, item 257, as amended). Quoting after E. Ura one of the more synthetic definitions of an official it should be said that: "the criterion for singling out a civil servant is the performance by him of substantive activities within the scope of state administration" (1995: 45–46).

In general, the statutory regulations mainly apply to the former group, i. e. civil servants, while the provisions of the Labour Code are applied to the others, occasionally using the provisions of the Act. The scope of the subject matter of the Act was as broad as that of the 1922 regulation. Initially it covered chief, central and territorial offices, the Sejm chancellery, the State Council chancellery and offices subordinate to the chief organs of state power and chief and central organs of state administration (art. 1). Special provisions allowed the Act to be applied to other groups of civil servants not listed in Article 1. The reinstatement of appointment as a method of employing civil servants after almost forty years represented a "milestone" in the regulations defining the legal status of civil servants.

As mentioned earlier, an appointment has extensive consequences, both for the employee and the employer. Thus, the Act limited the possibility of terminating the employment of an appointed official to the strict conditions set out therein. An official could be dismissed in the event of a repeated negative qualification evaluation, the liquidation of an office or its reorganisation, an involuntary loss of entitlement, loss of physical or mental capacity to work. There was, of course, the possibility of termination of employment without notice, through the fault of the official, as well as by agreement of the parties. The notice period was three months. The act of appointment was preceded by an oath and an administrative apprenticeship lasting twelve months (with the possibility of reducing it by half, which was left to the discretionary power of the head of the office). One can clearly see here a reference to the 1922 State Civil Service Act, in which the preparatory service also played an important role in the professional development of civil servants. It has been alleged in the doctrine that the administrative application refers only to those already employed (Korczak 2006: 294).

The scope of civil servants' duties was specifically standardised, obliging them, inter alia, to: protect the interests of the state, the law and the legitimate interests of citizens, observe the Constitution of the People's Republic of Poland and other laws, uphold the authority of the People's Republic of Poland, be guided by the principles of justice, respond in a matter-of-fact manner to the critical remarks of citizens, act promptly and impartially, behave with dignity both at work and outside work, observe the principles of social co-existence, observe work discipline, maintain state and official secrets, deepen their knowledge and improve their qualifications (Article 17). At this point, it should be mentioned that the Act has undergone profound changes since 1982 until today. With the political and social changes, it was adapted to the new system, the archaic provisions were eliminated, adjusting it to the newly introduced regime.

The original version of the Act also did not forget to impose an obligation on the official to conscientiously carry out official instructions (Article 18), with the exception of instructions leading to the committing of an offence. It also formulated a prohibition on taking up additional employment without the prior approval of the head of the office (Article 19), as well as a prohibition on participating in a strike or action disrupting the normal functioning of the office. Every appointed official was subject to a compulsory qualification assessment every two years by the head of the office, against which there was a formal appeal procedure (Article 20). The nature of the civil servant's work consisted of full availability, which can also be found in the statutory regulations, including the possibility for the civil servant, for a period of three months in a calendar year, to be commissioned to do other work than that provided for in the employment contract or the appointment letter, but in line with his or her qualifications. In addition, it included the possibility of being transferred to work in another office, another locality or even being transferred to another post also lower down (Article 10). In exchange for an extensive catalogue of duties, civil servants received, apart from the stabilisation of the employment relationship expressed in the form of an appointment, a number of other rights as compensation for their dedication, while at the same time having the task of rebuilding the corporate character of this professional group, and above all making employment in the administration more attractive (Boć 2004: 228). It was necessary to change the image of the civil servant profession (using the terminology of the time for a government office employee), which had largely lost its value and quality between 1945 and 1982. The Act provided for a wide catalogue of additional entitlements: the possibility of promotion, long-service allowance, jubilee awards, awards from the prize fund, 50 % concessions for rail and bus travel, allowances from the company's social and housing fund, reimbursement of travel expenses, travel allowances, one-off allowances on retirement or disability. In addition, various types of awards and distinctions were provided for, including the one established by the Decree of the Council of Ministers of 8 November 1982 on detailed rules for the award of the badge of honour "Distinguished State Employee", the procedure for submitting applications for the award of the badge, the determination of the specimen of the badge and the procedure for its presentation and the manner of its wearing (Journal of Laws 1982. No. 39, item 262), the specimen of which, in an unchanged form in the form of a medal with the inscription "Distinguished State Employee of the People's Republic of Poland" engraved on the reverse, is still in force to this day. This regulation was issued on the basis of Article 31, section 4 of the Act of 16 September 1982 on State Officials' Employees (Journal of Laws 1982, No. 31, item 214, as amended), still in force, however, the legislator "forgot" to derogate the regulation.

The 1982 Act was passed when martial law was still formally in force, perhaps as an attempt to strengthen state institutions and the tasks performed by the state. The turbulent history of Poland (political, social and economic changes) caused the Act to be amended more than forty times in the twenty-six years between its enactment and the present day. The most serious amendment, introducing the most significant changes, was that of 2 December 1994. This amendment was commonly referred to as 'lex Strąk' and owes its name to the applicant (Mikułowski 2003a: 79). This amendment is seen in the literature as the beginning of the second stage of the Act. Stage one began when the Act came into force and lasted until 26 January 1995, after which stage two began (Ura 2004: 52). The basic novelty in the December amendment was a change in the way officials were employed, the institution of appointment was repealed and replaced by a contractual form of employment relationship or the use of an appointment letter indicated in the Act in certain cases. At the same time, without breaking the principle of acquired rights, it was decided that persons who had been appointed earlier would retain this status (Article 2 of the Act of 2 December 1994 amending the Act on civil servants) (Journal of Laws 1994, No. 136, item 734). The possibility of employment on the basis of appointment was also retained in the case of transfer of an official to work in another office, promotion or reinstatement on the basis of a final court decision (Liszcz 2005: 118–119). These changes are not controversial, as already since the beginning of the 1990s there have been works on the establishment of a civil service corps and the creation of a comprehensive regulation concerning government administration employees.

It should be borne in mind that when the Civil Service Act of 5 June 1996 entered into force, transitional provisions set a deadline of 31 December 2007 for the expiry of employment relationships for civil servants appointed under the 1982 Act on Civil Servants. In December 1998, another Civil Service Act was enacted, at the same time changing this deadline to 31 December 2003 (and subsequently extending it by an amendment in December 2003 to 31 December 2010). The subsequent Civil Service Act of August 2006 on the civil service returned to the deadline of 31 December

2007 as the final date until which employment relationships entered into on the basis of appointments can remain in force. When the 1998 Act was in force, a problem of interpretation arose, as Article 137 concerning the above matter was not very clearly drafted. It seems that the will of the legislator was that the termination of employment relationships by appointment should apply only to those officials who, at the time of the entry into force of the Civil Service Act, were included in the corps, while this provision did not apply to officials appointed on the basis of the 1982 Act (before the amendment of 27 January 1995) who were not included in the structures of the civil service corps (e.g. employees of the Chancellery of the Sejm, the Senate, the President or the Office of the Ombudsman). Accordingly, the employment relationships of appointed officials employed in the offices listed in Article 1(1) of the 1982 Act on Civil Servants, provided that they were appointed before 27 January 1995, remain in force (Galińska-Rączy 2003: 62–65; Jagielski&Rączka 2001: 366–369). As a result of the amendment, appointed and non-appointed officials employed on the basis of an employment contract can be distinguished in administrative offices. The formal and legal status of the two groups is different, especially with regard to the termination of the employment relationship, while at the same time there are no contraindications to holding identical positions. In the amended Act we find a kind of lex specialis concerning the termination of the employment relationship with an appointed official in the form of an enumerative catalogue of premises referred to in Art. 13–151, namely: receipt of a negative evaluation of qualification, confirmed by a new negative evaluation, which cannot be made earlier than after three months, liquidation of the office or its reorganisation if it is not possible to transfer the public servant appointed to another position in the same office, non-culpable loss of qualifications required to perform work in the occupied position, permanent loss of physical or mental capacity to work in the occupied position, established by a ruling of the medical commission for disability and employment, if it is not possible to employ the public servant appointed to another position, the age of 65, if the period of employment makes it possible for the civil servant to obtain the right to an old-age pension, a valid sentence of deprivation of public rights or the right to exercise the profession, validly punished with the disciplinary penalty of expulsion from work in the office, culpable loss of entitlements necessary to perform work in the occupied position, loss of Polish citizenship, absence from work due to illness lasting longer than one year or isolation due to contagious disease, excused absence from work for other reasons.

The norms of the general labour law will apply to other civil servants employed under a contract of employment. However, with regard to civil servants' duties, the legislator did not make such a distinction. The amendments (not only the one of 1994) adjusted the provisions of the Act to the new conditions of the political system, modifying obsolete formulations while leaving in place essential institutions such as: rights and duties, disciplinary liability, establishment, change and termination of the employment relationship. Employees of the political cabinets of the prime minister, deputy prime ministers and ministers, as well as advisors to other state managers, employed under the Act, constitute a separate category. An employment contract is concluded with these persons for the duration of the office of the holder of a state managerial position, with the possibility of early termination with two weeks' notice (Article 471). The provisions of the Act do not apply to these employees as, in the light of the implementing provisions, they are to be classified as so-called "other employees of the office" and their positions are not official positions. The solution applied is fundamentally correct, as the trust on which cooperation between members of the political cabinet and advisors with those in power must be based is a cardinal element in the efficient management and functioning of administrative structures. The closest collaborators, which include members of the political cabinet and advisors, must enjoy the full confidence of their superiors (Liszcz 2005: 123–124).

It is evident that the legislator, at least in some aspects, was motivated by the idea of returning to the pre-war regulation. By combining elements characteristic of administrative law with labour law institutions, a special legal status of state administration employee was created, regulated both by official pragmatics, as well as general labour law. However, it should be remembered that the employment of civil servants during the PRL was subject to an additional factor in the form of party subordination (the party-bureaucratic apparatus was the decision-maker). Thus, a characteristic feature of the system at the time was a significant level of politicisation of official positions, regardless of the level of administration (Górzyńska 2005: 4–6). A similar trend can also be observed today, for instance, in the local government sector, with the difference, however, that the filling of official positions depends in many cases on several co-governing groups. Due to the system in place at the time, there was no possibility of a full return to inter-war solutions, as this was prevented by the doctrine of a socialist state in which labour relations (according to the assumptions) were to be governed by general labour law. An administrative employee, on the other hand, had to be fully committed to the doctrine of the time (so-called ideological commitment) and to society, as it was for society that he or she performed his or her service. During the communist period, the administration, being fully subordinated to the party, performed various types of roles. This was aptly put by J. Itrich – Drabarek: "In the forties and fifties it was the armed arm of the state, in the sixties it fell into blissful stasis (…), while in the seventies it was supposed to be an inspirer and active participant in social life" (1998: 14).

Chapter 3
Rationale for the creation of a modern civil service corps in Poland after 1989

The system transformation, social, political and economic changes after the 1989 breakthrough were also the beginning of work on changes in the structure of public administration. The idea of a return to the interwar institution of the civil service had been germinating since the early 1990s, starting with the formation of the first non-communist government under Prime Minister Tadeusz Mazowiecki. It should be remembered that as early as 1990, local self-government was established at the municipal level, which was the first step in reforming the administration of a socialist state. The necessity to undertake an initiative in the form of a reform of public administration resulted from the need for changes in the system of state management, improvement of its effectiveness, improvement of the quality of services provided to citizens and, above all, system changes resulting directly from the system transformation (Domańska 1997: 49).

Work on reforming government administration began with the establishment, by Resolution No. 74 of the Council of Ministers of 30 May 1990, of the National School of Public Administration (KSAP). The work on reforming government administration began with the establishment, by Resolution No. 74 of the Council of Ministers dated 30 May 1990, of the National School of Public Administration (Monitor Polski No. 21, item 167) modelled on the French Ecole Nationale d'Administration, initially as a research and development unit, later transformed by the Act of 14 June 1991 on the National School of Public Administration (Journal of Laws No. 63, item 266 with amendments) into a state organisational unit. The legislator explicitly stated that the task of the School was to educate and prepare civil servants and senior civil servants of the Polish administration for public service (Art. 1, para. 2 of the Act), at the same time indicating an intention to create a civil service corps. It should be noted that, in 2009. The National School of Public Administration was the winner of the UN Award in the category: "Developing capacity for knowledge management in state institutions".

The first Director of KSAP was Associate Professor Maria Gintowt-Jankowicz, on whose initiative and under whose leadership, work began in September 1990 on a draft Act on the National Civil Service, which following international consultations (in France, the USA and the UK) was submitted to the Sejm in 1991 by Jan Krzysztof Bielecki's Government. The drafting team included, among others e. g. J. Łętowski and T. Górzyńska (Zonn-Pasternak 1993: 5). In 1991, Prime Minister Bielecki appointed two teams to develop a comprehensive reform of the administration. The task of one of them, the seven-member Team for the Reform of the State Administration, was to develop assumptions for the reform of central administration. At the same time, draft laws were being prepared in the Office of the Council of Ministers on the creation of a Ministry of Public Administration, a Chancellery of the Council of Ministers and a State Public Service.

Unfortunately, the plans were thwarted by the change of Cabinet and the appointment of Jan Olszewski's Government in December 1991, which, as early as in January 1992, created a Team for the Reorganisation of Public Administration, consisting of eleven people and headed by Senator Jerzy Stępień. The Team was tasked with drafting, among other things, a regulation of the status of public administration officials. The co-ordinator of the work on the new draft law on the State Civil Service was, as before, M. Gintowt – Jankowicz. After two months, the Team presented Preliminary assumptions for the reconstruction of public administration, and in May 1992 a preliminary version of the Act on the State Civil Service was ready. A version advised, among others, by experts from the UK Royal Institute of Public Administration RIPA International Ltd. (Zonn-Pasternak 1993: 5; Izdebski 2001: 231–232).

Another change of government in July that year stalled the reform work. In October 1992, Prime Minister Hanna Suchocka appointed Michal Kulesza as Plenipotentiary of the Council of Ministers for the Reform of Public Administration. Council of Ministers Plenipotentiary for Public Administration Reform – Michał Kulesza, leaving the Team appointed by Prime Minister Olszewski as temporary experts. The Plenipotentiary and his office functioned at the Office of the Council of Ministers. The result of the Plenipotentiary's work was the presentation in March 1993 (the third version) of the Assumptions and Directions of Reform of Public Administration, which in fact continued the work of previous groups and teams, as M. Kulesza had been an active participant in work on the reform of the entire public administration, including the Civil Service (Izdebski 2001: 232). Despite the fact that the then President Lech Wałęsa dissolved Parliament on 31 May, the government of H. Suchocka adopted a draft Act on the State Civil Service (7 September), and then submitted it to the Sejm for debate, additionally attaching an urgency clause to it (Zonn-Pasternak 1993: 6). It should be noted that work on the Law on the State Civil Service was conducted in the manner and within the timeframe previously established (Kulesza 1993: 70). In an April 1993 publication discussing Założenia i kierunki reformy administracji publicznej it was assumed that in the second quarter the draft, together with the implementing acts, would be sent to the Sejm and would become effective on 1 January 1994. The basic premise of the reform was the creation of an efficiently functioning civil service corps isolated from the influence of political decision-makers. The state civil service was to constitute an efficient executive element, carrying out tasks in a professional, informed, professional and politically neutral manner, while at the same time being a loyal servant of the state, which provides a large measure of stability in the employment relationship through appointment. The proposed amendments were aimed at creating the legal basis necessary for building professional public administration staff. At the same time, it was wanted to ensure equal, transparent and clear access to the service for all citizens. The building of administrative staff was to be based on a modern, managerial orientation, moving away from the traditional bureaucratic style of management. The aim was to recruit new staff while at the same time changing the way in which existing employees functioned (Kulesza 1993: 64–65).

The 1993 draft defined a very broad scope of subjects. Not only government administration employees were subject to the Act, but also employees employed in the Chancellery of the Sejm, the Senate, the President, the Office of the Ombudsman, the Supreme Chamber of Control, among others. The project envisaged the derogation of the previous 1982 regulations on civil servants and the creation of management structures for the entire civil service. It was planned to establish a Directorate General of the State Civil Service in the form of an office subordinate to the Prime Minister, headed by a Director General. State employees were divided into two categories: appointed civil servants and contract employees. Four civil servant categories were established, for which the examination was to be conducted by the State Civil Service Examination Commission. The draft was based on the principles of equal, transparent and open access to the service for all citizens. Appointment was introduced as an element of stabilisation of the employment relationship and a number of privileges for civil servants, which were of course compensation for their dedication. Elements related to the professional development and training of state civil servants were not omitted either. It should be remembered that the project was preceded by a survey on the public's opinion of civil servants. The results of a survey conducted in February 1993 were alarming, as only about 30 % of respondents described civil servants as competent and courageous, about 20 % thought they were politically independent, while 14 % said they were not susceptible to corruption (Zonn-Pasternak 1993: 77).

The parliamentary elections held on 19 September 1993 changed the balance of power on the political scene. A parliamentary majority was formed by the SLD-PSL coalition, which meant the formation of a new cabinet with Prime Minister Waldemar Pawlak. He decided to withdraw all bills from the Sejm, including those with an urgency clause. The result of the accelerated elections and the change of ruling team was the halting of work not only on the Civil Service Act, but on the entire reform of public administration. The Plenipotentiary appointed by Prime Minister H. Suchocka continued to function formally until May 1994, and by the time M. Kulesza resigned from the post, no new Plenipotentiary had been appointed. The Public Administration Reorganisation Team, on the other hand, functioned until 1995 as a body which, in practice, took no action (Izdebski 2001: 234). With the benefit of hindsight, it seems less important that the new Cabinet halted work on the reform, while the change of optics "(...) of the reform as a process of working out comprehensive solutions concerning the whole system of public services and only gradual implementation of its individual elements". – as H. Izdebski states, was a mistake that caused many years of delay and stagnation in this area.

The comprehensive assumptions for the reconstruction of the administration system developed in 1990–1993 were not used by the SLD-PSL coalition. In December 1994, the 1982 Law on Civil Servants was amended (as mentioned above) and a new draft Law on the State Civil Service was introduced, which no longer envisaged the elimination of the 1982 Law, but rather the coexistence of both pieces of legislation (Izdebski 2001: 234). Such steps clearly indicate a departure from the developed assumptions of the system reform and the introduction of ill-considered, chaotic changes nullifying the hitherto attempts at system transformation. Reluctance to change, perhaps a lack of ideas, or fear of socially unpopular decisions resulting in a drop in support among the electorate caused such an important process to be stalled. During its term of office, W. Pawlak's cabinet only used the draft law on public procurement and led to the enactment of the law on the system of the capital city of Warsaw.

In March 1995, there was another change of government team, with Józef Oleksy becoming Prime Minister, with the same balance of power in Parliament. The programme premise of the new government was to carry out the so-called "reform of the Government Economic Centre'. Later that same month, the Plenipotentiary of the Council of Ministers for the Reform of the Government Economic Centre, former Minister of Industry and Trade Marek Pol, was appointed. In June 1995. In June 1995, the Plenipotentiary presented the assumptions of the reform using projects and proposals prepared in 1990–1993 and established cooperation with the authors of earlier solutions, which had been interrupted by the government of W. Pawlak. In the course of work on the preparation of the reform, it turned out that it actually had to be extended. The reason for this was the impossibility of reforming some ministries without reorganising the Office of the Council of Ministers. One of the proposed solutions was to abolish the URM, replace it with the Chancellery of the Prime Minister and establish the office of the Minister of Public Administration. It turned out that, in essence, the reform was about the 'Administrative and Economic Centre of Government, and this is what it came to be called. The fruit of this work was the adoption by the Council of Ministers in November 1995 of a package of reform projects, which the Sejm began to deal with in March 1996 (Izdebski 2001: 235). In the meantime, on 15 February 1996, the new Cabinet of Włodzimierz Cimoszewicz came into office (with no change in the configuration of forces in Parliament). On 5 July 1996 the Law on the Civil Service (Journal of Laws 1996, No. 89, item 402) was passed as the first post-war regulation which regulated the functioning of the Civil Service Corps, but only within the government administration. The law, whose legal existence, for purely political reasons and partisan party interests, came to an end on 1 July 1999 with the entry into force of the subsequent Civil Service Act of 18 December 1998 (Journal of Laws 1996, No. 49, item 483).

The success of passing the Civil Service Act after many years of work and huge political disputes must be described as half-hearted. By 1 January 1997, when the Act came into force, a comprehensive reform of public administration had not been implemented. The creation of a civil service corps (a very elite and narrow group of officials – as envisaged by the 1996 Act) left a whole host of administration employees outside its structure. Their legal status was defined by the 1982 Act on State Office Employees. The solutions worked out in 1990–1993 were abandoned, without deciding to unify the principles of operation of individual segments of the administration through the introduction of a common legal act. The 1994 amendment of the Act on State Office Employees revealed the legislator's real intentions and his reluctance to introduce a thorough, systemic change in administration. The chaotic and haphazard creation of new solutions complicated the picture of organisational structures in the administration. The lack of political will, consensus and the very high instability of the political scene (frequent changes of government) caused the reform to be delayed and used during political bargaining as a kind of bargaining chip.

The state of the Polish administration in 1989 did not inspire optimism. Its shortcomings included: a great deal of organisational and technological backwardness, distorted relations between the two segments of the executive sphere (political and strictly administrative), a rigid bureaucratic style of administration, over-elaborate formalism characterised by protraction, inefficiency, over-expenditure, wasteful spending of public money, lack of a personnel management system, instability of staff employment, and the habits and stereotypes of administration employees. It is important to note the huge influence of the political decision-makers of the communist period when it comes to staffing or the decision-making process itself.

The situation therefore called not so much for ad hoc changes, but for systemic changes remodelling the entire administrative structure. It became necessary to create new institutions and methods of interaction, to improve the flow of information and the decision-making process, to introduce behaviours, attitudes, customs and values corresponding to the civil service, and above all a managerial approach. The administration should be based on a system of efficient management, smooth interaction of its individual levels, distribution of tasks, competences and responsibilities in a clear and transparent manner. Another problem of the Polish administration was the negative image of officials in the eyes of citizens. The designed system reform also aimed to change this area. Its absence not only entrenched negative stereotypes about civil servants, but also failed to strengthen the organisationally weak, nascent young democracy, while the focus on decommunization of offices failed to produce the expected results. The development of a legal framework for the construction of a civil service could have been at least the beginning of a path towards the creation of a (to a limited extent) apolitical, professional civil service. The process of shaping the idea of a civil service corps in Poland has its roots in the Second Republic.

The efficiently designed State Civil Service Act (1922) laid the foundations for the construction of the Corps, which was brutally interrupted by the Second World War. From today's perspective, it should be acknowledged that the framework of institutions that were created in 1922 provided a solid basis for the construction of a modern Civil Service Corps. In the period of the People's Republic of Poland, the existence of civil service corps structures as developed was negated. The new communist order, drawn from Soviet Union solutions, introduced revolutionary changes. During the period of systemic transformation, models from the Second Republic began to be sought. The institutional solutions of the Third Republic refer to the achievements of pre-war Poland, building contemporary structures on the model of those times. Of course, taking into account the changed social, political and economic environment, the new European and international situation, as well as different standards, EU membership and the experience of other countries. The People's Republic of Poland was institutionally a very different period, guaranteed by force and received with reluctance, as a foreign model. It is worth recalling, at this point, that after regaining independence in 1918, we also benefited from models, but they lacked the ideals of the Russian partition. The models used by the Polish state after the First World War were to be found in the Prussian and Austrian partitions. Institutionally, the People's Republic of Poland cut itself off from the solutions of the Second Republic, but it left its consequences in the form of problems with the reconstitution of the civil service corps after 1989.

Chapter 4
Political and legal conditions for the creation of the Civil Service Corps in Poland after 1996

The entry into force of the Civil Service Act of 5 July 1996 on 1 January 1997 was intended to mark the beginning of a new stage in the building of a professional, vocational and, above all, politically neutral administrative staff. The Act was intended as a kind of remedy for a politicised administration. Its purpose was to attempt to reconcile the political neutrality of civil servants with their subordination to the executive. The extended vacatio legis period was intended to prepare the implementing acts necessary for the functioning of the newly established organisational structures. The Act clearly referred to its pre-war predecessor of 1922, laying the foundations for the construction of an elite corps of civil servants with a separate legal status. Assuming that the process of creating the corps is a long-term one, the legislator envisaged, as of 1 January 2008, the transformation of employment relations on the basis of appointment (concluded on the basis of the 1982 Act on State Office Employees) into employment relations on the basis of an employment contract for an indefinite period (Article 95 of the 1996 Act).

It should be borne in mind that the 1996 Act, with its narrowed scope of subjectivity, complicated the already intricate matter of civil servant law in Poland. As a result of its entry into force, while at the same time failing to derogate from earlier regulations, too many categories of civil servants and employees of state offices were created. Z. Cieślak, J. Jagielski and K. Rączka in their commentary to the Act list the four most important categories, pointing out that:

> they do not exhaust the set of employees of the state administration apparatus, they include: civil service appointed officials, officials appointed on the basis of the 1982 Act on State Office Employees, contractual officials employed on the basis of an employment contract on the basis of the 1982 Act on State Office Employees, after its amendment of 1994, and officials appointed to positions on the basis of separate regulations (1998: 20–21).

It is an indisputable fact that seven years after the Round Table, the Third Republic, despite much turbulence on the political scene, lived to see a belated regulation of this matter. From the moment of its creation, the Act had many opponents, also in political circles. It was accused of having too narrow a scope of subjects, introducing an additional legal regime without tidying up the entire regulation, as well as the lack of a competitive procedure for filling posts and leaving this to the discretion of the director general of the office. Attention was also drawn to: the lack of introduction of judicial control over the rulings of disciplinary commissions; the exclusion of judicial control over decisions not to admit interested persons to the qualification procedure; and the exclusion of control over decisions on a candidate's failure to meet the requirements for admission to service in a particular category. According to B. Kudrycka: "(…) such a regulation raises doubts as to whether, in this very way, the legislator does not leave a gateway allowing for the informal application of non-substantive criteria (e.g. political) to the filling of posts, professional training and promotion of officials" (1997: 33–34).

Opponents of the Act also stressed that it introduced an excessively strict requirement of seven years' seniority for Category A officials (thus giving preference to those with a communist background, which was an obstacle to the formation of a young administration elite trained at KSAP), and failed to introduce any preferences for KSAP graduates (Kornaś 2001: 27–28). When the Act on the Civil Service was passed, there were great hopes and prospects for the creation of modern, educated and prepared human resources and public administration structures. It was very often heard among the political elite of the time that, thanks to the new regulations, at the beginning of the 21st century Poland would have a fully modern cadre, whose experience and professional qualifications would be systematically improved and put to new tests. Moreover, the objectives and tasks to be fulfilled by the Civil Service, as implemented, will place our country in the ranks of resilient and efficient administrations, oriented towards responsive service of the state and society. As can be seen, the expectations and assumptions surrounding the entry into force of the new civil service legislation have not been realized (Szachułowicz 1997: 40).

Today, years later, it can be concluded that the 1996 Act, despite the assumptions of its creators, has not become the basis for the creation of a civil service corps. According to the vast majority of doctrine, the main reason for this was not legislative or conceptual incorrectness, but the way in which the assumptions of the Act were implemented and realised in contact with political 'appetites' and the desire for absolute subordination of the service to political factors (Jagielski&Rączka 1998: 15). These accusations were formulated mainly by the then opposition, which, having seized power after the parliamentary elections, exploited them, impeding the process of building the civil service. The shortening of the legal existence of the Act was undoubtedly accelerated by the parliamentary elections of 1997 and the seizure of power by the Right. As a result of differing views on the organisation of the civil service, on 17 December 1997 Prime

Minister Jerzy Buzek appointed a team headed by Zbigniew Derdziuk, Secretary of State in the Prime Minister's Office. The team was tasked with analysing and summarising the results to date in creating an impartial, reliable and neutral civil service. The report, published in February 1998, paints a frightening picture with a whole range of shortcomings, infringements and flaws, but most importantly with a conclusion in the form of preparing a new law on the civil service as soon as possible (Raport 1998: 5–12). The team analysed the implementation of the Act's provisions by the responsible bodies, i.e. the Prime Minister, the Head of the Civil Service and the Qualification Commission. The Prime Minister was accused of taking as long as six months to appoint the Head of the Civil Service, and of appointing a person whose candidacy had been negatively assessed by the Civil Service Council. In contrast, it took him more than 8 months to appoint the Qualification Commission. Moreover, the Prime Minister failed to issue a number of normative acts, which the law obliged him to issue, e.g. with regard to determining the periods taken into account when determining the period of service of a civil servant. To the Head of the Civil Service, the team led by Derdziuk accused, inter alia, the following: failure to prepare, prior to the announcement of the recruitment, the classification of positions in the civil service within the categories of civil servants, as he was obliged to do by Article 24(1)(3); failure to disseminate information about the service; failure to conduct any information campaign; publishing the announcement of the recruitment procedure only once and that in the middle of the holiday season (25 July 1997). The Head of the Civil Service admitted 514 persons to the qualification procedure who had certificates from the A. Pushkin Institute of the Russian Language in Moscow, which testify to knowledge of the language at a basic level, while according to the Resolution of the Qualification Commission of 16 July 1997, at least an intermediate level of proficiency was required. Between 1 October and 24 November, 26 persons holding a certificate from the Pushkin Institute were appointed. The Qualification Commission was pointed out that it had violated Article 30(1) of the Act by failing to verify the knowledge of a foreign language, but merely contenting itself with the information that the relevant certificate was in its possession. No provision was made to exclude the participation of the members of the Qualification Commission, the Civil Service officials involved in the preparation of the procedure and the authors of the examination questions in the qualification procedure. This resulted in the appointment of six members of the Qualification Commission and two directors and two general councillors from the Civil Service Office, who were admitted to the proceedings despite their participation in the preparation of the proceedings. Among the 115 appointees (between 1 October and 24 November) were 50 persons who, by political appointment of Prime Minister W. Cimoszewicz, held office by entrustment (Article 93), including: 18 directors-general in ministries and central offices, 32 directors-general of provincial offices. These are just some examples from a long list of allegations made by Derdziuk's team, accusing the service bodies of carelessness and unreliability, bias and partisanship (Raport 1998: 5–12).

In response, in the Civil Service Bulletin No. 5(11) of May 1998 there were published Notes to the "Report on the Analysis and Assessment of the Creation of the Civil Service" by the former Head J. Szachułowicz and a Position to the "Report on the Analysis and Assessment of the Creation of the Civil Service (August 1996-September 1997)" regarding the assessment of the functioning of the Civil Service Qualification Commission by the former Commission Chairwoman Z. Stawowiak. The authors of the comments accused Derdziuk's team of being biased and unreliable and of making unfounded accusations. They denied any violations considering the allegations as frivolous. Without prejudging whether the Derdziuk-led team's report was prepared in an honest or biased manner (as the audit would have to be carried out again), the effects it has had on the Polish administration are not optimistic. The construction of the Civil Service Corps that began at the beginning of 1997 was put on hold until July 1999. The lack of consensus among the various political options as to the shape of the corps, as well as the attempt by all political parties to dominate the nascent administrative cadre, certainly caused even greater inhibition in this already significantly delayed matter. Moreover, as noted in the doctrine, the change after such a short period of time of the model assumptions is a completely unprecedented phenomenon, "violating the principle of permanence and predictability of the democratic legal order", as well as causing destabilisation and introducing considerable elements of uncertainty (Mikułowski 2003: 81).

The elections, which resulted in a change in the political scene, led to the acceleration of work on a new civil service regulation. At the same time, the Prime Minister, as head of the corps, halted the qualification procedures for the service, de facto, stopping recruitment. The new government team accused the previous one of politicising the higher positions in the civil service in particular, undermining the credibility of the qualification procedures and appointments carried out so far. The opposition, on the other hand, believed that the new government, by amending the law and halting the recruitment and appointment process, wanted to appropriate the service, filling positions on a political basis (Szachułowicz 1998: 12–14; Stawowiak 1998: 14–16; Gąciarz 1998: 16–20). This period also saw a change in the position of Head of the Civil Service, with J. Szachułowicz replaced by J. Pastwa, and on 12 November 1997 Prime Minister J. Buzek dismissed the Head of the Civil Service. On 12 November 1997, Prime Minister J. Buzek dismissed the Chair of the Qualification Commission – Z. Stawowiak, which at the same time meant the suspension of the qualification procedure for those already admitted to it. The reason for this state of affairs was the fact, as reported in the press at the time, that:

> (…) shortly before the elections, Prime Minister W. Cimoszewicz appointed 18 directors general of departments in a number of ministries and several central offices. The administration supervisor L. Miller in turn appointed 49 directors-general in provincial offices.

> Some of them had left the SdRP or the PSL just before receiving their appointments, as under the law a high civil servant must be non-partisan (Andrzejewski 2000)[1].

On 21 April 1998, an inter-ministerial team was set up by the Prime Minister to prepare new solutions in the civil service. On 9 June 1998, the Council of Ministers adopted the document prepared by this team despite the negative opinion of the Civil Service Council of 15 May. The Civil Service Council determined that it was inadvisable and premature to enact a new Civil Service Act, recommending an amendment to the existing Act. Consultation of the Council was provided for as a statutory requirement (Kornaś 2001: 22).

In November 1998. In November 1998, the CSC passed another negative opinion on the implementation of the new law on the civil service (Kornaś 2001: 23), but the Sejm on 18 December 1998 passed a new law without any consultation with either civil servants' representatives or the scientific community. Even before the enactment of the new law, the National Assembly passed the 1997 Constitution, which in Article 153 of the Act on the Civil Service. Constitution, which in Article 153 defined the basis for the functioning of the civil service, narrowing its subjective scope to government administration only. The fate of the 1998 Act on the Civil Service (Journal of Laws of 1999, No. 49, item 483, as amended) began with an application to the Constitutional Tribunal by the then President of the Republic of Poland, A. Kwaśniewski, for an examination of the compliance of certain provisions of the Act with the Constitution. The President's request concerned Articles 2(1)(6) and (7), 15(3), 82(3), 83(3), 87(3) of the Act. Apart from Article 2(1)(6) and (7), the remaining provisions of the Act were found by the Court to be compatible with the Constitution. In doing so, it clarified that the challenged provisions of Article 2 are not inseparable from the entire Act. Therefore, there will be no legal obstacles to the entry into force of the Act (Judgment of the Constitutional Tribunal of 28 April 1999, Sign. K. 3/99). In its judgement of 28 April 1999, the Constitutional Tribunal stated that the provisions of the Act incorporating into the civil service corps persons employed outside the offices of government administration (i.e. employees of regional chambers of audit and local government appeal colleges) were unconstitutional. In the case of the remaining contested provisions, the Court did not find any irregularities.

The new Civil Service Act came into force on 1 July 1999. Many questions and doubts arise when the legislator decides, after such a short period of time, to enact a new act, rather than merely making corrections and adjustments through an amendment. The fundamental question is, of course, whether the new act was intended to improve the existing situation and was dictated by substantive considerations or was

---

1 Between January 1997 and January 1998, more than 200 articles on the establishment of the civil service corps were shown in the national press (including Rzeczpospolita, Gazeta Wyborcza, Polityka, Wprost, Gazeta Prawna, Życie) – most of them critical of the ways and effects of the implementation of the Act.

merely a political decision pursuing the partisan interest of the group currently in power. Furthermore, the question arises as to whether, after such a short period in force, it is possible to reliably assess how the objectives of the law have been achieved. The official argumentation supporting the introduction of the new act was as follows – to put in order and standardise legislation concerning all civil servants, to ensure equal, open and competitive access to the civil service, to harmonise regulations on the civil service with the Constitution of the Republic of Poland, to introduce norms converging with EU standards in view of accession to the EU, and also to adapt the administration to the forthcoming administrative reform of the country (Urząd Służby Cywilnej 1999). Indeed, there were many shortcomings, gaps and issues that needed more precise regulation in the 1996 Act, but the method of solving the problems in the form of eliminating the Act from legal circulation instead of amending it raises doubts.

The civil service model that was proposed in the 1998 Act differed from the one developed two and a half years earlier. Above all, the subject scope of the Act changed. The corps included all persons employed in government administration, regardless of the manner in which the employment relationship was established (in contrast to the previous regulations, when the corps was narrowed down to appointed officials only). As a result, the number of members of the Civil Service Corps increased from 104 persons on 1 January 1999 to around 116,000 on 31 December 1999 (Ura 2007: 115). It seemed that the 1998 Act would be the basis for building a civil service corps in Poland. Despite its imperfections and shortcomings, as well as the successive unfavourable changes introduced by successive government teams, it continued to function until 2006, at the same time creating hope for the stabilisation of service regulations and the realisation of the goal of building the corps. After the 2005 elections, when Law and Justice won the election and formed a government and coalition with Self-Defence and League of Polish Families, a significant, albeit negatively assessed amendment of the 1998 Civil Service Act was made. By the Act of 10 March 2006 amending the Act on local government employees, the Act on the Supreme Chamber of Control and the Act on the civil service (Journal of Laws No. 79, item 549), provisions were introduced allowing for the transfer to the civil service of former employees of the Supreme Chamber of Control and local government administration. In addition, the obligation for the Director General to inform the public about vacant positions if they are filled by, for example, a local government employee or a person from the Supreme Audit Office was dropped. The amendment received harsh criticism, the then Head of the Civil Service Council, Marek Rocki commented on it as follows:

> The amendment to the law adopted by the Senate means first and foremost the decentralisation of the management of the civil service. It is the result of the head of the civil service losing control over what happens in his subordinate units. It is also wrong that the appointment of civil servants will be on the basis of transfers rather than competitions. During the debate on the amendment, the Civic Platform put forward an amendment that

> would have provided that the director general would inform the head of the civil service of transfers made to individual posts. However, this proposal was rejected (Urzędnik bez konkursu 2006).

The amendment resulted in two motions to the Constitutional Tribunal, dated 17 and 19 May 2006, submitted by the parliamentary club of the Democratic Left Alliance and the Civic Platform club to examine the compatibility of the amending act with the Constitution. In decisions of 27 November 2007 (Ref. K 14/06) and 28 November 2007 (Ref. K 41/06), the Constitutional Tribunal discontinued the proceedings due to the inadmissibility of adjudication, as on 7 September 2007 the 5th Sejm passed a resolution on shortening the term of office, thus, in accordance with the principle of the discontinuation of the works of the Sejm, the right to appear before the Tribunal was also lost for the applicants, so the Tribunal could not adjudicate on the merits of the case.

According to J. Jagielski, the amendment of March 2006 entails unfavourable transformations in the corps involving the entry into the structure of the corps of persons who do not meet the statutory criteria, and this constitutes an easy way to fill posts according to various "keys, recommendations, party affiliations", leading in consequence to personnel management in the civil service in a subjective manner in response to short-term political needs (2006: 214). On 24 August 2006, another Act on the Civil Service (Journal of Laws No. 170, item 1218) and a closely correlated Act on the State Human Resources and High State Positions (Journal of Laws No. 170, item 1217) were passed. Again, the successive ruling team changed the conception of the civil service corps (the term public service began to be used – understanding it as the civil service and the State Personnel Resources). It should be remembered that the new laws were preceded by another parliamentary election in 2005 and the alternation of power. The legal acts of 2006, which are not currently in force, changed the idea of the civil service to a large extent, in a way disrupting the formula developed so far. The basic change was the exclusion of senior state positions from the Civil Service Act and their inclusion in the State Personnel Pool – a special 'pool' of persons with whom senior state positions can be filled, based on appointment by decision of the Prime Minister or a specific minister. The wave of criticism that followed the enactment of the new laws and the subsequent accelerated parliamentary elections caused the new government of the Civic Platform and the Polish People's Party to begin work on another law on the civil service (at the same time a parliamentary draft amendment to the Civil Service Act was also tabled). By a resolution of the Council of Ministers of 22 January 2008 on the completion of the public administration reform, it was decided to start work on amending the Act on the Civil Service and the State Personnel Resources. Earlier, on 15 November 2007, the Left and Democrats parliamentary club submitted a parliamentary bill on amending the Civil Service Act. Consequently, the two draft amendments were considered together. As a result, on 21 November 2008, a new Act on the Civil

Service was passed (Journal of Laws No. 227, item 1505, as amended), at the same time derogating from the Acts of 2006, abolishing the State Human Resources. The Act came into force on 24 March 2009. From March 2009, i. e. from the entry into force of the 2008 Act, until January 2016, i. e. until the latest amendment to the legislation (of December 2015), there was continuous work on the construction of the corps position. During this period, in principle, there were no major amendments that changed the concepts of the civil service or radically affected the way it operated. This time was undoubtedly conducive to "rooting" the introduced solutions. The laborious building of permanent mechanisms for the operation of government administration, based on decent normative foundations. The most recent amendment to the Civil Service Act of 2015 was also preceded by an alternation of powers. In the October 2015 elections, Law and Justice won a landslide victory. A success big enough to enable it to form a government on its own without the need for a cabinet coalition. One of the first decisions, already announced during the election campaign, was a change concerning the civil service. However, as in 2006, it was not decided to create a new normative act, but only to amend the existing solutions. Ten years later, Law and Justice, while in power again, modified the concept of the civil service, albeit in a milder way than in 2006. However, the solutions implemented in 2016 refer to the concept from 2006. The legislator made changes both in the structural dimension (Head of the S. C., S. C. Council), but above all in the conceptual one, which concerns mainly the filling of higher positions and their location in the structure of the corps. By the Act of 30 December 2015 amending the Civil Service Act and certain other acts (Journal of Laws 2016, No. 0, item 34), few changes were introduced, however of fundamental importance. The legislative process itself, due to its speed, was questionable. On 15 December, the draft was brought by a group of MPs, hence there was no obligation to hold public consultations as in the case of government drafts. On the same day, it was referred for the first reading at the session of the Sejm, which took place on 17 December 2015, the project was then referred to the Committee on Administration and Internal Affairs and on 22 December the Committee presented a report with a proposal for the Sejm to pass the law. On 29 December, the draft was referred to the second reading at the Sejm and then again to the Committee on Administration and Internal Affairs. Work in the Committee continued on 29 and 30 December, during which time the government's position was also received. The third reading in the Sejm also took place on 30 December and ended with the passing of the law. On 31 December, the Senate expressed its position with no amendments and the law was forwarded to the President of the Republic of Poland on the same day. On 7 January 2016. The President of the Republic of Poland signed the amending act and, after a vacatio legis of 14 days, the legislation became effective. The first of the doubts raised during the work in the Commission was the mode of bringing the bill as a parliamentary bill, which is not subject to the obligation of public consultation. In the main, it was argued that a change in the concept of filling senior positions by eliminating competitions, with momentous consequences for the functioning of the entire structure, should be preceded by a widespread public consultation. During the meeting of the Commission on 21 December 2015, Marek Wojcik, Member of the Civic Platform, submitted a request for a public hearing (Pełny zapis przebiegu posiedzenia Komisji Spraw Wewnętrznych i Administracji 2015) addressed, inter alia, to the representation of employees and civil servants and to trade union headquarters. The request was rejected. Another objection to the amendment was the pace of the work – 15 days from the moment the bill was brought to the floor. Too much haste, according to the opposition, did not allow for a thorough analysis of the proposed solutions. The draft was also accused of having too short a vacatio legis period – 14 days. It was argued that due to the importance of the changes, this period is insufficient to implement the new solutions. Since the statutory requirement to consult the Civil Service Council (Article 19 of the Act) had not been fulfilled, on 18 December 2015, the Civil Service Council adopted the draft. The Civil Service Council passed a resolution on the proposed solutions, criticising the omission of the statutory obligation. The Council also drew attention to the fact that the materiality of the matter should have influenced a broad public debate with various circles: experts, members of the civil service corps or academia (Civil Service Council Resolution 135 of 18 December 2015). The most serious objection to the amendment is the abandonment of open and competitive recruitment for senior positions. Competitions have been replaced by the institution of appointment. Between 1996 and 2016, successive governments introduced new legislation regulating the functioning of the service four times, not to mention multiple amendments to laws.

In retrospect, it can be seen that the Polish government administration is subjected to constant change, which makes it impossible to consolidate any solutions that would create stability. Staffing it with so-called "own people" seems to be the first and most important step after winning an election. Regardless of political hue, each political option in power "tinkers" with the civil service. As a result, thirty years after the change of political system, Poland does not have an educated civil service corps, and the prospects for further new solutions do not inspire optimism. The impression can be gained that successive governments fear disloyalty on the part of civil servants, believing that governing will be possible only with the help of civil servants they themselves employ. It seems to me that the Polish political class does not grasp the idea of a civil service, behaving as if it did not know the principle developed already during the Third French Republic that "governments and parliaments leave and administrations remain". One gets the impression that Polish politicians do not treat the administration as a guardian protecting the public interest while maintaining loyalty to any government.

4.1 Personal scope of civil service acts

The 1996 Act stipulated that: "In order to ensure professional, reliable, impartial and politically neutral performance of the tasks of the state, a civil service is established". This provision was found in essentially unchanged form in the subsequent Service Acts of 1998, 2006, 2008 and also in the 2015 amendment. Most importantly, however, this kind of formulation is reflected in Article 153 of the 1997 Constitution. The constitutional empowerment testifies to the importance of the matter, the validity of the institution. The Constitution prejudged that the corps operates only in government administration thus narrowing its subject scope considerably. In none of the post-war laws will we find a definition of the civil service (nor was there one in the law of 1922). The legislator defines the essence of the corps by indicating its purpose, which is to perform the tasks of the state (but in an appropriate manner indicated by it, i. e. – neutrally, professionally, reliably and impartially). It treats it objectively, as stated by Z. Cieślak, J. Jagielski, K. Rączka: "(…) as a category signifying a peculiar, special formula for the performance of state tasks by the staff" (1998: 11). In other words, it defines the corpus by indicating the ways in which state tasks are performed by a particular category of employees.

In contrast to the public-legal nature of the employment relationship as introduced by the 1922 Act, all laws after 1989 did not have such an arrangement. Persons employed in the civil service are in an employment relationship, and the employing entity is a specific government administration office. This is particularly evident in the 1998 and 2006 Acts, in which identical-sounding Article 7 refers to the Labour Law regulations in matters not regulated. Also the 2008 Act, in Article 9, refers to the Labour Code, covering all members of the corps, both employees and civil servants. It should be remembered that we will also find here a specific manner of regulating certain elements of the employment relationship, separate from the typical Code one (Liszcz 2005: 24). In the case of the 1996 Act, on the other hand, the situation was not so clear-cut, as the employing entity was the state and not a specific administrative office. This introduced a certain element of the public-legal nature of the employment relationship. Its combination with elements of labour law meant that, under the 1996 Act, the service did not constitute a uniform institution. In turn, the legislator itself did not explicitly define the category of the civil service relationship (Cieślak at al. 1998: 15–16).

Most changes over the ten years concerned the scope of the subject matter of the civil service corps. The first Service Act after the political breakthrough considerably narrowed the subject scope. The Act specified that the members of the corps were officials employed in government administration offices only on the basis of appointment. Outside the cognisance of the Act remained contract civil servants, service employees and political advisors, as well as local government administration and part of the state administration (chancelleries of the Sejm, the Senate, the President, the Office of the Ombudsman for Civil Rights, the Constitutional Tribunal, the National Broadcasting

Council, the National Electoral Office, court administration and the Main and Field Inspectorates of the State Labour Inspectorate and the Supreme Chamber of Control). The 1982 Act applied to these groups. Thus, the Act covered only a narrow group of officials performing tasks in offices subordinate to the President of the Council of Ministers, chief state administration bodies, central administration bodies and field bodies (Cieślak at al. 1998: 18–19).

Two and a half years later, the legislator changed the subject concept of the corps to include all employees employed in government administration, regardless of the fact of having the status of a civil servant. At the same time, two categories of corps members were distinguished: employees and civil servants, and higher positions in the civil service were defined. As a result – as I have written about it – the corps grew from 104 members (as at 1 January 1999) to approximately 116,000 people, including 99 civil servants (as at 31 December 1999). In the light of Art. 2 of the Act, the corps was made up of employees of the Chancellery of the Prime Minister, offices of ministers and chairpersons of committees making up the Council of Ministers, central offices, voivodeship offices, offices constituting auxiliary apparatus of territorial bodies of government administration, the Government Centre for Strategic Studies, commands, inspectorates and other organisational units constituting auxiliary apparatus, managers of voivodeship and some poviat joint services, inspections and guards.

Since, at the time the 1998 Act came into force, Article 153 of the Constitution narrowing the civil service to government administration was already in force, an amendment to the Constitution would have been necessary to widen the subject scope. Legal expert opinions on the extension of the civil service corps to other organisational units performing public administration tasks (i. e. local government) in the light of Article 153 of the Constitution, are mostly negative (Radziewicz 2005: 27–29). Which means that without a constitutional amendment there is no legal possibility to extend the civil service corps to other units not belonging to government administration. This was also the view of the Constitutional Tribunal, which on several occasions repealed regulations which included in the civil service corps employees who are not hierarchically subordinate to the Prime Minister (e. g. officers of local government appeals boards). In connection with the fact that the then President of the Republic of Poland, A. Kwaśniewski, in 1999 challenged certain provisions of the Civil Service Act to the Constitutional Tribunal, the CT in its ruling of 28 April 1999 stated that:

> The constitutional location of the civil service corps in government administration offices and the establishment of its subordination to the President of the Council of Ministers as its superior excludes the statutory extension of this corps to segments of the state not belonging to government administration. Article 153 of the Constitution limits the scope of the civil service, subject to the authority of the Prime Minister, to government administration offices. The provisions of the constitution that normalize the scope of activities and competences of government bodies must be interpreted strictly. Extension of the civil

> service corps to segments of the state other than government administration by the ordinary legislator would be an unacceptable modification of the constitutional system. For one thing is government administration and another is self-government or state administration, although all three may be regarded as public administration.

This did not in any way prevent the coalition government of PiS, LPR and Samoobrona from introducing in March 2006 an amendment concerning the transfer to the civil service corps of local government employees and employees of the Supreme Chamber of Control – Act of 10 March 2006 amending the Act on local government employees, the Act on the Supreme Chamber of Control and the Act on the civil service (Journal of Laws. No. 79, item 549). The justification states that the amendments aim to "to introduce a mechanism allowing for a flexible and rational personnel policy in public administration" – draft Act amending the Act on local government employees, the Act on the Supreme Chamber of Control and the Act on the civil service, together with an explanatory memorandum addressed to the Speaker of the Sejm on 6 January 2006 (Uzasadnienie 2006: 6).

The transfer was to be made by the director general of the office in agreement with the current employer. From the outset, these provisions raised constitutional doubts, as they allowed the status of a member of the civil service corps (civil servant and employee) to be obtained without meeting the selection rigours provided for in the Service Act. The above solutions seemed to contradict Article 60 of the Constitution, which provides all Polish citizens with the right of access to the service on equal terms. Meanwhile, these changes created preferences for two groups of administrative employees. Recruitment to another office does not necessarily have to meet the prerequisites of openness and competitiveness in the same way as recruitment to the civil service. (Działocha&Łukaszczuk 2006: 12–15; Bronowska 2006: 2–3).

Conceiving of flexibility and rationality as a possibility to create mechanisms allowing for the circumvention of regulations may consequently indicate attempts to fill the positions with specific people, and above all raises concerns about the purity of the legislator's intentions and suspicion of an attempt to politicise the positions.

A few months after the aforementioned amendment, the legislator decided to implement different solutions in the form of new legal acts significantly changing the previous regulations. The subjective scope of the civil service corps was narrowed as a result of the elimination of senior positions from it and their transfer to the newly created State Personnel Corps. What remained in the corps, therefore, were employees employed in middle-management, coordinating, independent, specialist, and support clerical positions (Article 2(1) of the 2006 Act). The term that the corps operates in government administration was removed from Article 1 of the Service Act. On the other hand, the following were included in the PZK – i. e. the set of candidates for high state positions (Article 4 of the Act): heads of central offices and their deputies, presidents of state agencies and their deputies, presidents of boards of state funds and their deputies, the Secretary of the Council of Ministers, provincial veterinarians and their deputies. In addition, the following were included in the PZK: managers of state organisational units with their deputies reporting to the Prime Minister, managers in the foreign service, directors general of offices and managers of departments or equivalent units in ministries, central offices, offices serving the chairpersons of committees that make up the Council of Ministers, the Chancellery of the Prime Minister, provincial offices. The Act introduced a kind of dualism, subjecting the PZK to a separate legal regime, singling out a special category of officials (incidentally, the highest, or most important officials) from the civil service corps. At the same time, it resulted in the fact that, in principle, in every organisational unit of the administration (e.g. an office, a committee, a ministry) we have to deal with persons employed in the civil service and persons belonging to the State Personnel Corps (PZK). In the light of Article 153 of the Constitution, discussed above, the Service operates in government administration and there is no possibility of limiting the operation of this provision to only a part of that administration by casually excluding certain (and in addition the most important) posts. This view is expressed by the vast majority of the doctrine (Izdebski 2006; Działocha 2006; Ura 2006). At the turn of June and July 2006, commissioned by the Office of Analyses of the Sejm Chancellery, well-known specialists, scientists, experts analysed the proposed solutions. Opinions were expressed, inter alia, by: Prof. Dr. Elżbieta Ura, Prof. Dr. Hubert Izdebski, Prof. Dr. Kazimierz Działocha, Prof. Dr. Grzegorz Rydlewski, Prof. Dr. Artur Nowak – Far, Prof. Dr. Helena Szewczyk, Prof. Dr. Jakub Stelina, Irena Galińska – Rączy (expert on legislation). All of the aforementioned persons subjected, inter alia, the solutions concerning the limitation of the personal scope of the civil service corps to severe criticism. In the justification of the law, reference was made to the possibility of flexible shaping of the employment relationship of senior civil servants due to the importance and scope of the tasks performed related to the implementation of government policy. According to the drafters, the exclusion of senior positions from the corps will ensure efficient cooperation between the civil service apparatus and the political sphere (Explanatory Memorandum to the Draft Law on State Personnel and High State Positions 2006). The above solutions lead to the conclusion that, in fact, the legislator's only intention was to politicise the most important part of the civil service, the managerial and decision-making staff.

The 2008 Civil Service Act abolished the State Personnel Resource by including senior state positions back into the ranks of the Civil Service Corps. The Corps is made up of employees of: the Chancellery of the Prime Minister, offices of ministers and chairpersons of committees making up the Council of Ministers, central offices, voivodeship offices, offices constituting auxiliary apparatus of territorial government administration bodies, commands, inspectorates and other organisational units constituting auxiliary apparatus, managers of complex services, inspections and voivodeship guards as well as some poviat and border veterinary doctors and their deputies (Article 2). Thus, the solutions adopted in 1998 were returned to, expanding the catalogue to include employees: The Office for Registration of Medicinal Products, Medical Devices and Biocidal Products, the Forest Seed Office, budgetary units servicing state special purpose funds, whose administrators are government administration bodies (Article 2, paragraph 1, points 5, 6, 7). In the course of work on the Act, the scientific community postulated that the situation of public servants should be tidied up by eliminating the Act of 16 September 1982 on employees of public offices from legal circulation and subjecting them to the regime of the Civil Service Act, but the legislator did not decide on this step (Szewczyk 2008). Currently, both civil servant pragmatics are in force, one concerning persons subject to the civil service regime and the other on civil servants. The most recent amendment to the Act in December 2015 did not exclude senior positions from the corps, but changed the mode of filling them (by eliminating competitions). However, in the doctrine, we find contrary positions (Culepa 2016: 7).

At the same time, as rightly noted by the National Council of Legal Advisers, in its opinion to the amendment, a completely separate status of a person employed in a senior position in the civil service not subject to some of the statutory rigours was created (Position of the Centre for Research, Studies and Legislation of the National Council of Legal Advisers 2015).

4.2 Legal nature of the employment relationship of a Civil Service Corps member

4.2.1 Categories of members of the Civil Service Corps

As I have already mentioned above, the 1996 Act created the institutional and legal framework for the Civil Service Corps, which consisted only of civil servants employed on the basis of appointment (alternatively, on the basis of separate provisions, the legislator was able to apply the Act to civil servants of other offices – Art. 3, para. 2). At the same time, the Act created a catalogue of prerequisites that had to be met by a candidate for civil servant (Article 4); these included: Polish citizenship, enjoyment of full public rights, no criminal record for an offence committed through intentional guilt, possession of the qualifications and predispositions required for appointment to the civil service, impeccability of character, a state of health permitting employment in the civil service, and the possibility of full-time employment. Fulfilment of the above conditions only created the formal possibility of applying for employment in the civil service, i. e. the possibility of entering the qualification procedure. However, without a guarantee of appointment, as this was left to the discretion of the administrative authority even in the situation of positive verification during the qualification procedure (Cieślak at al. 1998: 31). The law introduced the division of civil servants into four categories (A, B, C, S), constructing for each of them characteristics only in the form of overly vague definitions of education, professional preparation, skills and personality traits (Article 28).

At the same time, it was left to the Prime Minister to establish, in the form of a regulation, additional qualification requirements for persons entering the procedure. It was alleged in the law that the criteria introduced were undefined, not very clear and ambiguous phrases (e. g. ability to cooperate, creativity, ability to lead large teams of people). The lack of a clear system for valuing posts could be the basis for subjective assessments and, consequently, lead to posts being filled in a way that deviates from the idea of the civil service (Ura 1998: 125–126; Cieślak at al. 1998: 92–93). In practice, it was not possible to ascertain whether the legislative imprecision would lead to abuse as the legislator changed the structure of the corps. The 1998 Act introduced a general division of members of the civil service corps into: civil servants – i. e. persons employed on the basis of an employment contract and civil servants – i. e. persons employed on the basis of an appointment.

The corpus was expanded to include all persons employed in government administration regardless of the method of employment relationship. At the same time, civil servant categories were abolished. The employment prerequisites listed in Article 4 had to undergo some modification. The qualifications and aptitude required for appointment were replaced by civil service qualifications. The indefinite phrase *impeccable character* was replaced by *good repute*. The rigour of adequate health and full-time employment was removed. The second category of members of the civil service corps – civil servants – was established on the basis of appointment. In this case the legislator also introduced selection rigours in the form of (Art. 28): current employment in the civil service with at least two years' seniority in the corps, completion of preparatory service, possession of a master's degree or equivalent, knowledge of at least one foreign language confirmed by a certificate, not being subject to compulsory national defence or being a soldier in the reserves. Fulfilment of the above requirements only entitled the candidate to take part in the qualification procedure, the successful completion of which did not necessarily result in an appointment. The 2006 Civil Service Act did not actually change much in this respect. It left the division between employees and civil servants. There were identical selection requirements for employees (Article 4), while for civil servants the obligation to complete preparatory service was dropped and knowledge of foreign languages was narrowed down to the working languages of the European Union. This solution was also subjected to a seemingly fair amount of criticism. Particularly when it comes to officials employed in local administration offices. It was requested that one of the criteria should be the introduction of a good command of the Polish language: "(…) which in Poland is the basic official language, with which some public administration employees unfortunately have problems" (Szewczyk 2006). The requirement of two years' seniority was replaced by three years' seniority with the possibility of earlier application to join the qualification procedure with the consent of the director general of the office, however, not earlier than after two years from the beginning of the employment relationship (Article 19). This solution has been criticised because of the wide discretion of the director general and the lack of definition of the circumstances giving rise to an exception to the rule (Galińska – Rączy 2006). The qualification procedure was also kept essentially unchanged, only the body responsible for its conduct changed (the Head of the Civil Service was replaced by the National School of Public Administration). The exclusion of senior positions from the civil service and their placement in the State Personnel Resources resulted in the emergence of yet another category – senior civil servants, to whom a separate legal regime applied. From the point of view of the executive sphere of the state, these are strategic positions, which in the previous legal state (the 1998 Act) belonged to the higher positions in the civil service. At the same time, the legislator did not include the principle of political neutrality in Article 1 of the Act, specifying that the PZK is created in order to ensure professional, impartial and reliable performance of tasks.

In the light of the Act (Article 6), the State Personnel Resources (PZK) were composed of: civil servants, persons who had successfully passed an examination, persons who had won a competition announced by the Prime Minister, persons appointed by the President of the Republic of Poland as Plenipotentiary Representatives of the Republic of Poland in other countries and at international organisations, persons holding a doctoral degree. As a consequence, civil servants have been subjected to two separate legal regimes, both the Civil Service Act and the State Personnel Resources Act. The State Personnel Resource was also formed by persons discharged from professional military service performed in an official position at the Ministry of National Defence or a local government administration body subordinate to the Minister of National Defence, if the last official position occupied by such persons during their service was a position related to the management of a department or an equivalent unit at that Ministry. Membership of the resource lasted for ten years, after which it was necessary to pass an examination authorising re-entry into the resource. In the original version of the law adopted by the Seimas, a five-year seniority requirement was additionally applied to officials entering the resource. In a short time, this provision was modified. In addition, with regard to membership of the resource, the legislator initially stipulated that this period would last only five years.

The third change essentially lowering the threshold of requirements for candidates for high-ranking state positions was the reduction of the required length of service from five years to three years for those taking the PZK examination. These changes introduced in a short period of time (during the rule of the Law and Justice – LPR – Self-Defence coalition) clearly indicate a tendency to lower the requirement threshold. One can conclude that the coalition in power at that time, lacking trusted, loyal and available cadres capable of supplying the PZK (meeting all the conditions), decided to lower the criteria. Among experts evaluating the draft law on state human resources, the prevailing view was that the exclusion of a group of top officials was contrary to Article 153(1) of the Constitution (Działocha 2006).

The 2008 Civil Service Act returned in this respect to the solutions of the 1998 Act by dividing members of the civil service corps into employees – contracted and appointed officials. The selection rigours concerning employment in the service also remained unchanged, with the exception of the limited possibility of employing persons who do not have Polish citizenship (Article 4 in conjunction with Article 5). The requirement of good repute was also left in place. The application of this criterion to employment must pose considerable difficulties, as it belongs to the so-called 'soft' prerequisites, which cannot be put into a rigid framework. In all laws, in addition to considerations of a substantive nature, one can find a premise that does not fall within the objective criteria, namely good repute or irreproachable character. This vague, general phrase must be considered on a moral, ethical level, which consequently causes problems in practical application. Moreover, the law does not specify this concept, does not indicate the criteria, which consequently leads to subjective assessments (Szewczyk 2006: 90–91). In the absence of an adequate procedure, the assessment of this premise seems to remain a dead provision. In the doctrine we find attempts to define it. According to H. Szewczyk: "(…) the concept of good repute covers all cases where a person has been convicted of unintentional offences, (…) but it also refers to certain negative character traits, such as excessive gambling, sexaholism, abuse of alcohol, drugs or other stimulants, 'lordly lifestyle' – because they do not guarantee the proper performance of the tasks entrusted to them" (2010: 84).

This premise is intended to show that stricter selection criteria should be applied to members of the corps because of the principles of ethical conduct in force in the service. Unlike the other premises, it is left to the discretion of the administrative authority establishing the employment relationship (Jagielski&Rączka 2001: 34–36). The December 2015 amendment left the division of corps members into categories: employees and civil servants while highlighting the third category (belonging to the corps) – persons employed in a senior position in the civil service. No changes were made in terms of the conditions of employment on the basis of employment contracts and on the basis of appointment. All three laws, both of 1998, 2006 and 2008, define recruitment (at least in the verbal sphere) to the service as open and competitive and ensure the right of every citizen to be informed about job vacancies. At the same time, it should be borne in mind that the openness and competitiveness of recruitment applies only to the employment of corps staff. The recruitment of civil servants is no longer fully of this nature (and the 2015 amendment exacerbates this situation). The 1996 Act, on the other hand, introduced neither openness nor transparency as principles for recruitment to the service. Nor did it create a preference for graduates of the National School of Public Administration, unlike the 1998 and 2006 and 2008 Acts.

4.2.2 Method of establishing an employment relationship

As I have already mentioned, the employment relationship with a civil servant (in the light of the 1996 Act) was established on the basis of a full-time appointment, on behalf of the State for an indefinite period of time or, exceptionally, for a fixed period of time. The law, in Article 65, allowed part-time employment at the request of the Director General with the approval of the Head of the Civil Service of a person who is at least 55 years of age and has at least 10 years of seniority in the civil service, who has custody of a child under eight years of age, who is an academic staff member with an academic degree of at least PhD and who has been transferred to work in another office in another locality.

In addition to the fulfilment of the statutory conditions discussed earlier, it was necessary for the Selection Committee to establish that the qualification procedure had resulted in the candidate being placed in one of the civil servant categories (Article 27(3)). The application for the procedure, together with documents confirming that the selection rigours had been met, was addressed by the persons concerned to the Head of the Civil Service, who determined the list of persons admitted to the selection procedure. In the course of this procedure, the Selection Committee checked and assessed the qualifications and aptitude to perform the tasks (for a specific category). The assessment included knowledge, experience, skills, personality traits, professional achievements, length of service in public administration and performance evaluations (Article 30(1)). There is, however, no specification of the criteria for the assessment in the Act or in the implementing acts. The Commission was also obliged to make public the list of persons meeting the requirements for each official category. The conduct of the selection procedure had to be preceded by the Head of the Service making public, in the daily national press, information on the number of vacancies, the deadline for the submission of applications, the date on which the procedure was to be conducted and the types of documents confirming the fulfilment of the selection rigours.

As a result of the Commission's positive verification, the candidate for service was placed in one of the official categories, which of course did not entail a claim for appointment to the service, as this decision was left to the discretion of the administrative authority (Cieślak at al. 1998: 99). In the case of a person lacking at least two years' seniority, the Act provided for a fixed-term (two years) appointment; in other cases, the appointment was for an indefinite period. Except when the Director-General agreed to reduce the two-year period after a positive evaluation and one year of service. The qualification procedure was conducted on the basis of two Commission resolutions of 16 July 1997 on the Rules of Procedure of the Civil Service Qualification Commission and on the determination of the scopes of the qualification procedure for official categories. It consisted of two stages, each of which was very extensive. The first part – written – involved solving a knowledge test, general intelligence being tested by psychologists, a biographical questionnaire and problem-solving situational tasks. Part two was an interview conducted by a five-member committee with each candidate individually. An important element was the results of the knowledge test which helpfully served during the interview. The proceedings concluded with a deliberation and vote by the Commission (Kornaś 2001: 29).

Appointments were made by the Head of the Civil Service on the proposal of the Director-General of the office in which the official was to be employed, or alternatively, on the authority of the Head, the appointment could be made by the Director-General. The Director-General also designated the official's position corresponding to his or her official category and determined the salary, except for the Secretary of the Council of Ministers, Directors-General in ministries and central offices, as this was at the discretion of the Prime Minister. The instrument of appointment was in writing and contained: the name of the official, the date on which the employment relationship was established, the official's category and the period for which the official was appointed. The official took an oath, which he confirmed with his signature. Appointment as the exclusive principle for the establishment of the employment relationship meant that, on the one hand, the official was guaranteed stability and permanence, but, in return, he or she was obliged to be highly available and to be particularly loyal to the employer – i. e. the state.

The implementation of the Act's principles did not begin until the second half of 1997, during the already ongoing election campaign in connection with the upcoming parliamentary elections. A total of 8558 people applied to join the qualification procedure (this is how many applications were received): 649 for category A by 22 August and 7909 for category B by 12 September. The Derdziuk Team's "Report" stated that, although applications had not been completed, the Head of the Civil Service had established the first two lists of persons admitted to the proceedings, the majority of whom were directors-general (31 persons, or 63 %), directors-general of ministries or central offices (10), directors-general of provincial offices (21), as well as three employees from the Civil Service Office and three members of the Qualification Commission (Raport 1998: 6).

Only 750 persons were admitted to the qualification procedure by the Head of the Civil Service, of whom only 307 had been examined by the Qualification Commission by 29 October. 286 persons were subjected to the procedure for category A, positively qualifying 156 persons, while for category B 466 persons were examined, with positive results in the case of 88. As a result, only 244 persons were positively verified. Finally, at the end of October 1997, the qualification procedure was discontinued (Raport 1998: 6).

Between 1 October and 24 November, 115 people were appointed, of which: 91 to category A and 24 to category B. This entire group included 18 persons who were already performing the duties of director-general in a ministry or central office under the provisions of the transitional period, and 32 directors-general of provincial offices. At this point it is necessary to point out that among the above-mentioned persons there were 24 directors general in ministries and central offices, 35 directors general in provincial offices, 60 directors and deputy directors of departments and equivalent units, 44 directors and deputy directors of departments in provincial offices and 77 persons employed in other positions in government administration offices (Rydlewski 2001: 34). The conclusion is that only 4 persons who passed the qualification procedure were not employed in key positions in the state in public administration. As a result, on 31 December, 109 persons had the status of a civil servant (seven persons resigned from the civil service), of which: 85 persons were in category A and 24 persons in category B. This group also included the Deputy Head of the Service, nine directors-general of ministries and central offices and 15 directors-general of voivodeship offices. It seems interesting, albeit surprising, that in 1998 the only appointment was that of Deputy Head of the Civil Service.

One of the recommendations of the Derdziuk report was to prepare and implement as soon as possible a new law on the civil service, which should also eliminate from legal circulation the 1982 law on civil servants (Raport 1998: 13–19). The parliamentary elections in 1997 and the alternation of power (the formation on 17 October 1997 of a coalition government of AWS and UW with Prime Minister Jerzy Buzek) undoubtedly did not do the newly formed civil service any favours. Firstly, political pressures could not be avoided when the service was constructed, and secondly, the new ruling team did not escape political revanchism. The result was the loss of several more years in the construction of the civil service corps.

The entry into force of the 1998 Act dramatically changed the ways in which the employment relationship could be established due to a change in the construction of the corps. This was due to the emergence of two types of members of the civil service corps recruited through different modes, using different methods. The Director-General was and remained responsible for organising recruitment to the civil service corps. To this end, he disseminated information on vacancies in the office he headed and in the Civil Service Bulletin, while specifying in detail the requirements for the post, the scope of tasks, the required documents and the deadline and place for their submission. In addition, the candidate had to enjoy full public rights, not be convicted of an intentional crime and have the qualifications required for the civil service. In both subsequent laws, these provisions remained essentially unchanged, with the exception of the replacement of the Civil Service Bulletin by the Public Information Bulletin of the Chancellery of the Prime Minister (obviously due to the abolition of the Civil Service Office in the 2006 law, which will be discussed more widely in the next part of the dissertation). The deadline for candidates to submit documents has also been shortened. From 14 days in the 1998 Act to 10 days in the 2006 and 2008 Acts. (Article 28(3)).

In principle, apart from minor adjustments, the recruitment procedure has been almost identical since 1998. After the information about the vacancy is made public, a list of candidates is announced and then a protocol of the recruitment is drawn up, which contains: the designation of the position for which the recruitment was conducted, the number of candidates and the names, surnames and addresses of no more than five best candidates, information on the methods and techniques of the recruitment, the justification of the selection made. The 2008 Act added two more elements to the minutes (Article 30): the number of offers submitted, including offers that do not meet formal requirements, and the composition of the selection committee. It also created, in contrast to previous regulations, a closed catalogue of the elements of the protocol, as the phrase that: "the protocol shall include in particular", which gave a lot of freedom and the possibility to supplement the protocol with additional information (Drobny at al. 2010: 192). However, the 2006 Act, in Article 2(4) in conjunction with Article 34, allowed for the employment in official positions (without a procedure – on the basis of a transfer), of employees previously employed on the basis of separate official pragmatics: of 16 September 1982 on employees of state offices, of 23 December 1994 on the Supreme Chamber of Control and of 22 March 1990 on local government employees. The transfer was carried out by the Director General of the office, who was excluded from the scope of the Civil Service Act and included in the State Personnel Resources. This solution was not introduced in the most recent Act.

None of the Acts included specific rules and methods for recruiting for a vacancy. Only at the time of the 2006 Act. Only when the 2006 Act was in force did the Prime Minister, on 28 November 2006, issue a letter DP.122-1(1)/06/JK on the establishment of standards of conduct in the employment of employees in government administration, for information and application, in which it was specified that employment should be decided only on merit, objective grounds, confirmed by the competences and qualifications of the candidate (Szewczyk 2010: 94–95). The 1998 Act introduced the rules for establishing an employment relationship with a corps employee on the basis of: an employment contract for a fixed term not exceeding 3 years or an employment contract for an indefinite term. The 2006 Act recycled the above solution, while in 2008 the specification of a maximum three-year period for a fixed-term contract was abandoned (Article 35). The novelty in the 2008 Act is the obligation to conclude an employment contract for 12 months in the case of persons taking up a job for the first time in the civil service (Article 35(3)). No changes were made in the 2015 amendment with regard to the conclusion of employment contracts. Appointment was left as the form of employment.

4.2.3 Preparatory service

One of the most important solutions serving the process of professionalisation of personnel in public administration is the institution of preparatory service. It was introduced by the 1998 Act (it also existed under the 1922 Act) as an element of obligatory, theoretical and practical preparation of an employee for proper performance of official duties. The table below (Table 2) summarises the similarities and differences in the standardisation of preparatory service in the civil service between 1998 and 2016.

Table 2 Preparatory service in light of the 1998, 2006, 2008 Civil Service Acts and the December 2015 amendments

Features of the preparatory service	1998 Act	2006 Act	2008 Act	2015 Amendment
Obligation of service	yes	no	yes	yes
Objective of the preparatory service	theoretical and practical preparation for the proper performance of duties	theoretical and practical preparation for the proper performance of duties	theoretical and practical preparation for the proper performance of duties	theoretical and practical preparation for the proper performance of duties
Entity in charge	Director-General	Director-General	Director-General	Director-General
Organising entity	Director-General, together with the Head of the Civil Service in consultation with KSAP	Director-General	Director-General	Director-General
Obligated entity	All employees taking up their first job at CS	Some employees taking up their first job at CS	All employees taking up their first job at CS	All employees taking up their first job at CS
Entities exempted by law	KSAP graduates	None	KSAP graduates	KSAP graduates Senior staff
Time limit	6 months	Maximum 3 months	Maximum 4 months	Maximum 4 months
Verification method	Assessment by the examination board Written work to be assessed by a reviewer	None	Examination	Examination
Possibility of withdrawal or reduction	Reduction or withdrawal from an employee who demonstrates the knowledge required by the service programme	None	Withdrawal at the reasoned request of the person in charge of the cell in which the employee is employed (does not at the same time exempt from the examination obligation)*	Withdrawal at the reasoned request of the person in charge of the cell in which the employee is employed (does not at the same time exempt from the examination obligation)

Source: Table by author. Based on Civil Service Acts 1998, 2006 and 2008 and the December 2015 as amendments

* From 24 March 2009 to 31 December 2009, in ministries, central offices, provincial offices and the treasury administration, a total of 580 persons were exempted from the obligation to undergo preparatory service on the basis of Article 36(7), accounting for 16.87 % of all persons employed in

accordance with Article 35(3) of the Act (excluding KSAP graduates). In 2010, in ministries, central offices, provincial offices and the tax administration, a total of 78 persons were exempted from the obligation to undergo preparatory service pursuant to Art. 36(7), a total of 782 persons were exempted from the obligation to undergo preparatory service, accounting for 18.5% of all persons employed in accordance with Article 35(3) of the Act (excluding KSAP graduates). Compared to 2009 (the period from 24 March 2009 to 31 December 2009), this number increased by 10%, which may be due, inter alia, to the fact that in 2010 the study period was longer by almost 3 months (Sprawozdanie Szefa Służby Cywilnej za 2009 and Sprawozdanie Szefa Służby Cywilnej za 2010). In successive Head of Service Reports, no information is available on the implementation of the preparatory service.

Arguably, the legislator's aim was not only to prepare the employee theoretically and practically to perform tasks on behalf of the state, but also to establish another element of verification. This type of selection can be found in other laws (e.g. legislative or administrative application). In the 2008 Act, the legislator returned to the obligatory completion of preparatory service by employees of the civil service corps. In contrast, the 2015 amendment did not change anything in this respect. The 2006 standardisation allowed directors-general to be completely free in this respect and was severely criticised by the scientific community. "The professionalism of human resources will be served neither by discretion in referring an employee to serve nor by reducing the service to three months (…)" (Galińska – Rączy 2006). In turn K. Działocha and A. Łukaszczuk drew attention to the reduction in professionalism of civil servants as a result of the lack of compulsory civil service (2006: 12). Currently, in standardising the institution of the preparatory service, quite a lot of freedom has been left to the director general of the office to shape it, without clarifying the provisions, which in the future may have consequences in terms of lack of objectivity or reliability.

4.2.4 First assessment in the civil service

A complete novelty in the 2008 Act was the first assessment in the civil service (Article 37). According to this provision, any person taking up a job in the civil service for the first time is subject to a first assessment, with the exception of KSAP graduates who have applied for appointment in the civil service (Article 37(3)). Detailed rules, the procedure, the template of the first assessment sheet, the scope and templates of the forms are regulated by the Regulation of the President of the Council of Ministers of 23 July 2015 on detailed conditions and manner of first assessment in the civil service (Journal of Laws 2015, item 1144). Previously, the Ordinance of the President of the Council of Ministers of 15 June 2009 on the detailed conditions and manner of making the first evaluation in the civil service (Journal of Laws No. 94, item 772) was in force.

The first appraisal should be made no earlier than 8 months after the employment relationship is established and no later than one month before the end of the employment contract. The legislator distinguished in Article 38(2) the following prerequisites for the assessment by the direct superior: the employee's attitude, commitment and progress at work, relations with colleagues, punctuality of tasks performed, the result of the preparatory service examination, the assessed employee's report on the tasks performed by the employee.

The attitude rationale was expanded and described in the annex of the aforementioned regulation, indicating assessment elements such as decision-making and responsibility, work organisation and achievement of results, communication and relationship building through cooperation, professional development. The annex also identifies examples of effective and ineffective behaviour, which obviously facilitates the assessment. The outcome of the appraisal determines whether or not the Director-General concludes an indefinite-term employment contract with the appraised employee. At the same time, the Director-General may not employ for an indefinite period of time a person who has received a negative evaluation (Dubowik 2010: 25). The changes introduced are to be welcomed, as the obligation to carry out an appraisal will allow the employer to make more effective selections with a view to employing the best people. Of course, from a human resources management point of view, there are some dangers in having the appraisal carried out by the direct supervisor. Table 3 presents a summary of the conduct of the first appraisals in the civil service. As can be seen from the table below, negative appraisals constitute a small percentage in relation to positive appraisals, which oscillate around 97.5 %, which undoubtedly testifies to the accuracy and effectiveness of the employee recruitment and selection processes, as well as the ineffectiveness, appearances and façade of the conducted appraisals.

Table 3 First assessment in the civil service between 2010 and 2016

Years	Total number of assessments	Positive assessments	Negative assessments	Ratio of positive to negative ratings %
2016	4446	4353	93	97,9
2015	3020	2948	72	97,6
2014	2963	2888	75	97,5
2013	3650	3568	82	97,8
2012	3418	3336	82	97,6
2011	4868	4731	137	97,2
2010	3549	3463	86	97,6
Total	**25914**	**25287**	**490**	**97,6**

Source: Table by author. Based on Reports of the Head of the Civil Service on the state of the civil service and the implementation of the tasks of the civil service for the years: 2010, 2011, 2012, 2013, 2014, 2015, 2016. No information available for 2009.

4.2.5 Appointment as a form of employment relationship

Appointment as the legal basis for the employment of civil servants was present in each of the Acts. However, over the years and changing concepts of the civil service corps, it has undergone significant modifications. In the 1996 Act, appointment was the basic and only form of employment of civil servants. Candidates for employment in the civil service corps had to, inter alia, possess the qualifications and aptitude required for appointment to the civil service (Article 4). The 1998 Act, while distinguishing two categories of corps members: employees and civil servants, specified the way in which the employment relationship with civil servants was established on the basis of appointment. Consequently, on 31 December 1999, the civil service corps had over 116 613 members, including 99 civil servants. The figure does not include civil servants employed in district services, inspections and guards in the Lubelskie and Pomorskie voivodeships due to lack of data (Sprawozdanie Szefa Służby Cywilnej za 1999: 8). Obtaining an appointment, in the light of the 1998 Act, entailed the following prerequisites: employment in the civil service, two years' seniority in the service, completion of preparatory service, a master's degree or equivalent, knowledge of one foreign language confirmed by a specific certificate, being a soldier in the reserves or not being subject to compulsory national defence (Article 28). An employee applying for appointment had, in the first stage, to send the necessary documents to the Head of the Civil Service for admission to the qualification procedure. In the next stage, the employee, having met the requirements, could proceed to the qualification procedure conducted by the Head of the Civil Service. A screening team of at least 5 people checked the knowledge, qualifications and aptitude necessary to fulfil the tasks of the service during the proceedings. On the basis of the statutory delegation contained in Article 36 of the Act, the Prime Minister issued a regulation on the qualification procedure (Journal of Laws. No. 79, item 549) on 28 September 1999, in which the manner of conducting the qualification procedure was specified in detail. The thematic scope of the procedure, the organisation and method of its conduct, the minimum number of points to be obtained, the types of documents confirming the fulfilment of the conditions, the amount of the fee, as well as the list of documents confirming knowledge of a foreign language were determined.

If the legal prerequisites were fulfilled, i. e. the required number of points was obtained, the right to receive an appointment was gained. The appointment letter was drawn up in writing. It contained the name of the official and the date of appointment. On the date of the appointment, the existing employment relationship was transformed into an employment relationship on the basis of the appointment. The appointment was made by the Head of the Civil Service on behalf of the Republic of Poland. In turn, the civil servant took an oath, which was confirmed by a signature. A limit of appointments was and still is created annually. The limit of appointments of civil servants in the civil service for a given financial year, as well as the limits and financial resources for the remuneration and training of members of the civil service corps, is determined by the Budget Act. Within 7 days from the date of appointment, the Director General of the Office would award the lowest of the 9 official ranks to the official. Official ranks are standardised in the Regulation of the Council of Ministers of 29 October 1999 on the definition of official positions, required professional qualifications, official ranks of civil servants, multipliers for determining remuneration and detailed rules for determining and paying other benefits to which members of the civil service corps are entitled (Journal of Laws No. 89, item 99, as amended).

It is noteworthy that the service rank was granted retroactively from the date of appointment. The limit on appointments is directly linked to the guarantee of funds for the remuneration of officials and also guarantees permanent, but limited for the best, access to the official sphere. One category of employees that received special treatment in the 1998 Act are graduates of the National School of Public Administration.

The National School of Public Administration (KSAP) was established on 30 May 1990 by a resolution of the Council of Ministers. It operates on the basis of the Act of 14 May 1991. The School was established on the model of the French National School of Administration (ENA) in order to train neutral and professionally prepared civil servants. Interdisciplinarity is the basis of education at KSAP (social, political, legal and economic sciences). In addition, emphasis is placed on practical preparation through domestic and foreign internships (Gintowt-Jankowicz 1997: 45–49). In accordance with Article 21 of the Act, the recruitment of candidates to the Civil Service Corps also concerned KSAP graduates, so they were subject to the same selection rigour. Graduates of KSAP, having commenced work in the government administration, were entitled to apply for appointment as civil servants without undergoing the selection procedure. In line with Art. 27, they were exempt from the obligation to undergo preparatory service, nor were they required to have two years' seniority in the civil service, as they had acquired the necessary knowledge and skills during almost two years of very intensive training at KSAP. There was no correspondence at all with the above provision in Art. 23, which stipulates that the Prime Minister shall indicate to graduates of successive years of the National School of Public Administration the first posts in the civil service presented by the Head of the Civil Service, with the exception of higher posts in the civil service. So far, however, KSAP has had relatively limited significance in shaping the conditions for administrative personnel. This is mainly due to the small number of its students. By 1999, the School had only 347 graduates (Rydlewski 2001: 40).

Although Article 21 (2) extended recruitment to the service also to KSAP graduates, Article 23 restricted the recruitment process to them. The designation of a post by the Head of the S.C. was of a binding nature, since KSAP's students made, and continue to make, an undertaking to perform work in administrative offices in the positions made available to them for a period of no less than 5 years from the date of graduation. This was due to the fact that the training of one KSAP student cost, in 2009, approximately PLN 180,000 (Radwan 2009: 7). For example, in 2000, 110 jobs were offered to 46 KSAP graduates, while in 2001 as many as 107 jobs were offered to 52 graduates. In 2003, as many as 118 offers were made to 51 graduates (five offers were later withdrawn). In 2004, 154 job offers were made to 50 graduates[2]. At the end of 2008 and the beginning of 2009, KSAP introduced changes in terms of organisation and full-time education, with the result that two years of students graduated in 2010. However, just two years later it was decided to reintroduce one intake per year, hence the lack of graduates in 2013. The 2013 Report of the Head of the Civil Service shows that at the end of 2013 there were 688 KSAP graduates working in the civil service, representing nearly 63 % of all those who had graduated there. As at 31 December 2012, 1 out of 67 graduates was unemployed. This graduate took up a job in the civil service in March 2013. Due to organisational changes at KSAP, there were no graduates in 2013. Approximately 21 % of KSAP graduates were employed in senior civil service positions, approximately 23 % in middle management and coordinating positions, over 36 % in independent positions and nearly 20 % in specialist positions. The vast majority of KSAP graduates employed in the civil service in 2013 were civil servants (nearly 99 %) (Sprawozdanie Szefa Służby Cywilnej za 2013: 22). It is important to note that KSAP graduates have priority in obtaining appointments, as the number of appointments envisaged is already announced taking into account the number of appointments of KSAP graduates. In 1999, for the first time, a draft of the three-year plan for the limit of appointments of civil servants in the civil service provided for by Article 6(2) of the Civil Service Act was prepared, constituting, after its adoption by the Council of Ministers, an annex to the draft budget law for 2000. The figures proposed in this plan were established taking into account the needs of the civil service (ultimately, for proper selection for the existing 1,630 higher posts in the civil service, about ten times as many civil servants are needed), with awareness of, on the one hand, the existing limitation in the form of a small (estimated at about 5 % of the entire corps) group of employees possessing certificates of knowledge of a foreign language required in the qualification procedure, and, on the other hand, the potential opportunities for obtaining them by a further 5 % of those declaring knowledge or study of a foreign language. The School trains a small number of students, but its intention is to prepare the elite of public servants. That is why no more than 40 students have left KSAP each year since 2013. Until 2013, when the School organised as many as two intakes in one year, there were more graduates.

The 2006 Act, in regulating appointments, tightened the criterion for knowledge of a foreign language to the working languages of the European Union. In addition, language certificates at the basic level – B1 – were not recognised. The civil servant examination consisted of three parts: a test of knowledge, skills and managerial aptitude.

2 The statistics were taken from the Head of Civil Service Reports for each year, starting in 1999 and ending in 2004.

Table 4 Appointments of civil servants after 1996

Year	Limit of appointments in the Budget Act	Date of appointment	Number of applications	Number of persons taking the examination	Applications of KSAP graduates	Qualification procedure (appointments)	Total appointed	Share of persons appointed of those taking the exam, excluding KSAP
1997						116	116	
2000	1300	1 III 2000	285	240	208	43	251*	17,92%
2000	2800	1 X 2000	274	214	53	161	214	75,23%
2001	500	1 X 2001	384	324	58	218	276	67,28%
2002	400	1 X 2002	412	374	62	229	291	61,23%
2003	450	1 X 2003	675	633	52	395	447	62,40%
2004	600	15XI 2004	1639	1406	48	552	600	39,26(59,03**) %
2005	1500	1 XII 2005	5104	4176	58	1440	1498	34,48(41,98**) %
2006	3000	1 XI 2006	3637	3455	61	1784	1845	51,64%
2007	3000	1 XI 2007	736	718	60	159	219	22,14%
2008	1000	1 X 2008	901	887	56	598	653	67,40%
2009	1000	1 XII 2009	1067	1059	59	530	589	50,05%
2010	1000	1 XII 2010	2495	2466	45	951	996	38,56%
2011	500	1 XII 2011	1785	1760	66	431	497	24,48%
2012	500	1 XII 2012	no data	2075	70	426	496	20,53%
2013	200	1 XII 2013	no data	864	33	164	197	18,98%
2014	200	1 XII 2014	no data	880	32	153	185	17,39%
2015	200	1 XII 2015	no data	828	36	162	198	19,56
2016	200	1 XII 2016	no data	607	34	120	154	19,77%
2017	280	1 XII 2017	no data	563	39	236	275	41,9%
2018	350	1 XII 2018	no data	no data	35	206	241	–

Year	Limit of appointments in the Budget Act	Date of appointment	Number of applications	Number of persons taking the examination	Applications of KSAP graduates	Qualification procedure (appointments)	Total appointed	Share of persons appointed of those taking the exam, excluding KSAP
2019	420	1 XII 2019	no data	876	34	381	415	43,49 %
2020	490	1 XII 2020	no data	cancelled	34	cancelled	34***	0 %
SUMA				**24 405**	**1 233**	**9 455**	**10 687**	

Source: Table by author. Based on Chancellery of the Prime Minister (www.kprm.gov.pl), Department of the Civil Service and Reports of the Head of the Civil Service on the state of the civil service and the implementation of the tasks of the civil service for the years for 1997–2020. No information available for 2009.

* includes the Head of the Civil Service who was appointed on 17 November 1999.

** if those who did not fit into the appointment limit were included, the percentage of new appointments would be higher.

*** In 2020 and 2021, only KSAP graduates were appointed while the qualification procedure was cancelled in the same way as in 2020, which was justified by the situation related to the COVID-19 pandemic.

The prerequisite for passing the examination was a score of at least 60% in each part and a total of more than 60% of the total possible score. This is a very demanding requirement, which is why the first qualification procedure under the 2006 Act did not inspire optimism: only 718 people took the exam and 159 passed. The 2008 Act remains essentially unchanged and is based on the same rules as in the previous Acts. Changes have been made with regard to the expansion of the list of foreign languages whose documented knowledge qualifies for the qualification procedure (including knowledge of Arabic, Belarusian, Chinese, Icelandic, Japanese, Norwegian, Russian or Ukrainian). Instead of managerial skills and aptitude, skills to perform civil service tasks will be verified, and the appointment will be made by the Head of the Civil Service and not by the Prime Minister, as before. Changes have also been made to the determination of the results of the qualification procedure. They were regulated in the Ordinance of the Prime Minister of 16 December 2009 on the manner of conducting qualification proceedings in the civil service (Journal of Laws. No. 218, item 1695). Is not the restriction of the possibility to apply for appointment only to employees of the civil service corps (condition of employment) at the same time a restriction of free, competitive recruitment? Applying such principles, the recruitment of a civil servant is an internal recruitment, closing the way to persons not employed in the civil service corps. The doctrine advocates the abandonment of the selection procedure for civil servant appointments in its current form (Szewczyk 2010: 127–128). Table 4 illustrates the appointments of civil servants over the period 1996–2020.

It should be noted that the establishment of a large quota for appointments in 1999 and 2000 was not in harmony with the number of applications and entrants to the selection procedure, the proportion of newly appointed officials in relation to the quota being very small. Between 2002 and 2003, the number of applications was already slightly higher than the quota, indicating a slow increase in interest in the selection procedure. It was not until 2004 that for the first time the number of applications exceeded the appointment limit by almost three times and for the first time, despite a successful procedure, a sizeable group of people did not fit into the modest appointment limit. In 2005, despite a significant increase in the limit, there were again many more applicants. At this point, it is important to mention the controversy surrounding the situation of those who did not meet the quota for appointments in a given year, but who successfully completed the qualification procedure. Unfortunately, they have to rejoin the qualification procedure in the following year. In 2006, the limit was raised to as many as 3 000, but only 1 784 people were appointed as a result of the procedure, which may be an indication of the complexity of the examination or the lack of knowledge and skills of those taking it. In 2007, the new civil service regulations were already in place and, in addition, the State Personnel Pool was created. Although the quota remained the same in 2007, the number of applications fell dramatically (about four times less than the quota) and there was an appallingly poor performance of candidates for civil servants in the selection procedure – only 159 out of 718 applicants were appointed (representing 22.14 %). The reasons, perhaps, can be traced to the possibility of applying to the State Personnel Pool (PZK) as a second promotion path and the low level of knowledge of those taking the qualification procedure. However, in 2007, only 304 persons were admitted to the examination for the PZK, which, together with applicants for appointments in the civil service, gives us 1040 persons – with an appointment limit of 3000. Consequently, it should be concluded that the appointment limit still far exceeded the number of applicants (Table 5 shows the results of examinations for the State Personnel Pool over the period 2007–2009). The brackets in the fifth column indicate the percentage of those who successfully completed the examination. The average percentage "pass rate" of the examination for the PAS was just under 60 per cent, which may indicate either poor preparation of candidates or an overly exorbitant level of examination tasks.

Table 5 State Human Resources examinations in 2007–2009

Order number	Year	Number of persons admitted to the examination	Number of persons who took the examination	Number of persons who successfully completed the examination
1.	2007/1	89	84	54 (64,28 %)
2.	2007/2	100	89	47 (52,81 %)
3.	2007/3	86	84	56 (66,66 %)
4.	2007/4	29	25	11 (44 %)
5.	2008/1	63	61	31 (50,81 %)
6.	2008/2	60	55	26 (47,27 %)
7.	2008/3	32	29	20 (68,96 %)
8.	2008/4	23	21	9 (42,85 %)
9.	2008/5	17	16	10 (62,50 %)
10.	2008/6	26	23	14 (60,87 %)
11.	2009/1	8	7	5 (71,43 %)
12.	2009/2	14	12	6 (50 %)
TOTAL		**547**	**506**	**289 (57,11 %)**

Source: Table by author. Based on summary information from the National School of Public Administration.

In 2010 (when the regulations on the State Personnel Reserve were no longer in force), a reversal of the trend can be seen. With a limit of 1,000 appointees, as many as 2,466 people take the qualification procedure, resulting in 951 appointees and 45 KSAP graduates. This represents an almost completely filled appointment quota. The three-year plan for the limit of appointments of civil servants in the civil service for 2011–2013, submitted by the Head of the Civil Service, amounted to only 500 persons per year. This was dictated by budget savings that were a rationalisation of budgetary expenditure. The limit for appointments of civil servants in the civil service for 2012–2014 was adopted by the Council of Ministers on 5 May 2011 and was also – 500 persons. However, already in September 2012, this assumption was corrected by setting the limit for 2013–2015 at 200. The PO-PSL government in September 2015 adopted the limits: 2016–200 people, 2017–280 people, 2018–350 people. In September 2018. a further three-year limit of appointments was set, which was in 2019–420 persons, in 2020–490 persons and in 2021–550 persons. In 2020. Cabinet planned that the limit for 2021–2023 would be as follows: in 2021. – 30 persons, in 2022. – 40 persons, in 2023. – 40 persons (which, of course, was related to the difficult situation of public finances and economic problems during the pandemic period – the aim of such a low limit was to reduce personnel costs in the administration). However, already in 2021. The Council of Ministers decided that the limit for 2022–2024 would be as follows: in 2022. – 245 persons, in 2023. – 275 persons, in 2024. – 300 persons, which increases the possibility of appointing more persons many times over and serves well the development of the corps as a whole.

Employment in the civil service maintained a steady upward trend until 2010, with few exceptions (as shown in Table 6). It was not an alarming picture, like the one often created by the media, that the administration was growing at an alarming rate. Growth was taking place, albeit slowly. On the one hand, with the development of modern "e-government", the development of electronic technologies, we expect a reduction in administrative employment due to the facilitation of work. On the other hand, it is necessary to bear in mind that the tasks of the administration are expanding, entering new areas of citizens' lives, which consequently generates increased staffing needs. In addition, complex procedures, the increasing number of legal acts (including EU legislation) and, in many cases, the lack of clarity of legal norms are additional difficulties.

From 2010 onwards, there has been a steady, slight decrease in the civil service corps. In 2011, by 1605 FTEs, or 1.3 %. In the following year (2012) by 1.1 %. In 2013, on the other hand, the decrease was only 0.4 % compared to 2012, and in 2014 the rate was 0.8 %. In 2015, the number of FTEs decreased by 1155, or 1 %, compared to 2014 – a total of 38 % of offices reduced staffing levels compared to 2014. 2016 marked the sixth consecutive year of staffing reductions. An analysis of the Head of Civil Service Reports shows that the decreases are the result of, among other things. natural staff turnover and incomplete replacement of vacant posts (e. g. due to retirements), the non-renewal of expiring fixed-term employment contracts, as well as reorganisations carried out within the structure of offices (e. g. consolidation of tax chambers and offices) (Sprawozdanie Szefa Służby Cywilnej 2009–2016). However, it should be noted that over the period 2016–2020, in principle, the level of employment did not fluctuate much. Again in 2018. there was a decrease in employment related to the exclusion from the civil service of the National Water Management Authority together with the regional boards. The reduction in staffing levels amounted to only 1.2 %, i. e. 1,418 FTEs. These employees were incorporated into the newly established State Water Management

Table 6 Employment in the civil service since 1999

Order number	years (as at 31 December)	number of employees (FTEs)	including civil servants	Percentage of civil servants to total number of employees
1.	1999	116613	90	0,08%
2.	2000	118212	530	0,45%
3.	2001	116597	796	0,70%
4.	2002	118841	1070	0,90%
5.	2003	120435	1503	1,25%
6.	2004	119963	2101	1,75%
7.	2005	120310	3599	2,99%
8.	2006	no data	no data	no data
9.	2007	113237*	5253	4,60%
10.	2008	117796	4692	3,98%
11.	2009	122110	5983**	4,90%
12.	2010	123651	6919	5,60%
13.	2011	122046	7170	5,90%
14.	2012	121699	7503	6,20%
15.	2013	121195	7598	6,30%
16.	2014	120412	7675	6,40%
17.	2015	119257	7744	6,50%
18.	2016	118848	7728	6,50%
19.	2017	119382	7544	6,31%
20.	2018	117964	7593	6,43%
21.	2019	119750	7890	6,58%
22.	2020	118885	7659	6,44%

Source: Table by author. Based on Reports of the Head of the Civil Service on the state of the service for the years for 1999–2005 and for 2009–2020, and Reports of the Office of the Prime Minister, Department of the Civil Service and State Personnel Resources for 2007 and 2008.

* the difference is most likely due to the failure to include in the total number of persons all those belonging to the State Personnel Resource.

** of which 654 were civil servants who, as at 31.12.2008, were on unpaid leave granted for the duration of their appointment to senior state positions which are not state management positions. Report of the Head of the Civil Service on the State of the Civil Service and the Implementation of the Tasks of the Civil Service in 2009, p. 6.

Authority "Wody Polskie". Państwowe Gospodarstwo Wodne "Wody Polskie" was established by the Act of 20 July 2017 (Journal of Laws. 2017, item 1566) and began functioning on 1 January 2018. In general, the number of posts in the civil service corps has oscillated over the years just below or just above 120 000 and it should be said that it has remained fairly stable over the years.

Appointed officials, who are a kind of 'heart' of the entire civil service system, therefore represent a small percentage of all employees, currently less than 6.5 %. From 1999 onwards, there has unfortunately been a very slow increase in the number of appointed officials. In fact, as of 2015, it stands at around 6.5 %. At the time of the 1998 Act, it was estimated that 15 % of the total corps should be civil servants, as candidates for senior positions should be recruited from this category (Rydlewski 2001: 44). To date, since 1999, it has not been possible to reach the threshold of 15 % of appointed civil servants (i. e. to meet the original assumptions), and at the same time, given the pace, quality and quantity of changes in the civil service, this does not portend an improvement in the situation. It should be noted that in 2016, for the first time, there was a decrease in the share of civil servants in the corps. Compared to 2015, this share decreased by 16 posts (0.2 %). According to the 2016 Report of the Head of the Civil Service, one of the reasons for this was the low limit on appointments in 2016, as well as its incomplete implementation. The decrease was also due to civil servants leaving the service, in particular due to the acquisition of pension rights. However, it should be stressed that the decline in civil servants is part of a general trend of declining employment in the civil service. This may mean that employment in the civil service corps is becoming less attractive relative to offers from the private sector.

A variable showing the state of the civil service is the total number of offices where a civil service corps is in place. There has been a decrease of less than 3 % between 2016 and 2020, which means that the number of offices where civil service rules are applied has decreased slightly (in 2016 it was 1882 offices, while in 2020 it will be 1830 offices). It seems that those in power should rather seek to expand the scale of institutions covered by the civil service regime (of course, where this is possible and within the regulation of Article 153 of the Constitution). Firstly, this would eliminate, at least in part, the application of other legal orders concerning administration (e. g. the Law on Employees of State Offices – Act of 16 September 1982 on employees of state offices) (Journal of Laws No. 31, item 214, as amended). Secondly, it would make it possible to apply the identical principles contained in the Civil Service Act to persons employed in administration.

4.2.6 Senior positions in the civil service

The term senior civil service positions was introduced for the first time in the 1998 Act, which does not mean that it did not exist before. On the basis of the 1996 Act, civil servants in category A were capable of holding senior management positions, and were therefore presumably prepared to fill senior positions in the civil service. The 1998 Act singled out senior positions in the civil service in Chapter 4, including the positions of Director General of an office, Chief Internal Audit Inspector, person in charge of a department (equivalent unit) in central administration and their deputies, person in charge of a department and their deputies in provincial offices, provincial veterinarian and their deputies (Article 41). Senior positions were filled by means of a competition, which only a civil servant could enter. The Regulation of the President of the Council of Ministers of 3 November 1999 on the manner of organising and the detailed rules of conducting competitions for senior positions in the civil service (Journal of Laws No. 91, item 1028) regulates the detailed procedure for conducting competitions.

An exception to the above rule was the situation where, following a competition held twice, no candidate was selected from among the civil servants, it was possible for persons who were not civil servants to take part in the next competition. The Head of the Civil Service could admit persons who were not civil servants to a competition for senior positions if special professional skills or experience were required for the position. Competitions were conducted by the Head of the Civil Service, appointing a competition team of at least five persons. During the competition, the knowledge necessary to perform the tasks of the position covered by the competition was verified. In addition, predispositions and general abilities and managerial skills were examined.

The competition procedure was initiated by the Head of the Civil Service by announcing it in the Civil Service Bulletin, at the same time informing the directors general of the offices, whose duty it was to disseminate this information in the offices they headed. The basis of the competition was the drawing up of a job description, which served primarily to define the requirements. Each competition had to be tailored to the specifics of the post, but the overall scheme for conducting the competition was the same in all cases. Agreeing the requirements was the most difficult stage. The requirements for the position for which the competition was held were established by the head of the civil service in agreement with the minister, the head of the central office or the governor in whose office the position was located, taking into account, in particular, the type of tasks to be performed, the scope of managerial responsibility, the scope of authority to make decisions, the type and scope of contacts necessary to perform the tasks, the number of subordinate employees and the extent of their independence. It was necessary to indicate which requirements were essential and which were additional. The practice of filling senior positions was as follows. Since 13 July 1999. (i. e. from the time of the first competition) until 31 December 2004, there were 1,669 competitions for senior posts (that is how many were registered with the Civil Service Office), of which 130 were competitions for the post of Director General. In total, only 872 competition procedures were completed, resulting in only 635 senior civil service posts being filled: 1 post of Chief Inspector of Internal Audit, 82 posts of directors general of offices, 205 posts of directors of departments (or equivalent units), 112 posts of deputy directors of departments (or equivalent units), 119 posts of directors of departments (in provincial offices), 116 posts of deputy directors of departments. There were many reasons for this, certainly including problems in agreeing competition requirements for candidates. For example, for as long as 12 months in 2004 it was not possible to agree on the competition requirements for the post of director general at the Energy Regulatory Office, the Chancellery of the Prime Minister, and the Office for Substances and Chemical Preparations (Sprawozdanie Szefa Służby Cywilnej za 2005: 3). Throughout 2003, the Ministry of the Treasury, the Ministry of Foreign Affairs, the Chancellery of the Prime Minister, the Energy Regulatory Office, among others, also could not agree on the requirements for the posts of directors general (Sprawozdanie Szefa Służby Cywilnej za 2003: 3). It should be borne in mind that the competitions registered are very often second or third or fourth competitions. In 2005, as many as 182 (47 %) procedures were repeat competitions. This phenomenon is mainly due to a lack of candidates (in 2005, 78 competitions were not attended by any candidate) and the non-admission of any candidate to the competition (Sprawozdanie Szefa Służby Cywilnej za 2003: 3–4). In 2003, there were 5 persons remaining in the positions of directors-general in 15 ministries, which is only 1/3 of the total. In turn, 15 director general positions were filled out of 30 central offices. The situation was worst in voivodship offices, as only 2 out of 16 offices were filled (Sprawozdanie Szefa Służby Cywilnej za 2003: 4).

Between 1999 and 2006 (until the introduction of the State Personnel Resources Act), the filling of senior posts remained at a very unsatisfactory level. Taking into account the total number of vacancies, i. e. without taking into account employment in the form of "acting duties", the percentage of vacancies ranged from less than 30 % to more than 50 %. The statistics look different when those employed as 'acting' are excluded. The level of vacant posts did not exceed 12 % under the latter assumption. In individual years, the percentage of cancelled competition procedures is surprising, e. g. 54 % in 2001 or 45 % in 1999. It should be noted that "acting officers" did not go through the competition procedure, which not only affected the efficiency of employment, but also made it possible for positions to be filled by people from the same political circle or with different dependencies. This situation was the result, inter alia, of the introduction in 2002 of a provision amending the rules for filling senior posts. Introduced by the Act of 21 December 2001 on amending the Act on the organisation and work procedure of the Council of Ministers and the scope of action of ministers, the Act on divisions of government administration and amending certain acts (Journal of Laws No. 154, item 1800), Article 144a added to the Civil Service Act allowed the Head of the Civil Service (at the request of the Director General) to fill senior positions bypassing the competition procedure. If justified by the needs of the office, duties could be entrusted to a person outside the civil service corps at any time. With such an enigmatically worded and undefined premise in principle, any choice could be justified. It is significant that parliamentary elections were held in autumn 2001, in which the coalition of the Democratic Left Alliance and the Labour Union won a majority (41.04 % of votes – 216 seats), forming a cabinet together with the Polish People's Party, headed by Prime Minister Leszek Miller. This government, just two months after its formation, amended the Civil Service Act. The amendment had basically one objective: to politicise senior positions in the civil service. The constant changes resulting in the politicisation of the corps have been highlighted, especially in the press. In 2002 Janina Paradowska, a Polityka columnist wrote: "One of the largest armies in Poland – the civil service corps – today numbers over 110,000 government administration officials. It swings to the right or to the left to the rhythm of political change. Perhaps from this constant wobbling it will soon tip over …" (Paradowska 2002).

In December, the Constitutional Court ruled that Article 144a was unconstitutional because it undermined the idea of filling senior positions by introducing illegible rules for the functioning of the service. Disagreeing with the Ombudsman's conclusion, the representative of the Sejm reasoned that:

> (…) the contested solutions are only episodic in nature (they can be applied until the end of 2002) and are aimed, like the whole law that the amendment was introduced, at streamlining the work of the state apparatus. The abandonment for a certain period of time of the principle of competitive filling of senior positions in the civil service was aimed at rectifying the situation consisting in the existence of vacancies in these positions when the new government took power. This fact caused significant difficulties in the functioning of offices, which were to be managed by persons appointed through a competition. Such a solution was intended precisely to ensure 'uninterrupted continuity in the functioning of the civil service corps (Judgment of the Constitutional Tribunal of 12 December 2002, ref. K 9/02).

However, the Court's ruling did not entail the automatic loss of positions, so the persons in question were still in office in some cases. The effect of the unconstitutional provision of Article 144a being in force for a year was the employment of 16 persons as acting directors general of ministries, central and provincial offices and 70 department and division directors and their deputies. Six months after Article 144a was declared unconstitutional, there were still 13 top civil servant positions in the government administration filled on an acting basis, including in the Ministry of the Interior and Administration or the Public Procurement Office. The reason for this was the lack of agreed requirements for competitions, without which they could not be held. This appears to have been a deliberate effort to delay the start of competition procedures, driven by uncertainty and fear of change in senior positions. Consequently, as at 1 April 2003, there were 779 vacancies out of 1515 senior civil service posts, which were filled by 705 temporary 'acting'. In addition, there was an interpretation at the time that the six-month period providing for entrustment of duties applied only to heads of departments, employed by the Head of the Civil Service. On the other hand, it does not apply to directors general, whose contract is signed by the Prime Minister (Brunetko 2003: 42).

The results of the audit carried out in 2004 by the Supreme Chamber of Control in 33 offices were also not encouraging: 15 ministries, the Chancellery of the Prime Minister, the Civil Service Office and 16 provincial offices. One of the objectives of the audit was, inter alia, the filling of senior positions in the civil service. The audit covered the period from 1 January 2000 to 30 June 2004. The overall assessment of the NIK auditors was crushing, as:

> (…) despite 5 years of the Civil Service Act [the 1998 Act], the basic objective behind the establishment of the Civil Service, i.e. to ensure impartial, apolitical and competent performance of the tasks of the state, irrespective of the personnel changes taking place in political positions in government administration, has not been achieved (NIK 2005: 5).

The implementation of the law in terms of filling senior positions was also negatively assessed, accusing successive Prime Ministers, individual ministers and voivodes of: lack of their own initiative and action to fill senior positions through competition, lack of response in many cases to proposals addressed to them by the Head of the Civil Service to agree on the requirements, which made it impossible to hold competitions and resulted in the retention of temporary duty holders in their positions. The agreement between the Head of the Civil Service and the competent minister/voivode on the requirements to be met by candidates took from 6 days to 1 year and 8 months. The reason for the lengthy reconciliation of requirements was mainly due to the fact that the relevant ministers/voivodes did not respond to the requirements proposed by the Head of the Civil Service, despite repeated reminders (NIK 2005: 36–52).

The audit also found that in 2002 there was a significant decrease in the number of competition proceedings, which was undoubtedly linked to the introduction of Article 144a. At the same time, it was alleged that the auditors used non-substantive criteria in their hiring. In June 2004, out of the audited offices, in 5 of them the posts of director general of offices were still being filled on the basis of the non-applicable Article 144a. A total of 65.1 % of senior civil service posts – i.e. 499 (in the 33 offices audited) were filled on the basis of delegation. By contrast, as at 28 February 2005, one post of Director-General was filled on the basis of Article 144a of the Act. Between 2001 and 2002, the number of posts filled without competition increased from 315 to 544. Another post-audit conclusion was that:

> Delegation of duties to senior positions in the civil service, for long periods of time, has become a common practice which, in the opinion of the Supreme Audit Office, distorts the idea of the civil service. In addition, the entrusting of duties to persons, within a short period of time of their employment in the office, may also be indicative of non-substantive considerations, when deciding on the selection of persons entrusted with duties (NIK 2005: 5).

Furthermore, it has been rightly noted that personnel changes in these positions are natural, common in all democratic countries. When they are made too frequently and involve the professional, and not the political, staff of the office, they will, however, constitute a danger to the proper functioning of the office, and thus of the entire state structures. The introduction of the principles of competitive filling of senior positions in the Civil Service Act was intended to reduce this risk factor. The conclusion, after the audit, is that the opportunity to create an apolitical and professional civil service through the filling of senior positions was not used. During the audit period, in 2 offices (in the Ministry of Science and Informatisation and in the Ministry of the Treasury), directors general of offices were appointed under Article 144 of the Civil Service Act, without a competition procedure, in violation of Article 41, paragraph 2 of the Civil Service Act. The responsibility for this lies with Prime Minister Leszek Miller, who concluded the above contracts (NIK 2005: 36–52). During the audit period, the Head of the Civil Service conducted 709 competitions for senior positions in the civil service, which resulted in the selection of 592 persons. 296 appeals were filed against the results of 249 competitions. It is puzzling that the Head of the Civil Service found violations of competition rules in 30 cases and ordered a re-run of the competition. There were violations of deadlines, as well as unjustified refusal to admit a candidate to the competition and failure to notify the competition. The Supreme Audit Office was also critical of the rules governing the conduct of competitions, alleging a lack of detail and precision, resulting in violations and shortcomings in the application of the procedure (NIK 2005: 36–52).

In summary, the picture that emerges from the audit carried out by the Supreme Audit Office shows the indolence of the institutions, the lack of respect for the law, the lack of control measures for the Head of the Civil Service and, above all, the lack of understanding of the idea of the civil service. Political office-holders have not grasped, and do not seem to grasp to this day, that efficient, professional and politically neutral performance of the state's tasks does not have to involve a complete replacement of civil servants after winning an election.

The biggest changes occurred in connection with the 2006 laws. As a result of the enactment of the Civil Service Act and the Act on State Personnel Resources and High State Positions, senior positions were separated from the civil service corps and included in the State Personnel Resources, i. e. the set of candidates for high state positions. Only middle management, coordinating, independent, specialist and support positions were left in the civil service corps. The legislator abandoned the competition for senior positions, and they were filled by appointment from among candidates from the PZK by the competent authority, which was the President of the Council of Ministers or the competent minister, possibly the head of a central office and sometimes the Head of the Chancellery of the President of the Council of Ministers (Article 10 of the Act on p. z. k.). This resulted in a kind of dichotomy in the form of separation of persons employed in one office into those subject to the regime of the Civil Service Act and those subject to the regime of the State Personnel Resources Act. Both appointment and dismissal could take place at any time and in the same manner, which meant that there was total discretion and discretion in this respect. The prerequisite of having a good reputation, which a person appointed to a high-ranking state post should enjoy, was also applied (Article 11). Prerequisites for obligatory dismissal were singled out, i. e.: gross violation of the law, pursuit of an activity that is contrary to the duties performed, loss of the ability to perform official duties due to illness or other obstacle permanently preventing the performance of official duties, resignation from the post, conviction by a final sentence for an intentional crime or intentional fiscal crime, renunciation of Polish citizenship, loss of validity of a certificate confirming the qualifications for work on a high state post (art. 12 of the Act on p. z. k.).

In the doctrine, attention was drawn to the unconstitutionality of the above provisions (already at the stage of preparation of opinions to the drafts of both Acts) due to the narrowing of the subject scope of the civil service corps. Pursuant to Article 153, the civil service corps operates in government administration, this provision does not indicate the possibility of excluding certain positions from the scope of the service, which is precisely what the legislator has done. Only positions of a strictly political nature are excluded from the scope: ministers, voivodes, the Prime Minister. Also in countries with a well-established civil service structure, e. g. in France or Germany, we find such solutions (Działocha&Łukaszczuk 2006: 8–9). Narrowing the personal scope of the corps therefore leads to a breach of constitutional norms. In the course of giving an opinion on both drafts, it was pointed out that the introduction of such a solution would result in:

> (…) each time the rulers can fill all senior positions in the government administration at their political discretion. This mainly concerns the positions of directors and deputy directors of departments (and equivalents) in government administration offices and the positions of directors general – crucial for the functioning of the administration. The problem, therefore, concerns the legal position of a relatively small group of people – I think it is about 1,000–1500 people – whose role, however, for the functioning of public administration is crucial. By belonging to the civil service corps, they are its elite and create personal role models. Belonging to the political sphere, they are the party's 'soldiers' in the administration, executors of its programme mission, while for the rest of the administration staff they are a variable, external factor. M. Kulesza accused the draft laws in his opinion of promoting political servilism and promoting a career path to higher positions through political affiliation (2006: 5–6).

The explanatory memorandum to both laws emphasised that the civil service system was to be simplified and isolated from political influence, and the employment relationship adapted to the needs of implementing government policy, requiring rapid personnel decisions to be made at short notice and in a flexible manner. The managerial staff is to implement the policy of the government, the minister, the head of the central office or the provincial governor and should not have a permanent/stable employment relationship, as this negatively affects the quality of work (Explanatory memorandum to the draft civil service law 2006). There is no statutory guarantee of political neutrality in the Law on State Personnel and High State Positions. In turn, the explanatory memorandum reads: "The prohibition enshrined in the law on manifesting political views and being guided in the performance of duties by individual or group interests is a guarantee of the impartiality and integrity of the activities of persons in high state positions" (Explanatory Memorandum to the Draft Law on State Personnel and High State Positions 2006). The Constitutional Court has repeatedly dealt with the neutrality of members of the civil service corps, pointing out that political neutrality is the absence of the possibility of the influence of the world of politics on the activities of the corps, it is an order of political neutrality in the performance of state tasks. Thus, it is about maintaining neutrality with regard to the interests of political parties and conflicts generated by them or individual politicians. The Court pointed out that the public interest and the closely related tasks of the state and the need for objective adjudication of the duties entrusted to it are not always compatible with the interests of individual parties, coalitions or political groups. Guaranteeing the neutrality of the civil service corps consists in such a statutory solution that will guarantee: "(…) the absence of any, even temporary, possibility of interference in this area by politicians in power. The mechanism should therefore be free from the possibility of any interference from politics or attempts to impose specific decisions" (Judgment of the Constitutional Tribunal of 12 December 2002, ref. no. K 9/02, Journal of Laws no. 238, item 2025). Also in 2003 the Court ruled that Article 153 of the Constitution:

> (…) requires the legislator to shape the bodies functioning in the civil service in such a way as to eliminate influence of a political nature. The political neutrality of the civil service corps is to constitute a guarantee, indispensable for the proper performance of the tasks of the state, of the stability of the civil service staff in a situation of changing governments in a democratic state. One of the values arising from the establishment of a civil service corps is the prospect of ensuring a professional, stable and responsible service to the state apparatus and the administration's stakeholders (Judgment of the Constitutional Tribunal of 13 November 2003, ref. no. K 51/02, Journal of Laws. No. 199, item 1952).

On the other hand, in its judgment of 10 April 2002, the Court pointed out that political neutrality – or apoliticality – is the absence of an official's participation in a "widely understood political game". Freedom of functioning of an official means independence from political parties, ideology, religion. Ensuring political neutrality, according to the Court's judges "… is to be served by separating posts of a political nature, which are filled according to political criteria, from official, administrative posts, which are filled on the basis of considerations of a substantive nature" (Judgment of the Constitutional Tribunal of 10 April 2002, ref. no. K 26/00, Journal of Laws. No. 56, item 517). Furthermore, in the judgment of 12 December 2002, already cited, the Court drew attention to the professional performance of the tasks of the state (which is a premise arising directly from the Constitution), which is a necessary element within employment in the civil service corps. Persons employed must treat their duties as a permanent exercise of their profession and not merely a temporary occupation, as this would not reflect the idea of the civil service (Judgment of the Constitutional Tribunal of 12 December 2002, Case No. K 9/02, Journal of Laws No. 238, item 2025). The fact that both laws were passed in such a form demonstrates the political rationale of the legislator. However, it may also be an argument that we are witnessing a lack of respect for the rules of a democratic state of law granting the Constitution and its solutions the key place in the hierarchy of sources of law. It is also incomprehensible to underestimate the opinions of experts in this area, who unequivocally point to the unconstitutionality of some of the provisions on the one hand, and their divergence from the rules of a democratic state of law on the other. The introduction of rules that turn the most important official positions in the state into political spoils conflicts with the requirement to take care of the professional, pressure-free performance of state tasks. The construction of the Law on State Personnel Resources departed from the principles declared in the justification of the separation of the political and administrative spheres; on the contrary, it caused excessive interpenetration of the two spheres. The exclusion of senior positions from the civil service caused destabilisation and uncertainty for senior civil servants. One of the elements of building a loyal, professional civil servant cadre is to ensure its sustainability and its ability to perform its tasks reliably regardless of the turbulence and changes on the political scene. The exclusion from the corps and the dependence of appointments on the free decision of a political superior has shattered the sense of security and stability. The lack of trust between the new political sphere and the existing administrative sphere results in the immediate replacement of senior (and not only) civil servants. The overlapping lack of loyalty and the desire to capture government administration led to the enactment of the fourth Civil Service Act since the turn of 1989 (2008), with the simultaneous elimination of the Civil Service Act passed in 2006: Civil Service Act and the Act on State Personnel Resources and High State Positions. In September 2008, more than 7 500 persons were registered in the State Personnel Resource Register, while 264 persons passed the examination at the National School of Public Administration (Wyższe wynagrodzenia 2008).

The 2008 Civil Service Act reverted to the 1998 solutions, abolishing the state human resources and incorporating senior positions into the civil service corps. However, there was a marked change from the 1998 legislation. The filling of senior positions followed a competitive procedure, however, the Act allows persons from outside the service to enter the competition, making it an open and competitive competition. The Act did not provide for a centralised system of holding competitions for senior posts, as the 1998 Act did, since they were conducted by the Head of the Civil Service. In this respect, the competence was decentralised, granting it to the directors general of offices. The exception was the recruitment for the posts of directors general of offices, which is carried out by a team appointed by the Head of the Civil Service. A senior position in the service could be held by a person who fulfilled the following conditions (art. 53): had a professional degree of Master's degree or equivalent, had not been punished with a ban on holding managerial positions in offices of public authorities or performing functions related to the disposal of public funds, had managerial competence, had at least six years of work experience, including at least three years in a managerial position in units of the public finance sector – if applying for the post of director general of offices, had at least three years of work experience, including at least one year in a managerial position or at least two years in an independent position in a public finance sector unit – to another higher position in the civil service, met the requirements specified in the job description and in separate regulations.

The creation of a catalogue of prerequisites for eligibility to apply for a higher position in the civil service was necessary due to the elimination of the condition in the form of an appointment. Thus, the opening of recruitment to persons who do not have confirmation of their qualifications in the form of a civil service examination forced the legislator to create criteria confirming them (at the initial stage, of course – at the moment of joining the recruitment). In addition, in June 2009 the Recommendations of the Head of the Civil Service on the conduct of recruitment to senior positions in the service were issued. They constituted a general instrument for carrying out recruitment, of a preventive nature, introducing uniform rules for all participants in the process, clearly defined and communicated to all participants in the process (Rekomendacje Szefa Służby Cywilnej 2009: 20).

Article 54(6) explicitly prohibited the filling of a senior position by entrustment. The announcement of a competition for a senior position in the civil service is to be published in a publicly accessible place at the office, in the Office Bulletin and in the Bulletin of the Prime Minister's Office. The competition is to be carried out by a team composed of members of the civil service whose knowledge and experience warrant the selection of the best candidates. Competition teams are appointed by: by the Head of the Civil Service – in the case of competitions for directors general of offices and by directors general – in the case of competitions for directors and deputy directors of departments in the Chancellery of the Prime Minister, ministries and central offices, and competitions for directors and deputy directors in provincial offices, by the Chief Veterinary Doctor – in the case of competitions for provincial veterinarians and their deputies, or by the President of the Office for Registration of Medicinal Products, Medical Devices and Biocidal Products or the Director of the Forest Seed Office – in the case of competitions for heads of organisational units in these institutions and their deputies. In the course of the recruitment process for a senior position, inter alia, professional experience, knowledge necessary to perform the tasks related to the position, as well as managerial competence were assessed (Article 56(4)). In the course of the recruitment, the team selected no more than 2 best candidates and presented them to the relevant body, depending on the position (e.g. when the recruitment concerned the director general of offices, the candidates were presented to the Head of the Chancellery of the Prime Minister, the relevant minister, the chairman of a committee of the Council of Ministers, the head of a central office or a voivode – Article 57). The choice of the candidate is left to the discretion of the relevant body, and, as aptly noted in the literature on the subject, it does not have to be the candidate who has achieved the best result, which may be controversial even in the absence of any grounds for doing so. These solutions are accused that the subjective opinion of the competent authority may be decisive instead of substantive criteria (Stefański 2009: 19–20).

A protocol had to be drawn up of the recruitment. The novelty in the 2008 Act was, of course, the absence of the prerequisite of membership of the corps, which should be assessed positively due to the opening of the competition and going, *de facto*, beyond internal recruitment. There was also the possibility to fill a senior position without a competition by seconding a member of the civil service corps meeting the requirements for the position (Article 54, paragraph 4). The legislator introduced in Article 61 the rather controversial possibility of transferring persons occupying senior positions in the service. Transfer may be made at any time if the legitimate needs of the office or the interests of the civil service warrant it. A member of the corps may be transferred to an official position, in the same locality, at least equivalent in terms of salary to the position occupied prior to being employed in a senior position, but it must be in accordance with his qualifications and professional preparation. On the other hand, a member of the corps who was not employed in the civil service prior to being recruited to a senior position – to another official position in the same locality also consistent with the member's qualifications and professional preparation. The taking up of a post is usually associated with a relative, at least temporary, stabilisation of the employment relationship, which in the above situations has been considerably offset (Stefański 2009: 20). The introduction of undefined prerequisites in the form of the legitimate needs of the office and the enigmatic interest of the civil service must be controversial, as it allows in principle for unlimited transferability. There is no guarantee of work in the position occupied in this situation.

In view of the structural change through the abolition of the State Personnel Reserve, the legislator had to provide for various situations in the transitional provisions. Article 193 of the 2008 Act stipulated that within 30 days from the date of entry into force of the Act, a member of the civil service corps who is employed in the same office in which he holds a high state position becoming a higher position in the civil service shall be transferred, with his consent, to a higher position in the civil service corresponding to the high state position held. In turn, in Article 195, paragraph 1, the legislator stipulated that within 30 days from the date of entry into force of the Act, a person who is not a member of the civil service corps and who occupies, on the date of entry into force of the Act, a high-ranking state position becoming a higher position in the civil service, shall be offered employment in a higher position in the civil service corresponding to that position, or, if not accepted, in another position in the same office, in accordance with his/her qualifications and professional preparation.

Between 2009 and 2015, the provisions on filling senior positions in the civil service remained unchanged. In 2011, the Supreme Audit Office (NIK) conducted an audit: "Functioning of the civil service within the framework of the applicable legal regulations. The scope of the audit also examined the procedure for filling senior positions in the civil service". As a result, it was found that among the 676 recruitments for senior positions in the service that were carried out, irregularities were detected in only 2 proceedings and deficiencies in 11. In one case, the Head of the Civil Service ordered the Director General to re-run the competition: for the post of Director of the Security and Crisis Management Department of the Łódzkie Voivodship Office. In the NIK's assessment:

> (…) the Directors General, in filling senior positions in the civil service through open recruitment, ensured that the process was open and competitive. Recruitment was carried out in accordance with statutory rules and on the basis of internal regulations. The top positions were filled by persons who were selected by the recruitment teams and, in the case of internal promotion, by persons who met the requirements given to the position (NIK 2012: 34).

The Supreme Audit Office carried out this audit in 2011 in 21 offices, namely: Chancellery of the Prime Minister, 4 ministries, two central offices, 7 provincial offices, 7 tax offices and at the Head of the Civil Service. The audit covered the period from 24 March 2009 to 30 June 2011 with regard to the functioning of the civil service, and the period from 1 January 2009 to 30 June 2011 with regard to the filling of positions of heads of tax offices and directors of tax chambers. As can be seen, this was a time of slow implementation and strengthening of the provisions of the 2008 Act.

In 2010, after the abolition of the PZK and the integration of senior posts into the civil service, the number of senior posts was 1682 (as at 31 December 2010), of which 1569 posts were filled and 113 vacancies remained. This represents only 6.72 %. In 2010, the number of vacancies advertised for senior civil service posts was 283. Of the total number of vacancies advertised, 207 ended in the selection of candidates (representing approximately 73 % of the total number of completed vacancies). However, filling a position through a competition represents only about 17 % of all filled senior positions. Most, i. e. 767 (approximately 49 %) of the filled senior civil service positions were filled on the basis of Article 193(1) of the Civil Service Act, according to which a member of the civil service corps occupying a senior state position was transferred – with his/her consent – to a senior civil service position in the same office. The second most frequent basis for occupying a senior position was the so-called internal promotion, carried out only with regard to deputy heads of cells, on the basis of Article 54(2) and Article 204 of the Civil Service Act – 295 positions (i. e. about 19 % of all filled senior positions and about 35 % of positions (Sprawozdanie Szefa Służby Cywilnej za 2010: 21).

In 2011, 124 vacancies for senior positions in the civil service were conducted but does not apply to positions of directors-general (Sprawozdanie Szefa Służby Cywilnej za 2011: 21) Of all the vacancies conducted, 82 were concluded with the selection of candidates – i. e. 66 % of the vacancies conducted. The total number of vacancies for senior positions in the civil service in 2011 was 201 (of which 61 were still created in 2010). In the Report, vacancies for the positions of directors-general were classified separately. In 2011, there were 64 director general of offices positions in government offices (there were 62 director general positions in 2010). As at 31 December 2011, 53 of the above positions were filled. In 2011, work was undertaken to conduct and prepare 13 recruitments for the positions of directors general of offices as follows: Chancellery of the President of the Council of Ministers, Ministry of Culture and National Heritage, State Atomic Energy Agency, General Directorate for Environmental Protection, General Inspectorate of Road Transport, Railway Transport Office, Central Office of Weights and Measures, Central Office of Geodesy and Cartography, Office for Registration of Medicinal Products, Medical Devices and Biocidal Products, Ministry of Justice, Ministry of National Defence, Ministry of the Interior, Mazowieckie Voivodeship Office. Due to the resignation of the candidate selected during the recruitment, the resignation of all candidates during the recruitment, the termination of the recruitment without selecting the best candidate and, in particular, the non-completion of the recruitment procedure or the work related to the preparations for the recruitment – 10 of the above recruitments were continued in 2012. As at 30 March 2012, 4 recruitments had been completed. It is significant to note the words of the then Head of the Civil Service, who expressed concern about the lengthy process of vacancies for directors general of offices, in particular the failure of some relevant government authorities to comply with the statutory principle of promptness of their action to fill vacancies in these positions (Sprawozdanie Szefa Służby Cywilnej za 2011: 21–43).

In 2012, 172 recruitments for senior positions were carried out, excluding the posts of directors-general, of which there were also 64 in 2012. A significant increase in the number of incoming offers was noted – 1109 (2011: 767). The recruitment success rate for senior positions was 76 %, i. e. 131 vacancies were completed with a successful candidate. On 31 December, 55 posts were filled. In 2012, 22 recruitments were carried out for chief executive posts, of which 15 were filled. Identical to the previous year, the Head of the Civil Service expressed concern about the lengthy process of vacancies and the failure of some offices to follow the principle of prompt action to fill vacancies (Sprawozdanie Szefa Służby Cywilnej za 2012: 18–52).

In 2013, 192 vacancies for senior civil service positions were conducted, of which 73 % resulted in the selection and 68 % in the hiring of candidates. A total of 1 481 offers were received in response to advertisements for vacant senior positions (an increase on 2012 can be seen). There were 12 vacancies for directors general of offices. The recruitments completed in 2013 led to the filling of 9 director general of offices posts. As a result of the conducted recruitments, on 31 December 2013, 61(97 %) of the 63 positions of directors general of offices existing in the government administration offices were filled (on 27 November 2013, the Ministries of Transport, Construction and Maritime Economy and Regional Development were merged to form the Ministry of Infrastructure and Development) (Sprawozdanie Szefa Służby Cywilnej za 2013: 15–18). The analysis shows a significant increase in the effectiveness of the recruitments carried out.

In 2014, the staffing level for the positions of chief executive officers remained relatively high (at 31 December – 94 %, i. e. 59 out of 63 positions). At the same time, 83 %

of the recruitments for these positions resulted in the employment of a candidate. It is noticeable that there is a reduced turnover and a high efficiency of the recruitments carried out. At the same time, interest in senior positions in the civil service remained low compared to other positions, with an average of 6.5 offers per position. For one recruitment conducted for the post of director general of offices, an average of 6 offers were received in 2014. For the other senior positions in the civil service, an average of 7 candidates applied for one post. This may be related to the much higher requirements for these positions, as well as the much lower salaries compared to comparable positions in the private sector (Sprawozdanie Szefa Służby Cywilnej za 2014: 13–23).

In contrast, in 2015, interest in a senior civil service post remained almost identical (6.6 candidates on average). There were an average of 5.9 offers per recruitment carried out for the post of director general of offices. For the other senior posts, an average of 6.7 candidates applied for one post. In 2015, 9 people started working for the posts of directors-general and 23 finished (of whom 7 started as a result of vacancies that had already started in 2014). Overall, the occupancy level of these positions at the end of the year fell from 94 % in 2014 to 69 % in 2015. This was linked to the fact that a significant number of people ended up in these positions in the last quarter of 2015, which was of course linked to the December 2015 statutory changes. The Head of the Civil Service explains the low interest, compared to the other positions, in hiring for the higher positions by the considerably lower salaries in relation to the private sector while at the same time the requirements are very high (Sprawozdanie Szefa Służby Cywilnej za 2015: 12–23).

Overall, the number of higher posts fluctuated around 1,600 between 1999 and 2015 (from 1,430 in 2002 to 1,689 in 2005). Only since 2016 has there been a significant increase. As a result of statutory changes in October 2016, the catalogue of senior positions in the civil service expanded to include the positions of district veterinarian and deputy district veterinarian. Article 6 of the Act of 23 September 2016 on amending certain laws to combat infectious animal diseases, (Journal of Laws. 2016, item 1605).

These positions were previously in the group of middle management positions. In 2016, these positions were held by 515 people. The increase was as high as 32.4 per cent. In 2017, there were further statutory changes to the tax administration structures. The National Fiscal Administration was introduced at the same time as the following positions were established as senior positions: the director of the fiscal administration chamber, the director of the National Fiscal Information, the head of the fiscal office, the head of the customs and fiscal office and their deputies. In the case of the tax administration chambers and tax offices, these positions were previously middle management positions. The increase in senior positions in 2017 in relation to 2015 was as high as 101.32 %, while in relation to 2016 it was an increase of 52.02 %. In 2020, the posts of provincial inspectors of commercial quality of agri-food products and their deputies were included, increasing the number of senior posts to 3389. Article 13 of the Act of 23 January 2020 amending the Act on commercial quality of agri-food articles and certain other acts, (Journal of Laws 2020, item 285).

How sensitive senior positions in the civil service have been and continue to be is evidenced by the figures quoted above. From the point of view of ministers or heads of central offices, they are the most important element in the running of an institution, but at the same time (and this is often forgotten) they should be staffed by people with professional training. This leads to the conclusion that every time the political leadership of an institution (irrespective of its political colour) is afraid to work with officials who worked under their political opponents. On the one hand, it is difficult to disagree with some of this, but given the purpose of the civil service corps, such a thesis should not be justified.

In 2016, the competitive procedure for filling senior positions was abolished and replaced by the institution of appointment by authorised bodies (the amended provisions became effective on 23 January 2016). In addition, a statutory extinguishment of the employment relations of persons holding senior positions in the civil service was introduced. Pursuant to Article 6(1) of the amending Act, employment relations with persons holding senior positions in the civil service on the date the Act enters into force shall expire 30 days after the date of entry into force of the Act if, before the expiry of that period, they are not offered new conditions of work or pay for a further period of time or if they do not accept new conditions of work or pay. Civil servants are excluded from these solutions (Article 6(3)). With a single provision, the legislator provides itself with the possibility of replacing part of the staff occupying senior positions and this within a period of 30 days. Within the statutory period (30 days), 293 persons (19 %) were transferred to another position in the service, while employment relationships expired for 212 persons (13 %). During the period indicated, 1124 corps members (among whom were also those who had previously held senior positions) were appointed to higher positions. 131 persons were appointed from outside the civil service (about 12 %) (Sprawozdanie Szefa Służby Cywilnej za 2016: 29–30). In individual groups of offices, the figures are as follows: in ministries, out of 780 persons employed, employment relations expired for 105 persons, i. e. 13 %, in central offices, out of 432 persons, employment relations expired for 29 persons, i. e. 7 %, and in voivodeship offices and veterinary inspectorates, out of almost 370 persons employed in senior positions, employment relations expired for 78 persons, i. e. about 21 % (Sprawozdanie z 14 Posiedzenia Sejmu RP 2016). From the data presented, it appears that the greatest changes have taken place in the field administration. However, it seems to me that these changes will continue, because with such a legal basis, the temptation for politicians will be too great.

The most serious objection to the 2015 amendment is the abandonment of open and competitive recruitment for senior positions. Competitions were replaced by the institution of appointment. According to the new regulations (Article 53a), appointments (and dismissals) to senior positions in the civil service are made by the relevant minister, the head of a central office, the Head of the Chancellery of the Prime Minister and the provincial governor. Deputies and heads of organisational units are appointed by the director general of the office. The institution of appointment regulated by the Act of 26 June 1974 will apply here. Labour Code. At the same time, qualification requirements for persons occupying higher positions were relaxed by eliminating the condition of having six years of seniority in a managerial position (for general directors) and three years of seniority, including at least one year in a managerial position or two years in an independent position (for other higher positions). Abandoning recruitment in the form of a competition and replacing it with an arbitrary appointment that will de facto be made by politicians is a misunderstanding of the idea of the civil service. This solution undoes the still "fragile" and laboriously built Polish civil service. The legislator in the justification of the above changes states that:

> (...) the practice of application of the Civil Service Act indicates that the recruitment procedures have often been prolonged and ineffective, leading to delays in filling vacant positions. This phenomenon is particularly undesirable in the case of senior positions in the civil service, which are particularly related to the implementation of government policy and ensuring efficient administration and management of human resources. (...) Given the importance and scope of the tasks performed in senior positions in the civil service and the need to ensure the smooth functioning of the civil service carrying out government activities, it is proposed that hiring for the position should be done in a flexible and less formalised manner. The filling of senior positions in the civil service will therefore be by appointment by authorised bodies. This will enable the efficient employment in senior positions in the civil service of persons who meet the requirements provided for such positions in the Civil Service Act, and at the same time have the education, skills and aptitude adapted to the current needs of the office (Uzasadnienie 2015).

These solutions are mainly accused of being unconstitutional. On 1 February 2016. Ombudsman Adam Bodnar filed a motion to the Constitutional Tribunal to declare Article 53a of the Civil Service Act inconsistent with Articles 60 and 153(1) of the Polish Constitution, among others. According to the Ombudsman, the repeal of competitions introduces arbitrariness in the filling of senior positions and contradicts Article 60 of the Constitution, which ensures the right of citizens to access the public service on an equal basis. The Obdusman states that:

> Indeed, the abolition of the competition procedure also means the abolition of the procedural yardstick for checking whether this access takes place on an equal basis. Consequently, there is also no procedure to verify whether senior positions in the civil service are filled in a way that guarantees professional, reliable, impartial and politically neutral performance of state tasks (Article 153(1) of the Constitution of the Republic of Poland) (Ombudsman's application to the Constitutional Court 2016).

In addition, the amendment substantially violates Article 60 of the Constitution, according to which citizens are to have guaranteed access to the public service on identical terms. While providing in Article 6 of the Civil Service Act for the right to information about vacant positions and defining recruitment as open and competitive, the legislator at the same time excludes the provisions concerning higher positions. Thus, it differentiates equality of access for all citizens. In this regard, it is important to recall the judgment of the Supreme Court of 13 December 2010 (Judgment of the Supreme Court of 13 December 2010), in which the Court stated that:

> (…) the good protected by Article 60 of the Constitution is the transparency and openness of the rules applied in determining the requirements for taking up functions in the public service. The right guaranteed by this provision of the Constitution also includes the verifiability of the criteria used for recruitment to the service – the public authority is entitled to set specific conditions for access to a particular service, and thus selective recruitment to the public service. However, it is necessary to create adequate guarantees of the rule of law of decisions concerning access to the public service, so as to exclude any arbitrariness of action by the public authority.

In a similar vein, the Supreme Bar Council, the National Chamber of Legal Advisers, the Prosecutor General or Prof. H. Izdebski expressed their opinion, unanimously stating that the amendment violates constitutional rules and is aimed at politicising senior positions. In turn, the Supreme Court in its opinion of 7 January 2016 on the amendment stated that: "The principle of free filling of civil servant positions in the public administration organically contradicts the principles of a professional, politically neutral and stable civil servant corps in the state administration" (Opinion of the Supreme Court of 7 January 2016). And the 2002 Constitutional Court judgment discussed below will be fully applicable.

It is significant that the legislator does not draw conclusions from past practice and case law. In 2002, shortly after the parliamentary elections in autumn 2001, the victorious SLD and UP coalition, together with the Polish People's Party (PSL), introduced Article 144a into the then-effective law on the civil service (discussed above), allowing the Head of the Civil Service to fill senior positions bypassing the competition procedure. With such an enigmatically worded and undefined rationale in principle, any choice could be justified. The amendment had basically one objective: to politicise senior positions in the civil service. The Constitutional Tribunal found Article 144a to be unconstitutional, as it undermines the idea of filling senior positions by introducing illegible rules for the functioning of the service, and the abandonment of open and competitive recruitment means that there are no procedural guarantees for the verification of candidates. This is tantamount to arbitrary hiring decisions with a violation of the principles of the professional and apolitical nature of the service (Judgment of the Constitutional Tribunal of 12 December 2002). However, the Court's ruling did not entail the automatic loss of posts, so the persons in question were, in some cases, still performing their functions. Accordingly, as at 1 April 2003, there were 779 vacancies out of 1,515 senior civil service posts, which were filled by 705 temporary 'acting' persons (Brunetko 2003).

It is therefore impossible to agree with the legislator's rationale for lowering the qualification requirements for those occupying higher positions when speaking of the efficient functioning of the service. In his opinion, H. Izdebski draws attention to yet another extremely important element, namely that the legislator, in justifying this change, links higher positions with the "performance of government policy", whereas Article 153(1) of the Constitution provides for the "tasks of the state", the scope of which is undoubtedly broader (2016). These solutions clearly show a return to the 2006 regulations with some modifications, i.e. leaving the higher positions in the corps, but on separate terms. In 2006, these positions were excluded from the corps and were included in the State Human Resources.

Of a different opinion on the issue of eliminating the competitive recruitment mode are Z. Snażyk and M. Gintowt-Jankowicz. The former believes that the formula of appointment to senior positions may contribute to greater political loyalty of officials, whose primary task is to implement the political agenda of those in power. What remains debatable is the effectiveness of such a way of verifying qualifications, which remains at the disposal of the appointee (Snażyk 2016). M. Gintowt-Jankowicz, on the other hand, believes that there is little interest in competition proceedings, with only 2–3 people taking part "(…) it deprives these procedures of the nature of a competition and in fact remains a sham, a sham that is wasteful for a number of reasons (the time of the recruiters, the costs of tests and examinations, and the protraction in filling an important post, as raised in the justification of the project)". In addition, she notes that the possibility of filling a post without competition provided for in the law – Article 54, Articles 62–68 (so-called transfer; internal promotion), and the consequent frequent use of this procedure constitute a weakness of the competition mode. However, the author concludes that it will be necessary to develop a qualification verification procedure especially for directors general of offices and directors of departments (Gintowt-Jankowicz 2015). It is difficult to agree with the author on this matter, as the 2014 Report of the Head of the Civil Service shows that interest in senior positions oscillated at – 6.5 offers per place. With regard to the positions of directors-general in 2014, it was an average of 6 offers, while for the other positions it was 7 offers. Appointment to a senior position in the corps is also linked to the problem of granting unpaid leave for the duration of tenure. With the 2015 amendment, adjustments were also made in this regard. It was decided that a civil servant and an employee appointed to a position, the director general of the office or the head of the office (depending on the position) in which he is employed shall grant unpaid leave for the duration of the appointment. On the other hand, at the end of the unpaid leave, the civil servant or employee must be assigned a job position in line with his or her professional qualifications and skills (Article 53a(9)). Against the background of the Supreme Court's jurisprudence, this solution should not raise doubts, as in the judgment of 18 November 2014 (Judgment of the Supreme Court of 18 November 2014), the Supreme Court stated that it is permissible to grant an employee unpaid leave for the period of employment on the basis of appointment. At the same time, there will be no termination or transformation of the existing employment contract here, which runs concurrently with the employment relationship on the basis of appointment. And the mere revocation does not affect the existence of the employment contract under which the employee takes unpaid leave (Culepa 2016:13–14).

To sum up, the legislator in part of the solutions returned to the concept from 2006. Changing the optics of the civil service and treating it in terms of political spoils (in relation to sensitive – higher positions) is a misunderstanding of the idea of the corps. Lack of freedom from political influence in the course of carrying out public administration tasks may result in complete politicisation and acting for the benefit of those currently in power. The Civil Service Corps cannot be completely independent of political decision-makers, since in implementing the vision of the state of those currently in power, it has to follow the policy of the government. Hence, we cannot speak of complete independence, but at the same time we can put in place mechanisms to ensure that tasks are performed in the interests of the state and not in the interests of particular party politics. Competitions for senior positions in the civil service were undoubtedly such a mechanism. Positions that are sensitive in terms of the performance of state tasks and management in the civil service corps. The latest amendments to the law should be assessed unequivocally negatively. Firstly, they demolish the proverbial 'roof' of the corps – eliminating competitions for senior positions. By changing the formula created over a number of years, they negate good models implemented with great difficulty and resistance. They are opposing European civil service standards based on transparent, open and accessible procedures. As a result, they are destroying the achievements to date. However, Prof. M. Gintowt-Jankowicz is right when she writes that the claim often made in the public debate that the amendment abolishes the civil service is an abuse. Undoubtedly, it abolishes open and competitive recruitment for senior positions, which from many points of view constitute the 'heart' of the system, without which no organism is able to function properly. In the whole situation, the positive aspect is the possibility to occupy higher positions for persons who have gained professional experience outside the public sector (e.g. in the private sector). It is clear from the explanatory memorandum to the draft amendment that political preferences can/should be applied in the filling of senior positions, which raises the greatest doubts and concerns.

4.2.7 Change and termination of the employment relationship

One of the elements necessary in the formation of the employment relationship of a corps member are the issues of change and termination of the employment relationship. All normative acts have devoted considerable space to them. An elementary feature characterising work in the civil service is availability, hence all acts have provided for the possibility of transferring a member of the civil service corps to another post, to another office, or to another locality. The employment relationship of a person in the service is additionally encumbered by the possibility of unilateral and authoritative shaping by superiors, subject to the rules of law. Using the undefined premises: "the needs of the office" and "the interest of the service", the legislator allows a derogation from the rule of stabilisation of the employment relationship, doing so in the form of a unilateral, individual internal administrative-legal act (Cieślak at al. 1998: 118–119). The 1996 Act introduced the following possibilities for changing the employment relationship: transfer of a civil servant to another office in the same locality by the Head of the Civil Service, transfer of a civil servant to another office in another locality for no more than two years by the Head of the Civil Service, transfer of a civil servant to another office in another locality, once a year for a period of 6 months by the director general of offices, granting, at the request of an official, unpaid leave for the duration of an occupation, position or function outside the service, transfer of an official to inactive status for 1 year, with extension for 6 months in special situations, suspension of the employment relationship of an official under temporary arrest or against whom disciplinary or criminal proceedings have been brought. A transfer was made if the interests of the service or the specific interests of the service warranted it. The legislator graded the prerequisites and, although they appear to be ambiguous, it is possible, by applying the general provisions on the service, to make the concepts more specific. The interest of the service will thus be what the legislator included in art. 1 of the Act (reproducing Article 153 of the Constitution) defining the purpose of the establishment of the service – that is, to ensure the professional, reliable, impartial and politically neutral performance of the tasks of the state. Misappropriation of the above principles therefore constituted a violation of the interest of the service (Cieślak at al. 1998: 118–119). The transfer to another office in another locality could be for a period of up to 2 years. When transferring a civil servant to another locality, the Head of the Civil Service ensured that the civil servant had adequate housing, taking into account his/her family situation. Such a transfer could take place at most twice during the civil servant's employment relationship. It was not permissible to transfer without the consent of the civil servant a pregnant woman or a person who was the sole guardian of a child under the age of fifteen. It was also not permissible to carry out such a transfer when particularly important personal or family reasons of the civil servant stood in the way (Article 35). Where unpaid leave was granted, this period was counted – up to a total of five years – as part of the period of service on which the civil servant's employment entitlements depended (Article 38). This provision was a privilege designed to keep the civil servant in the corps regardless of a temporary change of activity. While remaining in a state of inactivity, the civil servant could not perform work but retained the right to the civil servant's category, salary and other entitlements and benefits, could not take up additional employment without the Director-General's consent and could not engage in activities or other occupations contrary to the civil servant's duties (Article 40 in conjunction with Article 51).

All subsequent Civil Service Acts have not brought radical changes in the above matter. Apart from a few significant changes, in many situations even the structure of the provisions was preserved, and some were even directly copied. The general change concerning the introduction of a category of corps employees in the 1998 Act forced the legislator to catalogue norms pertaining only to this part of the corps. Thus, in all laws, the institution of transfer of a civil servant corps official was left in place by introducing the premise: "legitimate needs of the office". At the same time, provision was made for the possibility of transferring a member of the civil service corps to another office in the same or another locality, at his/her request or with his/her consent by the director general of offices. In the 2006 Act. The Head of the Civil Service was replaced by the Head of the Chancellery of the Prime Minister. In addition, the 2006 Act introduced the possibility of transfer to a civil service position for persons previously employed in administrative offices functioning under the provisions of the Act on State Office Employees, the Act on the Supreme Audit Office and the Act on Local Government Employees. In the 1998 Act, there was still the possibility of transferring an official to a state of inactivity and granting him or her unpaid leave for the duration of his or her activities. These institutions applied only to civil servants; the next two Acts abandoned these solutions. Under the current law, unpaid leave can be granted to both an official and a corps member under Article 174 of the Labour Code. Unlike under the previous law, the period of leave does not count towards the period of employment on which the employee's entitlements depend (Szewczyk 2010: 203–204).

With the introduction of higher positions in the service in the 1998 law, the Head of the Civil Service was ordered to transfer officials from a group of higher positions to another office in the same locality or, with their consent, to another locality. He could also authorize the director general of the office to designate another position in situations of resignation from the position, the imposition of a disciplinary penalty of a ban on holding senior positions in the civil service, long-term illness of at least six months, and the elimination of a position as a result of a reorganization of the office.

This provision ceased to apply in the 2006 Act, due to the elimination of senior positions in the corps. However, the legislature did not reinstate it in the 2008 law, leaving only the optional nature of the transfer of a member of the civil service corps holding a senior position. If justified by the needs of the office or the interests of the civil service, a member of the civil service corps occupying a higher position in the civil service may be transferred at any time to a civil servant position in the same locality at least equivalent in salary to the position occupied prior to his/her employment in a higher position in the civil service, consistent with his/her qualifications and professional preparation. In turn, a member of the civil service who was not employed in the civil service prior to being hired in that position – to another official position in the same locality, consistent with his qualifications and professional preparation (Article 61 of the 2008 Act).

The last of the options for changing the civil service employment relationship was suspension. According to Article 41 of the 1996 Act, the employment relationship of a civil servant under temporary arrest was suspended by law. During the period of suspension, the civil servant received half the salary to which he was entitled up to the date of his temporary arrest. In addition, the director general of the office could suspend an official for up to 3 months, from his duties, if disciplinary or criminal proceedings were initiated against him. However, he retained the right to his salary and other civil service rights and benefits (Article 42). The legislature distinguished between two types of suspension: mandatory in Article 41 and optional in Article 42. In general, the suspension was intended to temporarily (possibly permanently – at a later date) remove the civil servant from performing public tasks, pending clarification of doubts about his integrity. In principle, the institution of suspension was regulated without significant changes in the next three civil service acts. In terms of mandatory termination of employment, one can distinguish: termination of the employment relationship by notice, without notice and by agreement of the parties. The norms concerning the termination of the employment relationship were found in Article 43 of the 1996 Act, which stated that the employment relationship of a civil servant terminates in the event of: refusal to take the oath of office, loss of Polish citizenship, a valid sentence of disciplinary expulsion from the civil service, a valid sentence of loss of public rights or the right to practice as a civil servant, the expiration of 3 months of the civil servant's absence from work due to temporary arrest, refusal to comply with the decision on transfer or failure to work in the office to which the civil servant was transferred, the expiration of the period for which the fixed-term appointment was made, failure of the civil servant transferred to inactive status to perform his/her duties despite a summons from the Head of the Civil Service. In the December 2015 amendment, only a linguistic change was made by replacing the term member of the civil service corps with civil servant and civil service employee.

In subsequent civil service acts, the legislature only slightly modified the prerequisites for the termination of an official's employment. In the 1998 act, loss of citizenship was replaced by renunciation. In 2008, on the other hand, the premise read: "loss of citizenship of a country that is a member of the European Union or of another country whose citizens are entitled to take up employment in the territory of the Republic of Poland on the basis of international agreements or provisions of Community law." The premise of a final conviction for an intentional crime was added and then in 2006 an intentional fiscal crime was added. The premise of loss of public rights was rewritten, which since 1998 reads "a final judgment of loss of public rights or a ban on practicing as a civil servant". In connection with the abolition of the institution of inactive status, this premise was also dropped.

With regard to the termination of the employment relationship, in the 1996 law there was the possibility of mandatory termination, which took place with three months' notice in the event of a permanent change in health that was established by a decision of the medical commission for disability and employment, as provided for by separate regulations, which made it impossible to perform the duties of a civil servant. A civil servant could be referred to this commission ex officio or at the civil servant's request in order to examine his health (Article 44). On the other hand, optional termination of employment could take place, with three months' notice, in the event of: reaching retirement age, if his period of employment enables him to obtain the right to a pension upon reaching that age, two consecutive negative evaluations, refusal to submit to examination by the medical commission for disability and employment.

A civil servant's employment could be terminated without notice in the event of absence from work due to illness lasting more than a year or seclusion due to an infectious disease during the period of receiving benefits for this, as well as in the event of excused absence from work for other reasons. It could also be done by mutual agreement of the parties or by three months' notice following resignation from the service. In the 1998 Act, in the case of optional termination of an official's employment, it occurs with three months' notice in the event of: reaching the age of 65, if the period of employment enables him to obtain the right to a pension, refusal to submit to examination by the Social Insurance Institution's medical examiner, liquidation of the office, if no transfer is possible (Article 61(2)). In addition, the premise of negative evaluation was transferred to the mandatory conditions for termination of employment.

In the 1998 Act, according to Article 61 (1), a civil servant's employment relationship was terminated, with three months' notice, in the event of: two consecutive negative evaluations, determination by the Social Insurance Institution's medical examiner of permanent incapacity to work making it impossible to perform the civil servant's duties; in order to examine the civil servant's health, the civil servant may be referred to the Social Insurance Institution ex officio or at the civil servant's request, loss of good repute, criminal proceedings pending for more than three months. The 2006 Act did not change anything in this regard, while the 2008 Act dropped the premise of mandatory termination of employment in the case of criminal proceedings pending against an official for more than three months. In the doctrine, this solution has been evaluated positively due to the lengthiness of ongoing criminal proceedings in practice (Stefański: 2009: 20).

The 2006 Act introduced for the first time the possibility of terminating the employment relationship with a civil servant, without notice, due to the civil servant's fault, in a situation of grave violation by the civil servant of the fundamental duties of a member of the civil service corps, if the fault of the civil servant is obvious. This provision remained unchanged in the 2008 Act. From the beginning of its introduction, it raised a number of legal questions. First, due to the level of generality of the condition, secondly, leaving to the immediate superior the right to decide on guilt (Dubowik 2007: 23–24). This may result in the instrumental use of this provision. As a result, there may be discretion in the termination of employment and a desire to use it to apply "political purges." Significantly expanded and detailed provisions for changing the employment relationship of a member of the civil service corps is the result of the philosophy of service (subordination during the performance of state tasks and availability). The nature of the employment relationship of a member of the civil service corps allows "unilateral and sovereign disposition by the competent body of the service of the place and time of work and decision on the type of tasks performed by the employee" (Sinkowska 2002: 74).

I have already mentioned the 2015 amendment to statutorily extinguish the employment relationship of senior civil service positions. According to Article 6(1) of the amending act, employment relations with persons holding senior positions in the civil service on the day the act enters into force shall expire 30 days after the date of entry into force of the act, if they are not offered new conditions of work or pay for a further period of time before that date, or if they do not accept the new conditions of work or pay. Civil servants are excluded from these solutions (Article 6, paragraph 3). Here we will not be dealing with the termination of the employment contract, but with its statutory termination in the form of expiration, by operation of law. This could mean the loss of employment within 30 days for those who have worked in the corps for a number of years. The creators of the amendment did not justify the introduction of such solutions. In this case, the Ombudsman also decided to send a request to the Constitutional Court, believing that the above provision is incompatible with the principle of citizens' trust in the state and the law under Article 2 and Articles 60 and 153 of the Constitution. The Ombudsman argued that the solution lacks substantive grounds for the verification of the hitherto employed, who, taking up higher positions through open and competitive recruitment, were hired because they met the relevant criteria. According to the Ombudsman, the reason for these changes is "(…) the desire to replace the existing constitutional requirement of impartiality, integrity and political neutrality with the free discretion of the appointing authority; a discretion under which political rather than substantive rationales will be decisive (…)".

The principle expressed in Article 2 of the Constitution is intended to provide citizens with legal security and a certain predictability, and to exclude situations of an arbitrary nature. The provision of Article 6(1) contradicts this principle by violating legal security without a legitimate reason, unless the reason can be considered: "failure to propose new working conditions or wages." Absent here is any reference to the substantive criteria that form the basis of the civil service corps (Ombudsman's petition to the Constitutional Court dated 1 February 2016). Particularly apparent is the violation of Article 153(1) of the Constitution, which, in providing for the reliable, professional, impartial and politically neutral performance of state tasks, includes a premise indicating the stability of the employment relationship. This stability, as stated in the judgment of 14 June 2011 Constitutional Court, is not absolute, but must be based on clear and transparent criteria. In addition, the permanence of the employment relationship is a barrier against the temptation to fill positions in the public service using political criteria, and is a sine qua non condition for maintaining impartiality and professionalism (Judgment of the Constitutional Tribunal of 14 June 2011). It is also rightly noted by the Supreme Bar Council that the legislator is introducing a kind of "mass dismissal" mechanism without giving its reasons. There is no justification for the necessity of such a possible replacement of personnel or any indication of the special needs of the state that would prompt the use of this type of procedure. Finally, there is no effort to present the financial aspect related to the possible necessity of paying severance payments (Opinia Naczelnej Rady Adwokackiej 2015). According to Prof. Izdebski, the amendment allowing the termination of labor relations is aimed at mass replacement of managerial cadres with political supporters of those currently in power (2016). Objections of a different nature are seen in the termination of labor relations by Prof. M. Gintowt-Jankowicz, who believes that 30 days is not enough time to make a real and reliable assessment. This is especially true in large-scale units. In addition, she believes that the identical treatment in this regard of the position of director general and department directors with their deputies is not rational due to the number of these positions in the offices, also Z. Snażyk thinks that the 30-day period for evaluation is unrealistic (Gintowt-Jankowicz 2015; Snażyk 2015).

In the course of the post-1989 transformation, there were already situations when the legislator decided to terminate employment relations by force of law. Referring to the jurisprudence of the Constitutional Tribunal, which has already ruled on the introduction of provisions terminating employment relations, it should be noted that in its judgment of 13 March 2000 (K 1/99), the Tribunal allowed for such a possibility in exceptional situations. (K 1/99), the Court allowed for such a possibility in exceptional situations. It must constitute a derogation from the principle, an extraordinary solution accompanying reform measures, connected with the necessity to realise other important legitimate constitutional values. In the cited case, the extinction took place in connection with the public administration reform implemented in 1999 (Judgment of the Constitutional Tribunal of 13 March 2000). In the case of the 2015 amendment to the Act on Service, there is no justification in the form of an extensive reform of public administration, hence, as Prof. E. Ura rightly notes, that the legislator has created for itself the possibility to get rid of persons with whom it does not want to cooperate – the "inconvenient" (2016: 56).

4.3 Scope of rights and obligations of a member of the civil service corps

The scope of rights and obligations of members of the civil service corps constitutes a specific catalogue for persons employed in government administration. Compared to other employee groups, the legislator imposes a number of obligations on the civil service, the observance of which is related to the performance of state tasks. In return, it proposes a catalogue of entitlements, the role of which is to compensate for the excessive obligations.

4.3.1 Statutory obligations

As far as statutory duties are concerned, the legislator in the 1996 Act created a catalogue which survived in an unchanged form until the 2008 Act. According to it, a member of the civil service corps (and in the 1996 Act only a civil servant) is obliged, in particular: to observe the Constitution of the Republic of Poland and other provisions of law, to protect the interests of the state and the rights of man and citizen, to manage public funds rationally, to perform entrusted tasks reliably and impartially, to perform entrusted tasks efficiently and on time, to observe statutorily protected secrecy, to develop professional knowledge, to behave with dignity in the service and outside it.

This catalogue should not be treated as a *numerus clausus*, since it contains only the basic and most important rules for members of the civil service (Jagielski&Rączka 2001: 225). The obligation expressed in the first point constitutes a kind of meta-principle. Attention is drawn to the duty to carry out the tasks entrusted to them in a reliable, impartial, efficient and timely manner. This obligation directly alludes to Article 1 of all the acts which stipulated that the tasks of the state should be performed by the civil service with integrity, impartiality and political neutrality. Reliability means such performance of the tasks entrusted to it that will show commitment and full use of one's skills, qualifications and aptitude. Impartiality will be the prohibition to be guided by one's political, religious convictions, individual or group interests (Jagielski&Rączka 2001: 228). The duty to behave with dignity in and out of the service also deserves special attention. It is an obligation that encroaches on the sphere of private life, obliging those employed in the corps to take special care of their own behaviour. Dignified behaviour is intended to reinforce the dignity and confidence of the post and the office. Situations in which a member of the civil service corps violates the principle of dignified behaviour may include the formulation of unflattering opinions concerning the public service or office, a disrespectful attitude towards state or local government institutions, inappropriate behaviour by a member of the corps in his/her place of residence, or alcohol abuse (Jagielski&Rączka 2001: 232).

Subsequent provisions of all the Acts bring injunctions or prohibitions that are almost identical in wording, in the form of: the obligation to carry out the official instructions of superiors (for corps members), the prohibition to be guided in the performance of official duties by individual or group interests (for corps members), the prohibition to publicly manifest political views (for corps members), the prohibition to participate in a strike or protest action disrupting the normal functioning of the office (for corps members, a provision added by the 1998 Act.), prohibition from holding office in trade unions (for civil servants, in the 1996 act only for category A). The 2008 act amended this prohibition by limiting it to a member of the civil service corps holding a senior position, prohibition from forming or participating in political parties (for civil servants, in the 1996 act only for category A). The 2008 act amended this prohibition by limiting it to a member of the civil service corps occupying a senior position, the prohibition on combining work in the civil service with the mandate of a councillor (introduced in 1998 for civil servants, since 2006 this prohibition also covers employees). The prohibition on forming and participating in political parties is intended to guarantee the political neutrality of civil servants. On the other hand, not combining work in the civil service with a mandate as a councillor is intended to separate the functions related to the exercise of public authority by local government bodies from the impartial performance of state tasks.

As of 1996, the legislator introduced provisions prohibiting the creation of a reporting relationship between spouses and persons related by blood or marriage up to and including the second degree of kinship or affinity of the first degree and by adoption, custody or guardianship. To ensure fairness and impartiality, provisions introducing restrictions on taking on additional work (also introduced in 1996) are in place. Since 1998, these provisions have stipulated that a member of the civil service corps may not take up additional employment without the consent of the Director General of the office or perform activities or occupations that are incompatible with the duties under the act or that undermine confidence in the civil service. A civil servant may not take up gainful employment without the consent of the director general of the office, since 2008 also a member of the corps holding a senior position in the service.

Another obligation imposed by the 1996 act was the evaluation of civil servants. According to it, a civil servant was subject to constant evaluation by his or her immediate superior with regard to the performance of the tasks entrusted to him or her, as well as for the purpose of determining the civil servant's professional development programme and individual career. Periodic written appraisal was drawn up at least once every 2 years, and its criteria, method of conduct and rules were established by the Head of the Civil Service by order. The 1998 Act differentiated this provision into members of the civil service corps, who were subject to a permanent evaluation by their immediate superior, and civil servants, who were subject to a periodic evaluation, at least once every two years, of the duties performed on the job, together with proposals for an individual development programme. The periodic appraisal was drawn up in writing by the immediate superior. It was public and should be served in full immediately on the official concerned. It was incumbent on the President of the Council of Ministers to lay down, by decree, detailed rules for the evaluation of officials. The 2006 Act specified that: "Not less frequently than once every 24 months and not more frequently than once every 12 months, the immediate superior shall prepare in writing a periodic evaluation of the civil servant, together with proposals concerning his/her individual professional development programme". The act omitted the provision that members of the civil service corps are subject to continuous evaluation by their immediate superior. On 5 April 2007, the Prime Minister issued an Ordinance on the detailed rules for conducting evaluations of civil servants (Journal of Laws No. 69, item 633), which clarified the rules for conducting evaluations.

The 2008 Act decided to regulate this issue more precisely and to introduce new regulations. Pursuant to Article 81, a civil servant and a civil servant employee employed on the basis of an employment contract for an indefinite period of time are subject to periodic evaluation carried out by a direct superior. The periodic appraisal concerns the performance of a member of the civil service corps of the duties resulting from the job description he/she occupies. It shall be drawn up in writing, every 24 months, and the appraised member of the civil service corps shall be immediately familiarised with it. It shall contain proposals for an individual professional development programme. In the case of first-time appraisees, the appraisal shall be drawn up if the period to be appraised is longer than 6 months. In the event of a negative periodic appraisal, a member of the civil service corps is subject to a new appraisal after a period of 6 months from the date of familiarisation with the appraisal. The President of the Council of Ministers will determine, by means of a regulation, the conditions and manner of carrying out periodic appraisals (criteria, specimen sheet, scale of appraisal and procedure) – Article 82. Appraisals, under the 2008 Act were also subject to persons holding senior positions in the civil service. Article 81 regulated these issues in detail (e.g. in the case of the director general, the evaluation was carried out by the Head of the Chancellery of the Prime Minister, the relevant minister, the chairman of a committee forming part of the Council of Ministers, the head of an office of a central government administration body or a voivode after consulting the Head of the Civil Service, while in the case of the head of a department or equivalent unit, it was carried out by the director general of the office).

The 2015 amendment abolished this obligation, as Article 81 does not apply to persons employed on an appointment basis. The absence of an assessment obligation may be of concern from the point of view of human resources management in the public sector. After all, the evaluation element is an immanent feature of human resources policy. The feedback obtained as a result of properly conducted appraisal influences the development and improvement of employees, the motivation to develop, the change of negative behaviour and, consequently, the quality of the functioning of the institution is improved. Staff appraisal has various functions. From analysing past work, future plans, correcting mistakes made, making superiors aware of expectations to planning areas requiring development (Penc 1998: 131). The appraisal system is a strategic element of management and, importantly, the results of appraisal should be the basis for personnel decisions. It undoubtedly translates into the smooth functioning of the institution in many areas (satisfaction of employees or customers of the administration) (Walenia 2015: 3). In 2013, work on the draft Human Resources Management Strategy was still underway in the Corps, and Order No. 3 of the Head of the Civil Service of 30 May 2012 on Human Resources Management Standards in the Civil Service was also in force. In February 2013, the Council of Ministers adopted the Efficient State 2020 strategy, which created an opportunity to finalise the draft Human Resources Management Strategy so that the two documents were consistent. In September 2013, the Head of the Civil Service submitted a draft resolution on the 'Strategy for Human Resources Management in the Civil Service 2020' together with the draft strategy to the Standing Committee of the Council of Ministers for deliberation (the Civil Service Council gave a positive opinion on the draft in September 2013). However, in December 2013, the Secretary of the Chancellery of the Council of Ministers returned the draft without consideration due to the resignation of the Head of the Civil Service (Sławomir Brodziński resigned in December 2013). In conclusion, several years of work on the Strategy were left without consideration, which undoubtedly shows the irresponsibility of policy-makers and the waste of public funds. It is hoped that the analyses prepared as part of the project will be used in the operation of the service.

In 2015, one of the priority tasks of the Head of the Civil Service was to simplify procedures in the civil service for human resources management. This objective was pursued through the introduction of new legislation simplifying human resources management procedures. 3 ordinances of the Prime Minister (on training, appraisals and first appraisal in the civil service) were introduced. 1 ordinance of the Prime Minister on job descriptions and job evaluation and 1 ordinance of the Head of the Civil Service on the conditions and modalities of interaction between the Head of the Civil Service and the directors-general of offices were introduced. Ordinance of the Prime Minister of 24 June 2015 on detailed conditions for organising and conducting training in the civil service (Journal of Laws, item 960), Ordinance of the Prime Minister of 4 April 2016 on the conditions for conducting periodic evaluations of civil servants and civil service employees (Journal of Laws, item 470), Ordinance of the Prime Minister of 23 July 2015. on the detailed conditions and manner of conducting the first evaluation in the civil service (Journal of Laws, item 1144), Order No. 57 of the Prime Minister of 24 July 2015 amending the Order on the principles of performing job descriptions and valuations in the civil service (M. P. Poz. 724), Order No. 5 of the Head of the Civil Service of 8 October 2015 on the conditions and procedure of interaction between the Head of the Civil Service and the directors general of offices.

The 2016 Report of the Head of the Civil Service stated that one of the elements that need to be changed in the area of human resources management is the evaluation process of members of the civil service corps. The problem is that the percentage of positive evaluations in 2016 was almost 100 % and this is another year with such results. Moreover, evaluations at the highest level accounted for almost two-thirds of the total. From this information, one should not conclude that members of the civil service corps have above-standard competences, but about the inadequacy of evaluations and the unreliability of their performance. In 2016, positive interim evaluations accounted for 99.7 %, in 2015.–99.8 %, in 2014.–99.6 %, in 2013.–99.7 %, in 2012. – 99,4 %. At the same time, in 2016 there were no individuals who were given a second negative evaluation (Sprawozdanie Szefa Służby Cywilnej za 2016, 2017: 6–33).

Another obligation imposed by the legislator (already in the act of 1996) is participation in training. The legislator devoted a separate chapter to this issue, and it should be inferred that it was and still is one of the important aspects concerning the civil service corps. According to the 1996 Act, a civil servant had the right to training and further training in the civil service, and was obliged to participate in training established individually for each civil servant. The National School of Public Administration and other units designated by the Prime Minister participated in the preparation and implementation of training programmes in the civil service. Detailed rules and conditions for organising and conducting training in the civil service were determined by decree of the Prime Minister. A civil servant did not pay fees for participation in training courses. The 1998 Act also devoted a separate chapter to training, specifying that a member of the corps participated in training, which included: central training – planned, organised and supervised by the Head of the Civil Service, general training – planned, organised and supervised by the Director General of the office, training within the framework of the individual professional development programme of a civil servant – planned, organised and supervised by the Director General of the office in agreement with the civil servant employed in a given office, study of strategic management for directors general of offices, specialised training – planned, organised and supervised by the Director General of the office, covering topics related to the tasks of the office. The detailed conditions for organising and conducting training were laid down in the Regulation of the Prime Minister of 22 March 2000 on detailed conditions for organising and conducting training in the civil service (Journal of Laws No. 22, item 280).

The 2006 Act did not include a provision for participation in a strategic management study for directors-general of offices, and the 2008 Act did not reinstate this form of training. The Head of the Civil Service determined and currently determines annually the plan for central training in the civil service (with the exception of the 2006 Act, when this was done by the Head of the Chancellery of the Prime Minister – e. g. in 2007 a Training Plan was created for persons belonging to the State Personnel Resources appointed to high state positions). To this day, cooperation with the National School of Public Administration is envisaged when establishing programmes. In addition, the central training plan is given an opinion by the Public Service Council. In all acts, the participation of a member of the civil service corps in the training provided for the civil service has been and is treated on a par with the performance of his/her official duties. This clearly demonstrates the importance that the legislator has assigned to training and the development of professional knowledge (Rydlewski 2001: 52). The latest Training Plan for 2023 provides for training on changes in labour law in light of amendments to the Labour Code, the operation of the office in a crisis situation and issues related to mental resilience. Traditionally, training on qualification proceedings, ethics, management, motivation is recommended (Plan szkoleń centralnych w służbie cywilnej na 2023). Since 1998, acts have provided for the possibility of directing a member of the civil service corps with a legal education to undergo a legislative application, ending with an examination. At present, the latest Regulation of the Prime Minister of 24 June 2015 on the detailed conditions for organising and conducting training in the civil service stipulates that the following training is organised: general, as part of an individual professional development programme, specialised and central training.

Another important obligation is to abide by the Civil Service Code of Ethics established by the President of the Council of Ministers, which is a set of rules of conduct for members of the civil service corps. A member of the civil service corps is to treat work as a public service, is always to have in mind the good of the Republic of Poland, its democratic system and is to protect the legitimate interests of every person. The Code was established by Order No. 114 of the Prime Minister of 11 October 2002 on the establishment of the Code of Ethics of the Civil Service (M. P. No. 46, item 683).

It is worth mentioning that the 2008 Act obliged the President of the Council of Ministers to define, by means of an ordinance, guidelines for observing the principles of civil service and the principles of ethics of the civil service corps (Article 15(10)). On 6 October 2011, the Prime Minister issued a relevant order, which became effective on 5 November 2011 (MP No. 93, item 953). In the light of § 1, a member of the civil service corps, while performing his/her official duties, is obliged to be guided by the following principles: legalism, the rule of law, fostering trust in public administration bodies; protection of human and civil rights, disinterestedness, openness and transparency, observance of statutorily protected secrecy, professionalism, responsibility for action or failure to act, rational management of public funds, openness and competitiveness of recruitment. The legislator further clarified the principles in detail in the order and empowered the Head of the Civil Service to resolve problems arising from the application of the principles, to monitor compliance with them, and to disseminate them. Chapter two sets out the corps' ethical principles, which include the rules of dignified behaviour, public service, loyalty, political neutrality, impartiality and integrity. The principles of ethics expressed in the Order refer to the 2002 Code of Ethics of the Civil Service, indicating the desirable behaviour of corps members. Here, the Head of Service constitutes the organisational, authority and supervisory element.

4.3.2 Powers

"Balance" to the obligations presented, is to be found in the broad catalogue of entitlements that members of the civil service corps have been and continue to be entitled to. In principle, throughout the period, the legislator has changed little in terms of the basic rights of corps members. Some of the changes resulted from the creation of categories of corps members, and the separation of entitlements was made accordingly. Most of the privileges established in the 1996 Act have survived legislative changes, and subsequent acts have enriched the catalogue. The exception is the 2006 Act, which reduced some of the entitlements (granting others instead). Table 7 shows the entitlements of members of the civil service corps from 1996 onwards.

In the 1998 Act, the legislator introduced a very favourable principle that all previous completed periods of employment and other proven periods of employment are included in the periods of work entitling to a long-term service allowance in the civil service if, under separate regulations, they are included in the period of work on which the employee's entitlements depend. Periods of employment in the Communist Party (Polish Workers' Party and Polish United Workers' Party) as well as in state security organs between 1944 and 1990 shall not be counted as periods of service.

The above provision has remained in force in basically unchanged form to this day. In the most recent act, an extension of rights has been made for officials transferred to another office in another locality. Accordingly, they are entitled to: housing provided by the office to which the civil servant has been transferred, or a monthly allowance to cover the cost of renting housing, paid during the period of transfer, a one-off transfer allowance of three months' salary, reimbursement of travel expenses for the civil servant and members of their family, reimbursement of the cost of transporting property, and a transfer holiday of a total of four days. A transferred official may receive the following maximum amounts in connection with the rental of a dwelling for himself and his family: for 1 person – PLN 1646, for 2 persons – PLN 1852, for 3 persons – PLN 2264, for 4 persons – PLN 2573 (these amounts concern Warsaw, Gdańsk, Gdynia, Katowice, Kraków, Poznań, Szczecin and Wrocław) (Drobny at al. 2010: 94–95).

In addition, pursuant to Articles 101 and 102 of the Act of 2008 authorising the Prime Minister to determine, by means of an ordinance, specific entitlements in terms of salaries and other benefits to which certain categories of members of the civil service corps are entitled, as well as other allowances to remuneration other than those provided for by the act. With the above in mind, the Ordinance of the Prime Minister of 19 December 2014 on special entitlements vested in certain categories of members of the civil service corps (Journal of Laws 2014, item 30) granting commission-based remuneration to members of the corps employed in the organisational unit of administrative enforcement of the tax office was issued. Members of the corps employed in maritime offices, taking part in technical tests of ships at sea after construction or repair or performing statutory tasks of the office during the work of the ship, are entitled to free board or a cash equivalent. Corps members employed in mining offices are entitled to entitlements related to Miners' Day: a day off work, a bonus of one day's pay and special monthly remuneration (e.g. 5 % of monthly basic salary – up to 5 years of service; 40 % of monthly basic salary – after 15 years of service).

Summing up the considerations so far, it can be said that the rights of members of the civil service, compared to the rights contained in the Labour Code for other employee groups, are very extensive, and in particular for civil servants (as indicated by the legislator, e.g. when transferring a civil servant). It is clear that the civil service is in a privileged position due to the various types of benefits and dues granted, aimed at creating compensation for the duties imposed. Privileges are intended to create an incentive for the brightest and best to take up the after all difficult work in the civil ser

Table 7 Entitlements of members of the civil service since 1996

Item	Entitlement	Act of 1996	Act of 1998	Act of 2008	Act of 2008 (with amendment of 2015)
1.	basic salaries	yes	yes	yes	yes
2.	ong-service allowance	yes	yes	yes	yes
3.	civil service allowance for official rank	allowance for classification in one of the official categories	yes – 9 official ranks for officials only	yes – 9 official ranks for officials only	yes – 9 official ranks for officials only
4.	possibility of advancing to the next step in grade	no	yes (officials)	yes	yes
5.	jubilee award	yes	yes	yes	yes
6.	prize fund	yes	yes	yes	yes
7.	one-off severance pay	yes (3 months' salary after 20 years' service)	yes (3 months' salary after 20 years' service)	yes (3 months' salary after 20 years' service)	yes (3 months' salary after 20 years' service)
8.	travel allowance	yes	yes	yes	yes
9.	Reimbursement of relocation costs	yes	yes	yes	yes
10.	additional annual leave	for officials only: 6 days – after 10 years, 12 days – after 20 years	for officials only: 6 days – after 10 years, 12 days – after 20 years	no	official, after 5 years (1 day per year – up to 12 days)
11.	paid health leave	one-off, max. 6 months	one-off, max. 6 months	no	no
12.	pension entitlements	yes	yes	yes	yes
13.	absence from work (incapacity due to illness)	pay for 1 year and sickness benefit	no	no	no
14.	protection as provided for public servants	no	yes	yes	yes

Item	Entitlement	Act of 1996	Act of 1998	Act of 2008	Act of 2008 (with amendment of 2015)
15.	working time – 8 hours per day and 40 hours per week	yes	yes	yes	yes
16.	part-time fixed-term employment	yes	no regulation in the act	no regulation in the act	no regulation in the act
17.	additional annual salary	no	yes	yes	yes
18.	special allowance	no	no	officials and other staff	yes
19.	activity allowance	no	no	officials and other staff	yes
20.	function allowance for senior post holders	no	no	no	yes

Source: Table by author. Based on Civil Service Acts 1996, 1998, 2006, 2008 and 2015 as amended.

vice. They are also intended to retain in the service employees to whom the private sector could offer more favourable financial conditions, hence the creation of an awards fund through which the Director General is able to reward special achievements and motivate commitment to the service.

4.3.3 Disciplinary liability

The disciplinary responsibility of the civil service corps was already shaped in the first Service Act as another important issue in terms of defining the status of corps members. Disciplinary responsibility is a constituent part of the status of many professional groups. It is a result of official subordination, which includes the right to issue official orders and enforce them, but also the possibility to apply disciplinary penalties (Jagielski&Rączka 2001: 320). All normative solutions specify that an official (1996 Act) or a member of the civil service corps (other acts) is liable for disciplinary action for breach of duty. Each of the acts identically stipulated that disciplinary proceedings may not be initiated after the lapse of three months from the date on which the Director General of the Office became aware of the breach of duties of the official/member of the civil service corps, nor after the lapse of two years from the commission of the act. If the civil servant/member of the civil service corps is unable to give an explanation due to absence from work, the three-month period shall not start and the period started shall be suspended until the date of his/her appearance at work. Each act distinguishes a wide range of disciplinary penalties applicable to both employees and civil servants. Table 8 shows the disciplinary penalties applied to members of the civil service corps from 1996 onwards. This catalogue was significantly modified in the 1998 act in connection with the change in the concept of the civil service personnel structure. At that time, a broad catalogue of penalties applied to employees was enacted, while the 2006 act, followed by the 2008 act, significantly trimmed the catalogue of penalties applied to employees and slightly modified the range of penalties for civil servants.

Since 1996, it has also been the rule that for minor breaches of the duties of a civil servant/member of the civil service corps, the Director General of the Office may punish him/her with a written warning. The punishment may be preceded by an investigation. If an objection was lodged, initially within 14 days (1996 Act) and then within 7 days (other acts), the case was initially heard by a disciplinary committee, which could uphold or revoke the punishment of a warning. From 1998 onwards, the director general of the office refers the case to the disciplinary ombudsman.

In the December 2015 amendment, Article 114(2) stipulates that the penalties provided for in the act also apply to a person holding a senior position in the civil service.

The procedure for disciplinary proceedings against officials has not changed since 1996, and is conducted in the second instance (in accordance with the general principle of two-instance proceedings). Disciplinary committees are entitled to hear cases: in the first instance, the Disciplinary Committee, and in the second instance, the Higher Disciplinary Committee.

The proceedings before the disciplinary committee are preceded by an investigation, which is conducted by the office's disciplinary ombudsman, and ends with the ombudsman's decision to forward a request for disciplinary proceedings to the disciplinary committee or, with the approval of the director of the office, to discontinue the investigation. The disciplinary ombudsman of the office is appointed by the director general of the office from among civil servants (1996 act) and now, since 1998, from among members of the civil service corps. The disciplinary committee initiates disciplinary proceedings from the date of the disciplinary ombudsman's request to hear the case. Proceedings before the disciplinary committee are open to the public and the accused has the right of defence. Disciplinary penalties shall be erased within a period of three years, and on the request of the punished person, the erasure may take place after a period of two years. The decision of the disciplinary committee of the office may be appealed by the parties to the Higher Disciplinary Committee within 14 days of the delivery of the decision. The acts of 1996, 2006 and 2008 contain a statutory delegation for the Prime Minister to determine, by means of a regulation, the manner of conducting the investigation and disciplinary proceedings and the organisation and functioning of the relevant structures. On 30 April 2009, the Ordinance of the Prime Minister of 9 April 2009 on explanatory and disciplinary proceedings in the civil service (Journal of Laws No. 60, item 493) entered into force.

Disciplinary committees adjudicate (and have adjudicated) with three or five members, depending on the punishment the accused faces (in the first instance), and with five members in the second instance. The disciplinary committee of the office, under the acts of 1996, 1998 and the current one, was and still is appointed by the Director General of the office from among the members of the civil service corps employed in the office. If necessary, the Head of the Civil Service could and still can establish a disciplinary committee for several offices. An exception was the 2006 act when the Head of the Chancellery of the Prime Minister created one disciplinary commission each for at least three offices. The commission had and still has 10 members, and its term of office is now 4 years (3 years in the 1998 Act, 2006 Act). The Disciplinary Board appoints from among its members a chairman of the board and his deputies.

The Higher Disciplinary Commission is appointed by the Prime Minister and consists of 15 members appointed by the Prime Minister for a period of six years, including 12 members appointed on the proposal of the Head of the Civil Service (in the 2006 act on the proposal of the Head of the Chancellery of the Prime Minister) from among civil servants and 3 members appointed on the proposal of the Director General of the Foreign Service from among diplomatic and consular staff. The members of the Higher Disciplinary Commission shall remain in office until their successors are appointed. The Higher Disciplinary Commission shall appoint a chairman and deputies

Table 8 Disciplinary penalties applied to members of the civil service corps since 1996

Item	Type of disciplinary penalty	Act of 1996	Act of 1998		Act of 2008		Act of 2008 (with amendment of 2015)		
		clerks	employee	clerks	employee	clerks	employee	clerks	senior positions
1.	admonition	yes	yes	yes	yes	yes	yes	yes	yes
2.	reprimand	yes	yes	yes	yes	yes	yes	yes	yes
3.	reduction of civil service bonus rate	yes	no	no	no	no	no	no	no
4.	disqualification from promotion to a higher rate of the civil service allowance or to a higher position for a period of two years	yes	no	yes	no	yes	no	yes	no
5.	disqualification from holding managerial positions in the civil service	yes	no	no	no	no	no	no	no
6.	owngrading of an official category	yes	no	no	no	no	no	no	no
7.	removal from the civil service	yes	no	yes	no	yes	no	yes	yes
8.	reduction in grade	no	no	yes	no	yes	no	yes	no
9.	barred from competing for a higher post for 2 years	no	no	yes	no	no	no	no	no
10.	prohibition from occupying a higher post for 2 to 5 years	no	no	yes	no	no	no	no	no
11.	expulsion from the civil service	no	no	yes	no	no	no	no	no
12.	reprimand with a warning	no	yes	no	no	no	no	no	no
13.	reprimand with disqualification from promotion to a higher grade for 2 years	no	yes	no	no	no	no	no	no

Item	Type of disciplinary penalty	Act of 1996	Act of 1998		Act of 2008		Act of 2008 (with amendment of 2015)		
		clerks	employee	clerks	employee	clerks	employee	clerks	senior positions
14.	downgrading	no	yes	no	no	no	no	no	no
15.	removal from service	no	yes	no	yes	no	yes	no	no
16.	reduction of basic salary, not more than 25 % – for not more than 6 months	no	yes	no	yes	yes	yes	yes	yes

Source: Table by author. Based on Civil Service Acts 1996, 1998, 2006, 2008 and 2015 as amended.

from among its members. Currently, the work of the Higher Disciplinary Commission is handled by the Prime Minister's Office (formerly the Civil Service Office). The diagram below shows how disciplinary proceedings are conducted against both employees and civil servants.

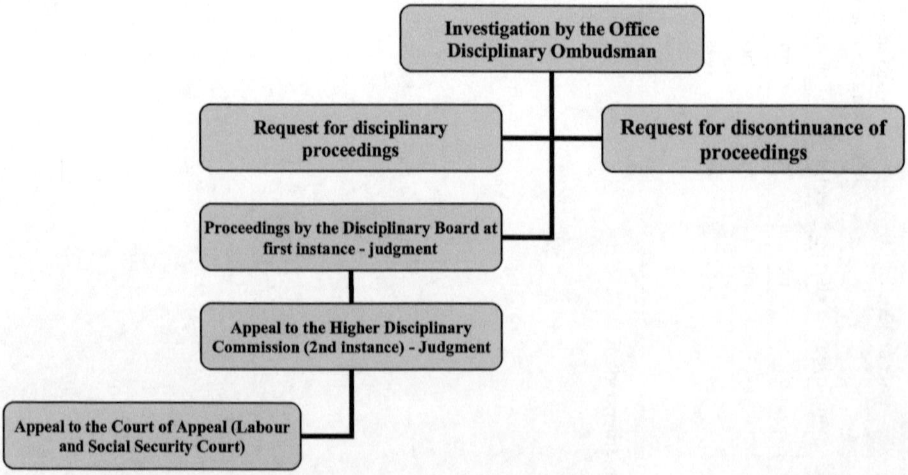

Diagram 1 Disciplinary proceedings at first and second instance
Source: Diagram by author. Based on Civil Service Act 2008

4.4 Organisation of the Civil Service

The 1996 Act on the Civil Service organised the internal structures of the corps. In establishing the bodies operating in the service, the legislator assigned to them roles and functions in the management of the service, the execution of tasks, powers and duties, the creation of the image and the mission and vision of the service, the execution of the powers and duties provided for in the act. The structure at the time of the creation of the service included: Head of the Civil Service, Civil Service Council, Directors General of the Offices, Higher Disciplinary Commission, Disciplinary Commissions of the Offices and an organisational and support apparatus in the form of the Civil Service Office. The 2006 Act abolished the institution of the Head of the Civil Service, together with the Office serving him, and his competences were taken over by the Head of the Chancellery of the Prime Minister and the Departments serving him in the Chancellery of the Prime Minister: Civil Service and State Personnel Resources. The 2008 Act restored the institution of the Head of the Civil Service, but without the Civil Service Office, leaving the Service Department in the Prime Minister's Chancellery. In addition, the Civil Service Council was replaced by the Civil Service Council in 2006, followed by a return to the Civil Service Council in 2008. The 2015 amendment also made significant changes to the status of the Head of the Civil Service and the Civil Service Council by transforming it again into the Civil Service Council.

4.4.1 Head of the Civil Service

The starting point for the creation of the Civil Service was of course the 1996 Act, and it was this Act that institutionalised the Corps, setting up the structures governing the Service. Within its framework, institutions were created, structures that were modified or changed in subsequent years, but which (obviously not all of them) continued to function for a long period of almost a decade. The creation of structures was necessary for the efficient management of the corps and for independence (to some extent) from the superior, who became the Prime Minister.

The Head of the Civil Service was established as a central organ of government administration, subordinate to the Prime Minister and appointed by him, competent in all matters of the service (Article 23 of the 1996 Act). The Head of the Civil Service and his deputies (also appointed by the Prime Minister) had to have the status of a Category **A** official, as provided for by the act. In view of the formation phase of the corps, the legislator stipulated that within two years of the act coming into force, the position of Head could be entrusted to a person who was not an official, with whom an employment contract was concluded (with the possibility of early termination with two weeks' notice). However, as Z. Cieślak, J. Jagielski, K. Rączka rightly point out, with regard to deputy Heads of Corps, the act does not allow for the temporary entrustment of duties to persons who are not Category A officials. From this, the conclusion is that until the first appointments it was not possible to fill these positions (1998: 71). However, the person appointed to the position of Chief, who was not an official, had to meet the conditions provided by law for all candidates for officials. In addition, a candidate for the position of Chief was required to have the knowledge, experience and moral authority to ensure that the tasks of the service would be fulfilled.

The first Head of the Corps, appointed only on 24 December 1996, was Jan Szachułowicz, who on 29 October 1997 tendered his resignation to Prime Minister Włodzimierz Cimoszewicz (which coincided with the parliamentary elections and the seizure of power by the right wing). The regulations on the organisational structures of the Service came into force on 25 August 1996 to enable the objectives of the act to be implemented as soon as possible. The appointment of the Head of the Service by the Prime Minister therefore took place only five months after these norms came into force.

His successor, Prime Minister Jerzy Buzek, appointed Jan Pastwa as Head of State on 7 November 1997, who held the position until the liquidation of the institution. According to J. Kornaś, Jan Pastwa was appointed without the opinion of the Civil Service Council, despite the statutory requirement (Kornaś 2001: 30). By an act of 18

December 1998, some of the provisions concerning the Head of the Civil Service were re-enacted, and he remained a central body subordinate to the Prime Minister and appointed by him from among the officials of the corps, with the establishment, as in the previous act, of a 2-year transitional period (Articles 8 and 9 in connection with Articles 145 and 146 of the 1998 act). Also the Deputy Chief (the act provided for only one deputy) was appointed by the Prime Minister, but on the proposal of the Head of the Civil Service.

However, the new act introduced a compulsory procedure for the Head candidate to be given an opinion by the Prime Minister's consultative and advisory body, the Civil Service Council. The Head of the Service became a tenure body, appointed for 5 years with the possibility of holding the post for further periods. As for the deputy, the term of office was not specified. The conditions for appointment and removal from office were also not specified, apart from the prerequisite of official status. An important change was the introduction of taxatively defined possibilities for the dismissal of the Head by the Prime Minister. While in the 1996 act. While the 1996 Act allowed the Prime Minister to dismiss him at any time and for any reason, under the 1998 Act he could do so in the event (Article 9(4)) of resignation from his post, loss of capacity to perform the duties entrusted to him as a result of a prolonged illness lasting at least six months or failure to fulfil any of the conditions of employment in the service.

The prerequisites for employment in the service, in the light of section 4 of the 1998 Act, were, inter alia: to have the qualifications required for the service and to be of good repute, conditions that were difficult to define unambiguously. Since, according to the act, the Prime Minister could dismiss the Chief if any of the above conditions were not met, this provided ample scope for free interpretation. The safeguard in cases of abuse was, of course, to be the Council's approval of the dismissal (Kornaś 2001: 51). Dismissal for loss of qualifications or loss of good repute (Article 4, points 4 and 5) additionally required the consent of at least 2/3 of the Civil Service Council. In both acts, the tasks of the Head of the Civil Service were largely similar. They mainly concerned the implementation of state policy towards the civil service, the collection of information, the use of financial resources, the preparation of draft normative acts, the dissemination of information about the service, the publication of the Civil Service Bulletin, and the presentation of annual reports on the state of the corps to the Prime Minister. The changes that were introduced in the 1998 act with regard to the powers of the Chief resulted from modifications in the conduct of the qualification procedure for the service, the introduction of a competitive procedure for filling senior positions and mandatory training. It also obliged the Head of the Civil Service to ensure compliance with the rules of the service and to guide the management process.

It is worth mentioning that the literature on the subject has repeatedly drawn attention to the ambiguity regarding the legal position of the Head of the Civil Service. The act defined him as a central body of government administration, elected from among civil servants. According to some theorists, however, he or she is not a member of the corps, but at the same time performs a number of activities and tasks related to directing, supervising and managing the corps (Sanetra 2001: 19–20; Szewczyk 2006: 20–21). The above comments can also be applied to the Deputy Head of the Civil Service (Liszcz 2005: 26). The 2006 Act, on the other hand, introduced almost revolutionary changes, abolishing this structure. Pursuant to Articles 119 and 120 of the 2006 Civil Service Act, the central body of government administration, which was the Head of the Civil Service, was abolished along with the liquidation of his office. The tasks and competences hitherto falling within their remit were carried out under the authority of the Prime Minister by the Head of his Chancellery, and with regard to qualification proceedings for employees applying for appointment, by the National School of Public Administration.

The tasks of the Head of the Prime Minister's Chancellery in the scope of the service listed in Article 8 of the 2006 Act were directly transferred from the 1998 Act with the exception of the competences concerning competitions for senior positions, which the Act eliminated. The scope of tasks was made more specific in the Prime Minister's Ordinance of 30 October 2006 *on the performance of civil service tasks by the Head of the Prime Minister's Chancellery* (Journal of Laws No. 198, item 1456). The 1996 Act also established the Office of the Civil Service, which is the executive apparatus of the Head, acting under his direction together with the Director General and the directors of individual departments. The organisation and modus operandi was determined by the Prime Minister by giving the Office a statute. The provisions concerning the Office were reproduced in the 1998 Act, while in 2006 the unit was liquidated and its tasks were taken over by the Chancellery of the Prime Minister, in which the Department of Civil Service and State Personnel Resources was established.

Undoubtedly, the post of Head of the Civil Service could not be categorised as a strictly clerical post. The legal status of this body clearly indicated a high degree of dependence on a political superior, with this being more evident in the 1996 Act. Although that Act limited the personal circle of candidates for the Head to civil servants, the manner of creation left no doubt as to its political character. Although the changes introduced by the 1998 Act limited the political influence through the element of tenure (a five-year term of office not coinciding with the term of office of the Parliament) and enumerative grounds for dismissal, they did not eliminate it entirely. The positioning of the Head as a central organ of government administration inscribes him, on the one hand, in the current political set-up, while, on the other hand, it obliges him to observe the principles of service, including the principle of political neutrality (expressed both in the Constitution and in the two laws).

The replacement of the Head of the Civil Service by the Head of the Prime Minister's Office, who, it should be remembered, acted only under the authority of the Prime Minister, clearly indicates a desire to make him completely subordinate to the Prime Minister. This is a straightforward path to politicisation. After all, the Head of the Prime Minister's Chancellery is one of the Prime Minister's closest co-workers, the position is filled from a political key, and there can be a personnel change in this position at any time. By definition, it is included in the political sphere, and does not benefit from guarantees of independence. In this situation, it does not provide the civil service with even a relative isolation from political influence (Stelina 2006). It is not characterised by the independence in decision-making that the Head of the Civil Service should have. The instability of the political scene at the time and the resulting frequent rotation of the government, the Prime Minister and consequently his Head of the Civil Service may also have been a concern. In addition, the Head of the Civil Service, under the act, was a central organ of government administration, while the Head of the Prime Minister's Chancellery did not have this status (Stelina 2006; Ura 2006). The majority of opinions on the new civil service regulations question the legitimacy of abolishing the institutions of the Head and the Office of the Civil Service and entrusting the performance of their tasks to the Head of the Prime Minister's Chancellery. A. Karwowska – Sokołowska believes that this regulation may raise constitutional doubts, as the Head of the Prime Minister's Chancellery under the Act on the Council of Ministers has a different scope of competence (2006; Izdebski 2006; Ura 2006). A 2008 Act restored the institution of the Head of the Civil Service, and Prime Minister Donald Tusk appointed Sławomir Marek Brodziński to the post on 14 April 2009 after consulting the Civil Service Council. The return to the 1998 solutions regarding the institution of the Head of the Civil Service is another statutory element intended to limit the possibility of political influence. The absence of direct authority from the Head of the Prime Minister's Chancellery, who is undoubtedly a strictly political entity, and his replacement by an apolitical official is a good step towards building a neutral civil service (starting, according to the rules, with the most important positions in the service). According to the latest Act, the Head of the Civil Service is a central organ of government administration reporting directly to the Prime Minister (who is the constitutional superior). The administrative service of the Head of the Civil Service is provided by the Chancellery of the Prime Minister, so the Civil Service Office has not been reinstated. In light of the Act of 2008. (art. 15), the tasks of the Head of the Civil Service include: ensuring compliance with the principles of the civil service, directing the process of human resources management, collecting information on the corps, preparing draft normative acts on the civil service, monitoring and supervising the use of funds for remuneration and training, planning, organising and supervising central training, disseminating information on the service, ensuring conditions for the dissemination of information on vacancies, conducting international cooperation in matters concerning the service.

In addition, the Head of the Civil Service prepares and presents to the Council of Ministers a draft strategy for the management of human resources in the service, which includes a diagnosis of the service and the definition of the strategic objectives, the implementation system and the financial framework. It is undoubtedly a good thing that the position of Head of the Civil Service has, at least in part, been excluded from current politics, if only through a ban on party affiliation that also covers the five-year period back (Article 11(1)(9)). Perhaps this will contribute to a partial depoliticisation of the position.

The 2015 amendment introduced changes with regard to the appointment of the Head of the Civil Service. Firstly, it will not be preceded by the opinion of the Civil Service Council, which will be abolished and replaced by the Civil Service Council (identical to 2006). The power of appointment is left to the Prime Minister, however, in the current state of the law, the Prime Minister has unlimited power to dismiss the Head. Articles 12 and 13, which establish obligatory and optional grounds for dismissal of the Head of the Civil Service, have been eliminated from the act. In addition, in the case of optional grounds, the Prime Minister consulted the RSC indicating the reasons justifying the dismissal. The reasons for dismissal and the opinion of the RSC constituted public information (Article 13(2)), which undoubtedly made the motives for the decision transparent. In addition, the requirements for candidates for the post were relaxed: the requirement for experience and party affiliation in the last 5 years was removed without obligation. Only the prohibition of party affiliation for the duration of the function was left in place. In addition, the candidate for Head of the Civil Service is no longer required to belong to the officials of the corps, and can in principle be from outside the corps. Unfortunately, in this case, the legislator did not indicate the rationale for the amendment of the existing solutions. The reasons for the change in the legal status of the Head of the S. C. should therefore be seen in the desire to politicise, to ensure unfettered influence of the ruling party on the staffing of this post. The elimination of substantive requirements for a body managing a sensitive element of the political system points to an attempt at total subordination. At the same time, it should be borne in mind that hitherto the post of Head of the Civil Service was protected by these elements from undue political interference. Currently, such factors are absent. After a deeper analysis, it should be concluded that the elimination of substantive grounds for appointment is de facto no different from the changes introduced in 2006. The incompatibility of the above solutions with the rules of a democratic state of law was pointed out by a number of institutions and experts. The Prosecutor General, in his position of 22 December 2015, wrote that:

> The abandonment of the prohibition of political party affiliation for a specific, sufficiently long period of time for the Head of the Civil Service and the constitution of only the requirement of no political affiliation at the time of appointment and holding office, must be seen as contradictory to the principle of political neutrality. For the proposed normative shape of the provisions under review does not protect the Civil Service Corps against an influx of persons involved in ongoing political activity, who only formally, immediately prior to appointment, renounce political activity. The function of the provisions under review is unambiguous – the civil service should be headed by a person who is not directly involved in political activity, and interference with that person by the political apparatus in

> the form of removal from office is possible in precisely defined cases (Opinia Prokuratora Generalnego z dnia 22 grudnia 2015).

In the opinion of the Supreme Bar Council, it was stated that the proposed changes reflect a desire to increase political influence over the Head of the Civil Service and constitute a straightforward way to change the concept of this body, which by definition was situated between the political and civil servant spheres. It constituted a kind of buffer between these spheres, designed to protect the corps from political interference, but at the same time should enjoy the authority and trust of those in power (Opinia Naczelnej Rady Adwokackiej z dnia 22 grudnia 2015). Identical demands were raised in his opinion by the National Chamber of Legal Advisers and H. Izdebski, who wrote explicitly that the change in the legal status of the Head of the Civil Service was to result in: *"he is to become an ordinary government functionary with political status"* (2016). However, this does not mean that the Polish Civil Service has not faced the problem of politicisation so far. As the literature on the subject points out, this has been a fairly serious problem over the past two decades (Gadowska 2015; Itrich-Drabarek 2012).

4.4.2 Civil Service (Public) Council

Another organisational link in the civil service is the Civil Service Council, a body established by the first Civil Service Act. It was established to perform tasks related to the establishment of the civil service and its functioning. There was no clear statement in the Act about the Council's legal position. From the tasks ascribed to the Council, it appears that it was to be a consultative and advisory body on civil service matters (Cieślak at al. 1998: 34). The 1998 Act on the Civil Service clarified the legal character of the Council, stating that it is an opinion-forming and advisory body of the Prime Minister. The same solution was adopted by the 2008 Act, while the 2006 Act did not contain any regulations concerning the Council, which was abolished and replaced by the Public Service Council, which is also an opinion-forming and advisory body (norms were placed in the Act on the State Human Resources and High State Positions). The tasks of the Council were partially modified, some of them were changed, some were eliminated, and completely new ones were introduced in their place. The Council's tasks under the 1996 Act included expressing opinions on civil service matters submitted to it by the Prime Minister or the Head of the Civil Service and on its own initiative, as well as giving opinions on draft normative acts concerning the civil service. In turn, giving an opinion on the criteria for assessments of civil servants and the manner in which these assessments are carried out was eliminated in the 2008 Act. This function was in force in the 1998 and 2006 Acts. Its absence is undoubtedly related to the specification at the level of the regulation of the criteria for evaluation of corps members. The opinion on the principles of promotion of civil servants was in force in the 1998 and 2006 Acts, and was removed in the 2008 Act. In all laws there was an opinion on central training programmes for civil servants and an opinion on the rules of professional ethics for civil servants. Another function of expressing an opinion on candidates for the post of Head of the Civil Service presented to it by the Prime Minister was absent under the 2006 Act, in the others it was functioning. The giving of an opinion on the draft rules of procedure of the civil service commissions, according to the 2008 regulations, is done only with regard to the rules of procedure of the Higher Disciplinary Commission. The giving of an opinion on the annual reports of the civil service commissions and the Head of the Civil Service in the 2008 Act only concerns the report of the Head of the Civil Service, identical to the 1998 Act, in the 2006 Act this was absent.

By the 1998 Act, the Council was allowed to give an opinion on the draft budget law in the part concerning the civil service and the annual execution of the state budget in this respect (this power is still in place today). In turn, the 2006 Act on State Personnel Resources and High State Positions added powers concerning: assessing the manner of conducting the examination and competitions for high state positions and qualification proceedings for civil servants applying for appointment. The 2008 Act significantly expanded the scope of the Council's activities to include: giving an opinion on the draft strategy for human resources management in the service; giving an opinion on the proposed rate of increase of salaries in the state budget sphere in the service; the possibility of requesting the Head of the Civil Service to take a position on matters determined by the Council in the application of the civil service rules, the possibility to send its representative to observe the course of the recruitment process carried out for a senior position in the civil service and the qualification procedure, the possibility to send its representative to observe the course of the recruitment process carried out for the position of the head of an organisational unit subordinate to or supervised by the Prime Minister or the competent minister, for which open and competitive recruitment is carried out under separate regulations. If irregularities were found in the course of the recruitment process conducted for a senior position, the Council could request the Head of the Civil Service to order a new recruitment. If irregularities were found in the conduct of the selection process, the Council could ask the Head of the Civil Service to order a fresh selection process. If irregularities were found in the recruitment process for the position of head of an organisational unit subordinate to or supervised by the Prime Minister or the competent minister, the Council could request the Prime Minister to order a new recruitment process.

The appointment and the term of office of the Council have in principle not been significantly modified (the changes in this respect resulting from the December 2015 amendment are discussed later). The first Council consisted of 27 persons (the appointments to the members of the first Council were handed over by the Prime Minister on 16 October 1996). In accordance with the regulation of the Prime Minister of 15 October 1996 on the number of members of the Civil Service Council and their remuneration (Journal of Laws No. 122, item 574), the Council consisted of 24 members and an additional 3 chairpersons of the Civil Service Commission (Cieślak at al. 1998: 40).

The 1998 Act set the number of members of the Council at 16 persons, the 2006 Act introduced a provision stating that the Council had between 15 and 24 members, while the 2008 Act established a 15-member body. Invariably over all years, the term of office of Council members has been 6 years, starting from the date of appointment, with half the number of members' terms ending every 3 years (this was amended in 2015). All members, from 1996 onwards, were appointed, and continue to be appointed, by the Prime Minister in part from among persons whose knowledge, experience and authority provide a guarantee that the Council's tasks will be carried out properly (experts in clerical matters) and from among representatives of parliamentary clubs. The 1996 Act provided only for the first of the groups, while other Acts included both groups in varying proportions. In the 1998 Act, the Prime Minister appointed 8 representatives each, in the 2006 Act: 1/3 were representatives of parliamentarians, while in the 2008 Act parliamentarians were represented by 7 members of the Council. Representatives of parliamentary clubs were appointed for the term of office of the Sejm and Senate. As a result of the December 2015 amendment, the Civil Service Council was again abolished and replaced by the Public Service Council (identical to the 2006 statutory solutions). The regulations in Articles 19–23 state that the Civil Service Council is an opinion and advisory body of the Prime Minister consisting of 7–9 members, who are appointed by the Prime Minister for a 4-year term. The chairman and vice-chairman are also appointed by the Prime Minister from among the members of the Council. The novelty is that members of the Council perform their functions socially. It should be added that, until now, the monthly salaries were between 1.3 and 1.5 times the minimum wage in accordance with the Regulation of the Prime Minister of 9 April 2009 on remuneration of members of the Civil Service Council (Journal of Laws of 2009, No. 60, item 491).

One may wonder whether the abolition of the remuneration will be a positive factor for the work of the Council members? After all, remuneration can be a motivating factor, which admittedly is not the most powerful motivator. The Prime Minister is not endowed with the power to dismiss a Council member at will. He or she does so when a Council member resigns, in the event of death, when he or she ceases to meet the conditions set by law or when a Council member fails to perform his or her duties for more than 12 months (excluding long-term illness). Until the 2015 amendment, the Prime Minister dismissed a member of the Council in case of non-performance of the duties of a member of the Council (at the request of the Council), non-performance of duties as a result of a long-term illness confirmed by a medical certificate (at the request of the Council), submission of a resignation when he/she lost his/her good repute (with the consent of at least 2/3 of the Council). In the 1996 Act there was also the premise of gross violation of the provisions of the Act, however, in 1998 this premise no longer existed, while the others have not been modified since 1998. In principle, the removal of a Council member in most cases had to be supported by a proposal from the Council, leading to the conclusion that the Council was a stable body and that the removal of Council members depended on the Council itself. At the same time, it constituted a barrier to possible steps by the Prime Minister, which were motivated only by political and not substantive considerations. The Council's independence from the Head of the Service and its subordination to the Prime Minister allows for a certain degree of autonomy and undoubtedly increases the level of objectivity in the assessment of the Head of the Service's activities. It should be borne in mind that the Council is only an advisory and consultative body, and not a decisive and decisive one. The Council's opinions are not binding, but their consultation by the relevant entities is necessary in certain situations and their absence may have serious legal consequences for the decision taken (Sinkowska 2002: 39–40).

Undoubtedly, a change in the method of creating Council members may result in the elimination of members representing the parliamentary opposition from its composition. In the previous legal status, the 7 members of the Council were appointed at the request of parliamentary clubs, representing all clubs, from among MPs, senators or non-parliamentarians whose knowledge, experience and authority gave the guarantee that the Council's tasks would be carried out properly. According to the Supreme Bar Council, parliamentary representation in the Civil Service Council constituted a kind of element of control of the legislature over the executive (Opinia Naczelnej Rady Adwokackiej z dnia 22 grudnia 2015).

Among the Council's competences, the amendment lacked the power to give an opinion on a candidate for the post of Head of the Civil Service and to give an opinion in the event of his or her dismissal. In addition, as a result of the elimination of competitions for senior positions, the Civil Service Council cannot direct its representative to observe the recruitment process for a senior position or for the position of head of an organisational unit subordinate to or supervised by the Prime Minister or the relevant minister. The current Council also cannot have the power to request the Head of the Civil Service to carry out a new recruitment process for a senior position when irregularities are found.

In conclusion, it can be said that the Council, while having only consultative and advisory functions, could in fact be an important element in the structure of the civil service corps. It deals with issues that are important from the point of view of the management of the service, both at a high level of generality and of a specific dimension and nature.

4.4.3 Director General

The last link in the civil service structure discussed is the post of director general of the office. It was created in the 1996 Act in order to ensure that in administrative offices there were personnel acting in an apolitical, professional manner, providing a guarantee of continuity in the functioning of administrative structures and performing human resources management tasks in administrative bodies. Such a formula was intended to separate administrative (professional) posts from political posts, which were filled from a party key, often on the basis of non-substantive criteria. In contrast to political positions (such as: voivode, minister), the position of director general was to be independent of the current balance of political forces. As time has shown, practice has run counter to theory, and the post has proved to be a proverbial 'morsel', so attractive to every government team that it has not failed to politicise it in various ways. The structure of the post of Director General has been the same since the inception of the Civil Service Acts (although the key element – their filling – has undergone modifications, due to the creation of the State Personnel Pool or the abolition of the competition mode).

The tasks of the Director General in subsequent acts were defined with increasing precision. In the 1996 Act, his or her tasks included ensuring the functioning of the office, the conditions of its operation, as well as the organisation of work, implementing personnel policy in the civil service, carrying out civil service tasks in the office, performing labour law actions with respect to civil servants. The 1998 Act specified that the Director General ensures the functioning and continuity of the office, the conditions of its operation, as well as the organisation of work, performs labour law activities with respect to persons employed in the office and implements personnel policy in the civil service, performs certain tasks of the head of the office, performs other tasks under the authority of the government administration body.

In the Act, we will also find a number of other competences provided for the general director, e. g.: organisation of recruitment of candidates to the civil service corps, appointment of an examination commission, conclusion of an employment contract with an employee, organisation of preparatory service or shortening of the period of preparatory service. In the next act – i. e. in the Act on the State Reserves and High State Positions, in principle no deeper adjustment was made in the scope of the tasks of the Director General (only the performance of certain tasks of the head of the office and the performance of other tasks under the authority of a government administration body were excluded). The change that took place was a systemic change, which I have mentioned many times before, this was done by excluding the Director General from the civil service system. In the course of the drafting of the State Personnel Act, it was pointed out that the exclusion of the position of Director General from the service entrusts important tasks to a person outside the corps, but, moreover, this person will be entirely available to the superior, since, in the light of Article 10(8), removal from the positions held may take place at any time, in the same manner as the appointment. In addition, the exclusion of the condition of neutrality with regard to high state positions has been criticised (rightly so). There would then be no stabilisation of the employment relationship and the political superior would be free to replace the director-general, making it a de facto political position (Stelina 2006; Izdebski 2006). There are also a few dissenting voices among the opinions (Fundowicz 2006). The latest Service Act reinstated two functions excluded by the 2006 Act, in addition to obliging the Director General to prepare a human resources management programme in the office, as well as to organise recruitment for vacant official positions, including senior civil service positions. The December 2015 amendment, while abolishing competitions for senior positions, at the same time dramatically changed the way these positions are filled. Currently, directors general are appointed and dismissed by the relevant minister, the head of a central office, the Head of the Chancellery of the Prime Minister or the provincial governor. The Labour Code will thus apply. At the same time, the key point is that appointment is an institution to which substantive recruitment criteria, such as in the case of the competition procedure (as mentioned earlier), do not apply. Appointment, and with it dismissal, depends on the will of the body authorised to make it. In addition, the relaxation of eligibility requirements constitutes a restriction of the professionalisation element.

The purpose of creating the post of director-general was undoubtedly to relieve *strcite* political bodies – ministers, voivodes, heads of central offices – of clerical work. It is created when the post of the head of an office is strictly political in nature and political criteria are used in filling it, while where filling it is based on substantive (professional) criteria, there is no need to create the post of director-general. The director general manages the civil service of the office in question (in terms of staff and material), and is the link between the administrative and political spheres. The idea behind the creation of this post was to ensure apolitical, professional, stable and sustainable civil servants in an administration separated from the political leadership. It should be noted that Article 38 of the Act of 8 August 1996 on the Council of Ministers (i. e. Journal of Laws 2003, No. 24, item 199, as amended) clearly and definitively indicates political positions by stating that if the President of the Republic of Poland accepts the resignation of the Government, the resignation shall be submitted by secretaries and undersecretaries of state as well as voivodes and deputy voivodes (Jagielski&Rączka 2001: 80–87).

The director is tasked with ensuring the smooth running of the office regardless of who is at the helm of power. The position of the Director General has undoubtedly

Table 9 Legal status of the director general of the office since 1996

Item	Feature	1996 Act	1998 Act	2006 Act	2008 Act	Amendment of 2015
1.	Position in the structure	Civil Service Corps	Civil Service Corps	State Human Resources	Civil Service Corps	Civil Service Corps
2.	Offices in which it functions	government administration offices	government administration offices	offices serving ministers, members of committees making up the Council of Ministers, in the Chancellery of the Prime Minister, in offices serving heads of central offices, in voivodship offices.	w Kancelarii Prezesa Rady Ministrów, w urzędzie ministra, urzędzie przewodniczącego komitetu wchodzącego w skład Rady Ministrów, urzędzie centralnego organu adm. rządowej oraz w urzędzie wojewódzkim	in the Chancellery of the Prime Minister the Chancellery of the Prime Minister, in the office of the minister, the office of the chairman of the committee that makes up the Council of Ministers of the Council of Ministers, the office of the central government administration body and in the voivodship office
3.	Offices where the following do not function	district offices and field offices of special administration (currently – non-associated administration)	field offices of government administration subordinate to ministers or central government administration bodies (special), commands, inspectorates and other organisational units constituting auxiliary apparatus of heads of combined services, inspections and guards	central offices of government administration in which, due to the specialised nature of tasks, the post of office general director is not created	in the General Headquarters the Police Headquarters, the Headquarters of the State Fire Service and the Headquarters of the Border Guard	in the Police Headquarters Police Headquarters, the Headquarters of the State Fire Service and the Headquarters of the Border Guard

Item	Feature	1996 Act	1998 Act	2006 Act	2008 Act	Amendment of 2015
4.	Direct subordination	To the competent administrative body, but also functional dependence on the Head of the ivil Service	directly to the competent minister, head of the central office or voivode	to the head of the office	to the head of the office	to the head of the office
5.	Purpose of establishment	apolitical, stable staff, separated from political superiors	apolitical, stable staff, separated from political superiors	adaptation of the employment relationship to the implementation of government policies requiring swift, flexible staffing decisions, more efficient interaction between officials and politicians	apolitical, stable staff, separated from political superiors	apolitical, stable staff, separated from political superiors
6.	Recruitment	selection procedure (appointment)	competition	appointment by competent authority	open and competitive recruitment	appointment by competent authority
7.	Job group	category A	senior positions in Civil Service	senior state positions (non-Civil Service)	senior positions in Civil Service	wyższe stanowiska w sc

Source: Table by author. Based on Civil Service Acts 1996, 1998, 2006, 2008 and 2015 as amended.

been strengthened by the provision of Article 37(1) of the Act on the Council of Ministers, according to which the Minister performs his/her tasks with the assistance of the Secretary and Undersecretaries of State, the Minister's Political Office and the Director General of the Office. In addition, Article 39(4a) makes him responsible for the smooth functioning of the office and the office's readiness to perform its tasks in the event of the resignation of the political leadership of the office (Article 38).

As mentioned above, the filling of director general positions in previous years was carried out with considerable difficulties. There were a variety of reasons for this. They ranged from the reluctance of political superiors to hire professionals not affiliated with any political party, to the attempt to politicise these positions on a normative level (Article 144a, discussed earlier), which is why the first Service Act included a provision (Art. 93) allowing, for a period of 2 years from the date of its entry into force, for the post of Director General of an office to be filled by a person who is not a civil servant, but who meets the general statutory conditions for appointment and whose knowledge, experience and moral authority will ensure the fulfilment of the tasks of the civil service. The two-year period did not have time to elapse, as the Sejm had previously passed another act on the service withholding appointments to the corps under the first act, which also entailed problems in filling the positions of directors-general. The 1998 Act provided for a longer term of five years, allowing for the hiring of a non-civil servant as director general. A different solution was adopted by the 2008 Act, specifying in Article 196, sec. 1 and sec. 2, that within one year from the date of entry into force of the Act, recruitment should be carried out for the positions of directors general of offices if these positions are occupied by persons employed on the basis of entrustment of duties (in the light of the Act on State Human Resources and High State Positions) and at the same time were not civil servants, did not pass the examination at KSAP, did not win the competition announced by the Prime Minister, were not appointed by the President as plenipotentiary representatives of the Republic of Poland in other countries and to international organisations (Drobny at al. 2010: 628–629). The effect of the 2015 amendment to the regulations is that both civil servants and employees of the civil service corps can be appointed as directors general. There are no requirements for prior experience in the public administration sector or the need to have previously held managerial positions. The requirements relate only to higher education, possession of managerial competence and the absence of a conviction by a final judgment prohibiting the occupation of managerial positions in offices of public authorities or the performance of functions related to the disposal of public funds (Article 53(1)). In the event of the appointment of a civil servant or civil servant to the post of Director General, unpaid leave shall be granted in the office in which he or she is previously employed (Article 53a(7)).

Conclusion

The changing conception of the role of the state generated inevitable changes in public administration. Its tasks and competences, as well as its organisational structure, depended, and still depend, on the conception of the functioning of the state. Over the years, transformations of the public administration resulting from changing ideologies and the evolving environment have been visible. In summary, social-political-economic changes generate changes in public administration, with administration generally being the element resistant to change, with the proviso that the political sphere partly sees these changes as partisan interests. The interaction between the political and administrative spheres should be based on 'peaceful' co-existence, as their activities are closely correlated. It seems to me that they are even 'genetically' linked, and a rigid 'demarcation line' will cause more losses than benefits. The ideal would be to allow the administrative sphere in particular to function in such a way that politicians, with a high degree of trust, limit their influence on the administration. However, from the point of view of politicians, with limited access to information and limited knowledge in relation to officials, their increased desire to exert influence is to be expected. Consequently, it is still an open question whether civil servants should be neutral, or indeed whether they can be neutral at all, in a situation where they are de facto pursuing the agenda of a particular government. Moreover, being specialists, they become in many cases the creators of specific statutory solutions, and this in turn generates a threat to the superior position of politicians in this respect.

The process of shaping civil service models has been determined by historical, geographical, cultural and social circumstances. Hence, we are dealing with differently shaped systems in different countries. They are clearly marked by the specifics of a particular country, but we can find common "elements" situating a country on the axis "open model – closed model". A clear trend is the convergence of models with the apparent predominance of positional system solutions. Contemporary socio-economic conditions seem to fit the open model, hence the hybrid models found in many countries.

The Polish circumstances were and still remain quite specific. The considerations contained herein lead to several conclusions. Firstly, the scale of the problems that emerged in the initial period of transition was the result of the obliteration of the model created in the Second Republic. The positive experiences of pre-war Poland were offset by the solutions of the People's Republic of Poland, thus complicating the process of corps creation. As a result, we can speak of a much reduced continuity of experience. Secondly, most of the former 'Soviet bloc' countries faced such problems. On the problems of post-communist countries in this matter (Public Administration in Post-Communist Countries. Former Soviet Union, Central and Eastern Europe, and Mongolia 2017).

Consequently, after the breakthrough of 1989, four acts on the civil service have already been enacted in Poland (and a number of amendments, including the last one – significant in its consequences – of December 2015), which is not conducive to the creation of apolitical, professional cadres and, on the contrary, undermines trust in state bodies. The process of creating a service is a long-term one, the need to 'root' the regulations, to get officials accustomed to the new conditions, while constant changes to the law do not contribute to this goal. After more than 25 years of trying to build the corps, we have certainly not lived to see our own model of civil service. The theoretical basis in the form of a normative layer does exist, but it is not sufficient for the formation of a corps that is supposed to fulfil the ideas of the service. Elements of both the career system and the positional system can be found in all laws. The 2006 Acts introduced quite a few elements of the positional system, but the declared "flexibility and mobility" was only a contribution to politicisation and partyisation, especially of senior positions. The 1998 and 2008 regulations (similar in concept) introduced many elements of a positional system. The 1998 and 2008 regulations (similar in their objectives) introduced the solutions used in both systems (with the predominance of the career model), with the 2008 law eliminating some of the shortcomings of 1998 by making recruitment to senior positions more flexible. The most recent amendment of 2015, introducing revolutionary changes in this respect, changed the previous philosophy of the service, as the state of the corps after the abolition of competitions for senior positions has not improved and, on the contrary, the situation of the service has worsened. The scale of appointments and dismissals especially during the first period of the new regulations reached almost 30 % – which is quite a high percentage. In addition, there is freedom to bring into the ranks of appointees people who have not been subject to the rigours of the Civil Service Act during their previous careers (in 2020 – around 30 %). There is a noticeable increase in the number of senior posts between 2016 and 2020. In 2015, there were 1588 higher positions, while in 2020 there were as many as 3389. This represents an increase of 113.41 %. If we combine this with the change in the way higher posts are filled, it appears that those in power have secured direct influence over the filling of a large number of posts. The share of civil servants in the total number of people employed in the civil service is declining – which means that the professionalisation process is slowing down. The elimination of open and competitive recruitment for senior positions, i. e. competitions, raises serious constitutional questions (related to

Article 60 and Article 32 of the Constitution). The lack of substantive premises in the filling of senior positions constitutes a negation of the idea of a professional corps and a weakening of legal guarantees of professional stability, which is an immanent feature of the professional performance of tasks by the administration (Pastwa 2016: 52–53). The lack of a kind of "anchor" stabilising the employment relationship of officials may lead to instrumental treatment of the work performed and a sense of insecurity. The lack of legal security (understood as the stabilisation of the employment relationship), and the constant fear of the possibility of dismissal, are certainly not conducive to the principle of impartiality and political neutrality that are the key ideas of the civil service. The relaxation of qualification requirements for those holding senior positions may result in a reduction in the quality of their work, which will undoubtedly have an impact on the professionalism of the tasks performed by the state and its structures. The exclusion of senior service positions from the periodic appraisal system and the abandonment of the establishment of an individual professional development programme may reduce these individuals to passive executors of political demands or guidelines/instructions. In addition, there is a lack of safeguards against political pressure when discretionary decisions on the filling of senior positions are taken by political decision-makers with a lowering of merit criteria. Guarantees of the apolitical character of the civil service, which is represented by the Directors General, will not be preserved, as there is no buffer to separate the political and administrative spheres. It should be remembered that, in line with Art. 153 of the Constitution, it is the Prime Minister who is the head of the Corps, while the duty of the Corps is to perform the tasks set by those in power (implementation of government policy). It is not possible to completely separate these two spheres (political and administrative). They must, by virtue of the tasks they perform, cooperate with each other. Hence, we cannot speak of complete independence. The creation of a civil service corps, and with it mechanisms protecting civil servants from undue interference from politicians, is an instrument of relative independence understood as freedom from political influence in the performance of tasks commissioned by those currently in power. However, these are carried out not in the partisan party interest, but in the public interest (Springer 2016: 124).

Senior positions have become de facto political positions which is in opposition to the constitutional principles of a democratic state under the rule of law. The position of Director General may have a negative impact on the functioning of the lower posts (being in charge of personnel policy is fundamental to the idea of an apolitical and neutral service). The Director General will not be a buffer to protect other staff from political pressure and influence. These changes represent a perversion of patterns of behaviour implemented over a number of years with considerable difficulty and resistance occurring in both the political and administrative spheres. It was rightly concluded by J. Itrich-Drabarek that: "Resistance to public administration reforms in Poland has occurred among the officials themselves, who are blamed for 'hand-holding', conservatism, self-interest, and the strengthening of bureaucratic barriers" (2010: 77).

Moreover, the amendment goes against European civil service standards based on transparent, open and accessible procedures. The message it sends to the entire corps is as follows: "political connections instead of substantive rationale are the way to fill senior positions". Such a mechanism is a straightforward route to the partisanship of key administrative positions in the state, which in turn leads to the degradation of the corps and the performance of tasks not in the state interest but in partisan party interests, which is organically contrary to the idea of service. All these elements will result in a lack of authority and a lack of leadership legitimacy for those holding senior positions which, in turn, is a sine qua non for the functioning of the corps as a whole. The result of the reforms is the politicisation of the civil service, and it may also be that there will be a permanent replacement of managers, as well as a reduction in the quality of those managers. This will undoubtedly lead to a reduction in the quality of the administration's services and its efficiency. Excessive fluctuation, the so-called "personnel carousel", is not conducive to professionalisation, reliability and, as a result, a deterioration in the quality of democratic processes. There is a fear that arbitrarily appointed positions will become party synecracies for party appointees. In the long run, it may turn out that the Polish civil service is facing unfavourable stagnation. Excessive politicisation of the Polish administration resulting in violations of legal and ethical norms (e.g. neutrality of officials) and strong politicisation during the development and implementation of public policies has been repeatedly pointed out in the literature (Gadowska 2010: 207; Bossaert, Demmke 2003: 17–21). The quality of the public administration's functioning depends on many diverse factors. An indispensable element of an efficiently functioning civil service is the creation of such operating conditions that allow it to develop and improve "in peace". Undoubtedly, it is not served by constant changes in legal regulations that bring with them instability and uncertainty.

An immanent feature of the service is its political neutrality, which does not imply total isolation from the political sphere. These spheres must cooperate, there must be communication, information flow. After all, the administration implements the development strategies adopted by those currently in power, so it cannot be definitively separated from politics. The crux of the problem lies in ensuring that the activities of the administration do not go beyond the accepted legal framework and, above all, that the administration does not favour and support political decision-makers in the struggle for electoral support. The better the quality of interaction, the more effectively the state functions. It should be remembered that interaction is not to be about blind subordination, but about performing tasks for the common good, never in the individual interest of a political party. We should agree with the widespread view that the civil service, as traditionally understood, must first be consolidated, and only then, slowly, should modern solutions be implemented. It is necessary to become accustomed to the essence of the civil service, to adopt certain canons, and this is much more difficult in a state where these ideas have been denied for 50 years. In principle, we have no tradition, the pre-war norms having undergone multiple changes, and the turbulence on the political scene in the inter-war period did not do much to "root" the Corps. Analysing the evolution of the Polish service after 1989, one may get the impression that the construction of an apolitical corps is only a catchy election slogan, while after the elections, the victorious parties begin to treat the entire corps as political spoils. The filling of posts after the elections is a kind of repayment of election commitments to political allies. There is a clear lack of trust and confidence in the loyalty and competence of officials. Each successive political team does not trust officials who worked under their predecessors. Beblavy rightly observes that until the political parties are convinced that the civil service 'will not stab them in the back' during their governments it seems doubtful the reform towards a professional and stable service (Beblavy 2002: 65). There is sometimes a suggestion in the doctrine that if the problem of creating a service is so great, then perhaps a reorientation to a different model is in order. The problem is that there are no concrete proposals. The construction of the corps should start with the restoration of its ethos. Despite the passage of years, T. Górzyńska's thesis remains to this day fully adequate, correct and reflective of reality:

> The right theoretical assumptions, good laws, well thought-out structures and meticulously developed working methods can only be truly effective in practice if they are implemented by personnel who understand the essence and objectives of the state service, and are professionally and morally prepared for the tasks entrusted to them (2011: 79).

The Polish state still faces the task of developing a strategy for implementing, on the one hand, the provisions of the Service Act, and on the other hand, for creating an ethos of service that cannot be guaranteed by normative acts alone. Furthermore, it should be borne in mind that, on a European scale, Polish civil servants are among the lowest paid, which undoubtedly has its impact on the quality of the tasks performed and on the significant turnover of staff. The situation in which the civil service found itself in 1989 was, of course, the result of more than 50 years of absence of democratic rules. Restoring a well-functioning service requires both systemic, but also, and perhaps above all, cultural and mental changes. Perhaps a public backlash against political clientelism in the administration and an increase in public awareness would work (Gadowska 2010: 207). However, it is not possible to completely replace the staff at one point in time. It must be remembered that the ranks of government administration were filled both by people formed under the previous system (with their habits and experience) and those educated after 1989. The process of change requires many years and considerable financial outlays, the creation of a system to teach and educate new staff. The very existence of well-structured regulations setting standards of behaviour is highly desirable, but it does not determine the existence of the civil service. Subsequent laws, starting from 1996, created different concepts for the construction of the corps. The 1996 Act created a system similar to the career model based on professional, reliable, impartial and politically neutral performance of state tasks. Another act (1998) changed the philosophy of the corps while reforming the structures of the state and, a year earlier, guaranteeing the constitutional status of the service (Article 153 of the Constitution). In principle, it came closer to a mixed model, variously assessed by the doctrine (for some with the predominance of the career system – e. g. J. Czaputowicz, for others with the predominance of the positional model – e. g. T. Górzyńska). The next two Acts of 2006 on the civil service and the state human resources were intended to make the service more flexible, bringing it closer to the positional model. Despite negative opinions on the unconstitutionality of the solutions and the clear political rationale for the changes, they were made, fortunately, for a short period. The creation of a state human resources pool evoked unambiguous associations with the human resources reserve for managerial positions in state administration and the national economy, established by a resolution of the Central Committee of the Polish United Workers' Party in 1973. The 2008 Act largely reverted to the legal status of 1998, applying a number of solutions familiar under it. The 2015 amendment demolished the proverbial 'roof' of the corps by abolishing competitions for senior positions.

Another of T. Górzyńska's statements, reflecting, in a sense, the essence of the work done over the past 20 years on the solutions forming the civil service, is symptomatic of the Polish civil service:

> Each of the laws to date has been "an act of a different government", of a different political party (SLD, AWS, PiS, PO). Each time they have pushed their concepts of the civil service, for themselves, and each time it has also turned out that they are in fact a "gift" to the next team, usually unwanted. This handling of the civil service is at odds with the basic principles of the performance of state tasks (sometimes more broadly of public tasks (2011: 77).

In conclusion, to this day it has not been possible to create a functioning corps, and the pre-war status and prestige of the civil service profession remains in the ambit of every government. Depoliticisation and de-partisanship are other unrealised demands. Most of the democratic countries of the former Eastern Bloc have struggled to create a well-functioning service, seeking a variety of solutions, not always the best from the point of view of socio-economic and historical circumstances. Poland's more than 20-year experience of re-establishing the civil service is not free of errors and shortcomings, particularly in the human resources (HR) management aspect. Characteristic of many of the changes is a recklessness and disregard for the importance of a well-functioning administration for the development of a democratic state under the rule of law. What prevails is a desire to "appropriate" and ruthlessly subordinate government administration officials to all successive ruling teams. The result is the absence, to this day, of a formed civil service corps in Poland. There are not even stable and tested legal regulations allowing for the slow building of human resources.

Concluding the discussion so far, the following doubts/questions arise: Are we as a State able to realise access to good administration for citizens? In the context of the degradation of the civil service (especially in the situation of the COVID-19 pandemic), can we speak of the efficiency of the State? The effectiveness of its action in the name of the common good of citizens? It seems to me that it is inadequate to ask whether to restore the principles previously in force. The question should be how to do this so that the social/administrative/structural costs are as little as possible for the efficient and effective functioning of the state, i. e. the well-being of citizens. What needs to be done immediately is to strengthen the guarantees of political neutrality of officials and to introduce mechanisms for professionalisation (substantive rationale for filling senior positions) and apoliticality.

Bibliography

1. Scientific papers

Antoszewski, A. (1999): Administracja publiczna w systemie politycznym, [in:] Administracja publiczna. Wprowadzenie. In: Ferens, A., Macek I. (eds): Administracja publiczna. Wprowadzenie. Wrocław, pp. 55–74.

Auer, A., Demmke, Ch., Polet, R. (1996): Civil Service in the Europe of Fifteen. Current Situation and Prospects. Maastricht.

Bach – Golecka, D. (2008): Służba cywilna a władza polityczna w administracji rządowej. Przykłady praktyki innych państw. In: Czaputowicz, J. (scientific ed): Administracja publiczna. Wyzwania w dobie integracji europejskiej. Warszawa, pp. 329–342.

Ban, C. (2014): Drawing the line between political control and politicization: an anlysis of public administration theory. Paper presented at the annual meeting of NISPAcee, Budapest, 1, pp. 1–12.

Beblavy, M. (2002): Management of Civil Service Reform in Central Europe. In: Peteri, G (ed): Mastering decenralization and public administration reforms in Central and Eastern Europe. Budapest.

Boć, J. (2004): Administracja publiczna. Wrocław.

Bossaert, D., Demmke, Ch. (2003): Służba cywilna w państwach akcesyjnych. Tendencje i wpływ procesów integracyjnych. Łódź.

Brunetko, K. (2003): Służba cywilna w III RP: punkty krytyczne. Warszawa. https://www.batory.org.pl/ftp/program/przeciw-korupcji/publikacje/sluzba_cywilna.pdf (accessed 2020/01/09).

Chrabąszcz, R., Hausner, J., Mazur, S. (2003): Administracja publiczna w wybranych krajach Europy Środowo-Wschodniej. Kraków.

Cieślak, Z., Jagielski, J., Rączka, K. (1998): Komentarz do ustawy o służbie cywilnej. Warszawa.

Culepa, M. (2016): Służba cywilna po nowelizacji. Kompendium służb zatrudnienia. Warszawa.

Czaputowicz J. (2005): Zarządzanie w administracji publicznej w dobie globalizacji. *Służba Cywilna,* 10, pp. 9–41.

Czaputowicz, J. (2001): Implikacje integracji z Unią Europejską dla polskiej służby cywilnej. *Służba Cywilna*, 1, pp. 22–49.

Demmke, Ch. (2004): Służba cywilna w krajach europejskich: między tradycją a reformą. Łódź.

Demmke, Ch., Moilanen, T. (2010): Civil Services in the EU of 27. Reform Outcomes and the Future of the Civil Service, Frankfurt am Main–Berlin–Bern–Bruxelles–New York– Oxford–Wien.

Dębicki, M. (2002–2003): Służby publiczne w świecie korporacji. Ograniczenia i niebezpieczeństwa menedżeryzmu jako narzędzia administracji publicznej. *Służba Cywilna,* 5, pp. 103–116.

Dębicki, M. (2001): Urząd i urzędnik XXI wieku. In: Kudrycka, B. (ed): Rozwój kadr administracji publicznej. Białystok.
Domańska, E. (1997): Kapitał nowoczesnej administracji. *Biuletyn Służby Cywilnej*, 1, pp. 49–51.
Drobny, W., Mazuryk, M., Zuzankiewicz, P. (2010): Ustawa o służbie cywilnej. Komentarz. Warszawa.
Dubowik, A. (2007): Wzmożona trwałość stosunku pracy z mianowania. Praca i Zabezpieczenie Społeczne, 9, pp. 18–26.
Dubowik, A. (2010): Podstawy nawiązania stosunku pracy z członkami korpusu służby cywilnej. Praca i Zabezpieczenie Społeczne, 1, pp. 22–30.
Działocha K., Łukaszczuk A. (2006): Nowa ustawa o służbie cywilnej (aspekt prawno – konstytucyjny). *Państwo i Prawo*, 11(729), pp. 3–16.
Ferens, A. (1999): Administracja publiczna. Wprowadzenie do nauki administracji publicznej. In: Ferens, A., Macek I. (eds): Administracja publiczna. Wprowadzenie. Wrocław, pp. 9–28.
Gadowska, K. (2015): Dysfunkcje administracji. Służba cywilna w perspektywie neoinstytucjonalnej. Kraków.
Gadowska, K. (2010): Law in Action: The Problem of Political Patronage in the Process of Appointing High-ranking Posts in Civil Service in Poland. In: Nemec, J., Peters, B. G. (eds): State and Administration in a Changing World. Bratislava, pp. 207–241.
Galińska – Rączy, I. (2003): Sprawa interpretacji art. 137 ust. 2 ustawy o służbie cywilnej. *Biuletyn Biura Studiów i Ekspertyz Kancelarii Sejmu*, 2(51)/03, pp. 62–65.
Gąciarz, J. (1998): Odpowiedź na zarzuty zawarte w „Raporcie z przeprowadzonej analizy i oceny tworzenia służby cywilnej (sierpień 1996 – wrzesień 1997)" przedstawiona na posiedzeniu Rady Służby Cywilnej w dniu 3 kwietnia 1998r. *Biuletyn Służby Cywilnej*, 5, pp. 16–20.
Gintowt – Jankowicz, M. (1997): Krajowa Szkoła Administracji Publicznej. Cele, działalność, zamierzenia. *Biuletyn Służby Cywilnej*, 1, pp. 46–51.
Gintowt – Jankowicz, M. (2000): Służba cywilna w wybranych państwach demokratycznych. Warszawa 2000.
Górski, A. (2000–2001): Ustawa o służbie cywilnej z 18 grudnia 1998 r. w świetle aktów prawnych o państwowej służbie cywilnej z lat 1918–1922. *Służba Cywilna*, 2, pp. 73–96.
Górski, A. (2001–2002): Civil servans czy politicus servans – w okresie międzywojennym i obecnie. *Służba Cywilna*, 3, pp. 70–97.
Górzyńska, T. (2005): Od koncepcji do stworzenia podstaw prawnych funkcjonowania służby cywilnej. Warszawa. Paper presented at the seminar meeting of the College of the Supreme Audit Office (NIK) of 20 April 2005 on the subject of Dobra administracja, pp. 1–22.
Górzyńska, T. (2011): Reformy statusu członków służby cywilnej w Polsce. Przyczyny – cele – oczekiwania. In: Mikułowski, W., Jezierska A. (eds.): Wyzwania rozwoju zasobów ludzkich administracji publicznej w dobie kryzysu ekonomicznego – jak działać lepiej mając mniej. Warszawa, pp. 62–80.
Grosse, T.G. (2000): Działania anty-korupcyjne w państwach członkowskich OECD, Florence. Raport w ramach programu Fundacji im. Stefana Batorego i Helsińskiej Fundacji Praw Człowieka „Przeciw Korupcji", https://antykorupcja.gov.pl/ak/analizy-i-raporty/oecd/3528,Dzialania-antykorupcyjne-w-panstwach-czlonkowskich-OECD.html (accessed 2018/08/24).
Hausner, J. (2007): Od idealnej biurokracji do zarządzania publicznego. In: Zuba, K. (ed): Biurokracja. Fenomen władzy politycznej w strukturach administracyjnych. Toruń, pp. 42–67.
Hekajłło, W. (1924): Ustawa o państwowej służbie cywilnej (pragmatyka służbowa) w brzmieniu obecnie obwoiązującem wraz z odnośnemi ustawami, rozporządzeniami, okólnikami i popularnym komentarzem, z uwzględnieniem orzecznictwa Najwyższego Trybunału Administracyjnego. Warszawa.

Herbut, R. (1999): Administracja publiczna – modele, funkcje, struktura. In: Ferens, A., Macek I. (eds.): Administracja publiczna. Wprowadzenie. Wrocław, pp. 29–54.
Herbut, R. (2008): Nowy styl rządzenia a tradycyjne mechanizmy sterowania polityką. In: Sroka, J. (ed): Wybrane instytucje demokracji partycypacyjnej w polskim systemie politycznym. Warszawa, pp. 26–54.
Heywood, A. (2007): Ideologie polityczne. Warszawa.
Heywood, A. (2009): Politologia. Warszawa.
Itrich – Drabarek, J. (1998): Etos polskiego urzędnika na tle historycznym. *Biuletyn Służby Cywilnej*, 6(12), pp. 11–15.
Itrich-Drabarek, J. (2010): Uwarunkowania, standardy i kierunki zmian funkcjonowania służby cywilnej na tle europejskim. Warszawa.
Itrich – Drabarek, J. (2012): Służba cywilna w Polsce – koncepcje i praktyka. Warszawa.
Izdebski, H. (1993): Współczesne modele administracji publicznej, Urząd Rady Ministrów, Pełnomocnik Rządu do spraw reformy administracji publicznej. Warszawa.
Izdebski, H. (2001): Historia administracji. Warszawa.
Izdebski, H., Kulesza, M. (2004): Administracja publiczna. Warszawa.
Izdebski H. (2007): Od administracji publicznej do public governance. *Zarządzanie Publiczne*,1, pp. 7–20.
Jabłoński, A.W. (1999): Tendencje przeobrażeń administracji publicznej na Zachodzie. In: Ferens, A., Macek I. (eds): Administracja publiczna. Wprowadzenie. Wrocław, pp. 75–94.
Jagielski J., Rączka K. (2001): Komentarz do ustawy o służbie cywilnej. Warszawa 2001.
Jagielski, J. (2006): Kilka refleksji w kwestii kadr administracji publicznej. In: Łukasiewicz J. (ed): Biurokracja – III Międzynarodowa Konferencja naukowa, 2–4 czerwca 2006 r. Krynica Zdrój. Rzeszów, pp. 210–219.
Jakubowska, E. (1998): Odpowiedzialność zawodowa w administracji. *Biuletyn Służby Cywilnej*, 10(16), pp. 24–29.
Jaśkiewicz, W. (1969): Stosunki służbowe w administracji. Warszawa.
Jełowicki, M. (1986): Instytucje prawa urzędniczego. Warszawa.
Kasznica, S. (1946): Polskie prawo administracyjne. Poznań.
Komar – Morawska, A. (1998): Profil etyczny urzędnika państwowej służby cywilnej w II Rzeczypospolitej Polskiej. *Biuletyn Służby Cywilnej*, 2(8), pp. 17–18.
Korczak, J. (2006): Procedury naboru do służby cywilnej – biurokratyzacja czy modelowa biurokracja. In: Łukasiewicz J. (ed): Biurokracja – III Międzynarodowa Konferencja naukowa, 2–4 czerwca 2006 r. Krynica Zdrój. Rzeszów, pp. 285–302.
Kornaś, J. (2001): Koncepcje polskiej służby cywilnej w świetle ustaw z 1996 i 1998r. Zeszyty Naukowe Akademii Ekonomicznej w Krakowie, 571, pp. 21–38.
Kościołek, J. (1947): Państwowa służba cywilna. Jednolity tekst pragmatyki i komentarz. Łódź.
Kudrycka, B. (1997): Podstawy kodeksów etycznych służby cywilnej w Polsce (na tle porównawczym). *Państwo i Prawo*, 2, pp. 24–37.
Kudrycka, B. (1998): Neutralność polityczna urzędników. Warszawa.
Kudrycka, B. (2001): Nowe wyzwania i trendy w reformowaniu administracji publicznej. In: Kudrycka, B. (ed): Rozwój kadr administracji publicznej. Białystok, pp. 26–48.
Kulesza, M. (1993): Założenia i kierunki reformy administracji publicznej, Pełnomocnik Rządu ds. Reformy Administracji Publicznej. Warszawa.
Liszcz, T. (2005): Prawo urzędnicze. Lublin.
Łętowska, E., Łętowski J. (1995): O państwie prawa, administrowaniu i sądach w okresie przekształceń ustrojowych. Warszawa.

Majcherkiewicz, T. (2008): Civil Service Reform in Poland: The Influence of Path Dependency. In: Killian, J., Eklund, N. (eds.): Handbook of Administrative Reform: An international Perspective. New York, pp. 139–158.

Malec, J. (2003): Studia z dziejów administracji nowożytnej. Kraków.

Matheson, A. (2003–2004): Modernizacja sektora publicznego: nowy program. Przegląd dwóch dekad modernizacji z perspektywy zarządzania zasobami ludzkimi. *Służba Cywilna*, 7, pp. 29–52.

Mazur, S. (2002): Od tradycyjnej administracji do zarządzania publicznego. *Zeszyty Naukowe Akademii Ekonomicznej w Krakowie*, 598, pp. 15–28.

Mazur, S. (2005): Historia administracji publicznej. In: Hausner, J. (ed): Administracja publiczna. Warszawa, pp. 41–62.

Mazur, S. (2007): Biurokracja jako dylemat. *Zarządzanie Publiczne* 2(2), pp. 99–112.

Mazur, S. (2016): Neoweberyzm i jego fundamenty teoretyczne. In: Mazur, S. (ed): Neoweberyzm w zarządzaniu publicznym. Od modelu do paradygmatu? Warszawa, pp. 15–27.

Mikułowski, W. (2003): Sprawna służba publiczna jako instrument rządzenia państwem (I). Współczesne Zarządzanie, 1, pp. 65–82.

Mikułowski, W. (2003a): Sprawna służba publiczna jako instrument rządzenia państwem (II). Współczesne Zarządzanie, 2, pp. 44–57.

Mróz, M. (2000): Służba cywilna w państwach Unii Europejskiej (system awansowy i pozycyjny w badaniach Europejskiego Instytutu Administracji Publicznej). Kancelaria Sejmu Biuro Studiów i Ekspertyz, 746, pp. 1–7.

Osborne, D., Gaebler T. (2010): Rządzić inaczej. Warszawa.

Zonn-Pasternak, K. (1993): Państwowa służba cywilna. Dział IV – Pracownicy administracji. Warszawa.

Pastwa, J. (2016): The challenge of civil service professionalisation: Lessons from Poland. In: Meyer-Sahling J. H. (ed): The professionalisation of the Civil Service beetwen Politics and Administration. Montenegro, pp. 48–58.

Penc, J. (1998): Motywowanie w zarządzaniu. Kraków.

Peters, G., B. (1995): Polityka i biurokracja państwowa. In: Selection and elaboration Szczupaczyński, J. (ed): Władza i społeczeństwo. Antologia tekstów z zakresu socjologii polityki. Warszawa, pp. 153–172.

Peters, G., B. (1999): Administracja publiczna w systemie politycznym. Warszawa.

Public Administration in Post-Communist Countries. Former Soviet Union, Central and Eastern Europe, and Mongolia (2017): Liebert, S., Condrey, S. E., Goncharov D. New York.

Radziewicz, P. (2005): Prawne możliwości rozszerzenia zakresu podmiotowego ustawy o służbie cywilnej na państwowe jednostki organizacyjne wykonujące zadania z zakresu administracji publicznej (inne niż organy administracji rządowej), w kontekście dyspozycji art. 153 Konstytucji. *Zeszyty Prawnicze Biura Studiów i Ekspertyz Kancelarii Senatu*, 2(6), pp. 27–29.

Raport z przeprowadzonej analizy i oceny tworzenia służby cywilnej (sierpień 1996 – wrzesień 1997), (1998). *Biuletyn Służby Cywilnej*, 4(10), pp.1–5.

Rubisz, L. (2007): Biurokracja a państwo. Z perspektywy współczesnych doktryn politycznych. In: Zuba, K. (ed): Biurokracja. Fenomen władzy politycznej w strukturach administracyjnych. Toruń, pp. 85–103.

Rexed, K. (2004–2005): Służba cywilna a modernizacja sposobu sprawowania władzy. *Służba Cywilna*, 9, pp. 47–54.

Rydlewski, G. (2001): Służba cywilna w Polsce. Przegląd rozwiązań na tle doświadczeń innych państw i podstawowe akty prawne. Warszawa.

Rydlewski, G. (2006): Polityka i administracja w rządach państw członkowskich Unii Europejskiej. Warszawa.
Rydlewski, G. (2007): Systemy administracji publicznej w państwach członkowskich Unii Europejskiej. Warszawa.
Sanetra, W. (2001): Strony stosunków pracy w służbie cywilnej i samorządzie terytorialnym. In: Sanetra, W. (ed): Stosunki pracy w służbie cywilnej i samorządzie terytorialnym. Białystok.
Sinkowska, L. (2002): Status prawny członka korpusu służby cywilnej. Toruń.
Smyk, G. (2004): Korpus urzędników cywilnych w Guberniach Królestwa Polskiego w latach 1867–1915. Lublin.
Springer, B. (2018): Vicious Cycle. A 20 Years' Perspective on the Changes in the Civil Service Model. In: Itrich-Drabarek, J., Mazur, S., Wiśniewska-Grzelak, J. (eds.): The Transformations of the Civil Service in Poland in Comparison with International Experience. Berlin, pp. 109–128.
Stawowiak, Z. (1998): Stanowisko do „Raportu z przeprowadzonej analizy i oceny tworzenia służby cywilnej (sierpień 1996 – wrzesień 1997)" – w zakresie oceny funkcjonowania Komisji Kwalifikacyjnej do Służby Cywilnej. *Biuletyn Służby Cywilnej*, 5, pp. 14–16.
Supernat, J. (2003): Administracja publiczna w świetle koncepcji New Public Management. Administracja publiczna. Studia krajowe i międzynarodowe. *Zeszyty Naukowe Wyższej Szkoły Administracji Publicznej w Białymstoku*, 2, pp. 28–46.
Stefański, K. (2009): Nowa ustawa o służbie cywilnej – reforma czy kontynuacja. *Praca i Zabezpieczenie Społeczne*, 5, pp. 18–22.
Stelina, J. (2005): Charakter prawny stosunku pracy z mianowania. Gdańsk.
Szachułowicz, J. (1997): Perspektywy Służby Cywilnej. Biuletyn Służby Cywilnej, 1, pp. 39–42.
Szachułowicz, J. (1998): Uwagi do „Raportu z przeprowadzonej analizy i oceny tworzenia służby cywilnej (sierpień 1996 – wrzesień 1997)". *Biuletyn Służby Cywilnej*, 5(11), pp. 12–14.
Sześciło, D. (2014): Administracja neoweberowska: biurokracja 2.0? https://www.academia.edu/8196749/Administracja_neoweberowska_biurokracja_2_0 (accessed: 2018/12/05).
Szewczyk, H. (2006): Zatrudnienie w służbie cywilnej. Bydgoszcz – Katowice.
Szewczyk, H. (2010): Stosunki pracy w służbie cywilnej. Warszawa.
Śledzińska – Simon, A. (2010): Prawa polityczne urzędników. Warszawa.
Ura, E. (1995): Pozycja prawna pracowników terenowej administracji rządowej i samorządu terytorialnego. Lublin.
Ura, E. (1998): Służba cywilna w Polsce. In: Antonowicz, L., Groszyk, H., Sawczuk, M., Skrzydło, W., Bojarski, T. (eds.): Polska lat dziewięćdziesiątych. Przemiany państwa i prawa. Vol 2. Lublin, pp. 117–131.
Ura, E. (2004): Prawo urzędnicze. Warszawa.
Ura, E. (2007): Ewolucja służby cywilnej w Polsce (zagadnienia wybrane). *Zarządzanie i Marketing. Zeszyty Naukowe Politechniki Rzeszowskiej*, 245/11, pp. 101–130.
Ura, E. (2016): Zmiany w regulacjach prawnych służby cywilnej – uzasadnione czy upolitycznione. In: Ura, E., Pieprzny, S. (eds): Problemy współczesnej administracji publicznej w Polsce. Rzeszów, pp. 41–57.
Verheijen, T., Rabrenovic, A. (2001): The evolution of Politico-Administrative relations in Post-communist states: Main Directions In: Verheijen, A. (ed): Politico – Administrative relations: who rules? Bratislava, pp. 17–33.
Walenia, A. (2015): Aspekty etyczne systemów ocenia pracowników w instytucjach publicznych. *Annales. Etyka w życiu gospodarczym*, 18/1, pp. 49–59.
Weber, M. (2002): Gospodarka i społeczeństwo. Zarys socjologii rozumiejącej. Warszawa.

Wiszniowski, R. (2005): Modernizacja europejskiej administracji publicznej. In: Wiszniowski, R. (ed): Administracja i polityka. Europejska administracja publiczna. Wrocław 2005, pp. 9–24.
Zieliński, E. (2001): Administracja rządowa. Warszawa.
Zieliński, T. (1984): Stosunek pracy i stosunek służbowy w administracji państwowej. In: Łętowski, J. (ed): Pracownicy administracji w PRL. Wrocław, pp. 89–155.
Zuba, K. (2007): Biurokracja jako podmiot polityczny w demokracji. In: Zuba, K. (ed): Biurokracja. Fenomen władzy politycznej w strukturach administracyjnych. Toruń, pp. 107–123.

2. Sources

A. Documents, programmes, plans, reports, opinions, positions

Bronowska, R. (2006): Opinia do ustawy o zmianie ustawy o pracownikach samorządowych, ustawy o Najwyższej Izbie Kontroli oraz ustawy o służbie cywilnej. *Kancelaria Senatu Biuro Legislacyjne*. Warszawa.
Działocha, K. (2006): Opinia o zgodności z Konstytucją RP poselskich projektów ustaw: o służbie cywilnej (druk 552) i o państwowym zasobie kadrowym, obsadzaniu wysokich stanowisk państwowych oraz o zmianie niektórych ustaw (druki nr 553 i 553-A). *Biuro Analiz Sejmowych (commissioned opinion)*. Wrocław.
European Governance a white paper Commission of the European Communities. (2001). Brussels.
Fundowicz, S. (2006): Opinia w sprawie projektów: ustaw o państwowym zasobie kadrowym, obsadzaniu wysokich stanowisk państwowych oraz o zmianie niektórych ustaw; ustawy o służbie cywilnej (druki sejmowe nr 552 i 553). Biuro Analiz Sejmowych (commissioned opinion). Lublin.
Galińska – Rączy, I. (2006): Opinia prawna na temat projektów ustaw o służbie cywilnej (druk 552) oraz o państwowym zasobie kadrowym, obsadzaniu wysokich stanowisk państwowych oraz o zmianie niektórych ustaw (druk 553 oraz 553-A). *Biuro Analiz Sejmowych (commissioned opinion)*. Warszawa.
Gintowt-Jankowicz, M. (2015): Opinia o projekcie ustawy o zmianie ustawy o służbie cywilnej oraz niektórych innych ustaw (print No. 119 of 15 December 2015 – commissioned opinion). Warszawa.
NIK – Najwyższa Izba Kontroli (2005): Informacja o wynikach kontroli organizacji i funkcjonowania służby cywilnej. Warszawa.
NIK – Najwyższa Izba Kontroli (2012): Informacja o wynikach kontroli Najwyższej Izby Kontroli: Funkcjonowanie służby cywilnej w ramach obowiązujących regulacji prawnych. Warszawa.
Izdebski, H. (2006): Opinia w przedmiocie zgodności z konstytucją projektów ustaw: o służbie cywilnej (druk sejmowy 552) oraz o państwowym zasobie kadrowym, obsadzaniu wysokich stanowisk państwowych oraz o zmianie niektórych ustaw (druki sejmowe nr 553 i nr 553-A). *Biuro Analiz Sejmowych (commissioned opinion)*. Warszawa.
Izdebski, H. (2016): Opinia prawa w przedmiocie ustawy z dnia 30 grudnia 2015r. o zmianie ustawy o służbie cywilnej oraz niektórych innych ustaw (Journal of Laws 2016, item 34). Warszawa.
Karwowska – Sokołowska, A. (2006): Opinia do ustawy o służbie cywilnej. Biuro Analiz Sejmowych (commissioned opinion). Warszawa.

Kulesza, M. (2006): Opinia zlecona na temat funkcjonowania służby cywilnej w obszarach projektowanych ustaw (druki 552, 553, 553-A). *Biuro Analiz Sejmowych (commissioned opinion)*. Warszawa.
Opinia Naczelnej Rady Adwokackiej z dnia 22 grudnia 2015r. w sprawie poselskiego projektu ustawy o zmianie ustawy o służbie cywilnej oraz niektórych innych ustaw (parliamentary print No. 119), (2015). Warszawa.
Opinia Prokuratora Generalnego z dnia 22 grudnia 2015r. w sprawie poselskiego projektu ustawy o zmianie ustawy o służbie cywilnej oraz niektórych innych ustaw. Warszawa.
Opinia Sądu Najwyższego z dnia 7 stycznia 2016r. o poselskim projekcie ustawy o zmianie ustawy o służbie cywilnej oraz niektórych innych ustaw (BSA III-021-525/15).
Plan szkoleń centralnych w służbie cywilnej na 2017r. (2017). Warszawa.
Plan szkoleń centralnych w służbie cywilnej na 2018r. (2018). Warszawa.
Plan szkoleń centralnych w służbie cywilnej na 2023r. (2023). Warszawa.
Rekomendacje Szefa Służby Cywilnej dotyczące przeprowadzania naboru na wyższe stanowiska w służbie (2009). Warszawa.
Urząd Służby Cywilnej, (1999): Służba cywilna – pytania i odpowiedzi. Warszawa.
Snażyk, Z. (2016): Opinia prawna do ustawy o zmianie ustawy o służbie cywilnej oraz niektórych innych ustaw (parliamentary print No. 119). Warszawa.
Sprawozdanie Szefa Służby Cywilnej o stanie służby cywilnej i realizacji zadań tej służby za rok 1997, (1998). Warszawa.
Sprawozdanie Szefa Służby Cywilnej o stanie służby cywilnej i realizacji zadań tej służby za rok 1998, (1999). Warszawa.
Sprawozdanie Szefa Służby Cywilnej o stanie służby cywilnej i realizacji zadań tej służby za rok 1999, (2000). Warszawa.
Sprawozdanie Szefa Służby Cywilnej o stanie służby cywilnej i realizacji zadań tej służby za rok 2000, (2001). Warszawa.
Sprawozdanie Szefa Służby Cywilnej o stanie służby cywilnej i realizacji zadań tej służby za rok 2001, (2002). Warszawa.
Sprawozdanie Szefa Służby Cywilnej o stanie służby cywilnej i realizacji zadań tej służby za rok 2002, (2003). Warszawa.
Sprawozdanie Szefa Służby Cywilnej o stanie służby cywilnej i realizacji zadań tej służby za rok 2003, (2004). Warszawa.
Sprawozdanie Szefa Służby Cywilnej o stanie służby cywilnej i realizacji zadań tej służby za rok 2004, (2005). Warszawa.
Sprawozdanie Szefa Służby Cywilnej o stanie służby cywilnej i realizacji zadań tej służby za rok 2005, (2006). Warszawa.
Sprawozdanie Szefa Służby Cywilnej o stanie służby cywilnej i realizacji zadań tej służby w 2009 roku, (2010). Warszawa.
Sprawozdanie Szefa Służby Cywilnej o stanie służby cywilnej i realizacji zadań tej służby w 2010 roku, (2011). Warszawa.
Sprawozdanie Szefa Służby Cywilnej o stanie służby cywilnej i realizacji zadań tej służby w 2011 roku, (2012). Warszawa.
Sprawozdanie Szefa Służby Cywilnej o stanie służby cywilnej i realizacji zadań tej służby w 2012 roku, (2013). Warszawa.
Sprawozdanie Szefa Służby Cywilnej o stanie służby cywilnej i realizacji zadań tej służby w 2013 roku, (2014). Warszawa.

Sprawozdanie Szefa Służby Cywilnej o stanie służby cywilnej i realizacji zadań tej służby w 2014 roku, (2015). Warszawa.
Sprawozdanie Szefa Służby Cywilnej o stanie służby cywilnej i realizacji zadań tej służby w 2015 roku, (2016). Warszawa.
Sprawozdanie Szefa Służby Cywilnej o stanie służby cywilnej i realizacji zadań tej służby w 2016 roku, (2017). Warszawa.
Sprawozdanie Szefa Służby Cywilnej o stanie służby cywilnej i realizacji zadań tej służby w 2017 roku, (2018). Warszawa.
Sprawozdanie Szefa Służby Cywilnej o stanie służby cywilnej i realizacji zadań tej służby w 2018 roku, (2019). Warszawa.
Sprawozdanie Szefa Służby Cywilnej o stanie służby cywilnej i realizacji zadań tej służby w 2019 roku, (2020). Warszawa.
Sprawozdanie Szefa Służby Cywilnej o stanie służby cywilnej i realizacji zadań tej służby w 2020 roku, (2021). Warszawa.
Sprawozdanie Szefa Służby Cywilnej o stanie służby cywilnej i realizacji zadań tej służby w 2021 roku, (2022). Warszawa.
Stanowisko Ośrodka Badań, Studiów i Legislacji Krajowej Rady Radców Prawnych dotyczące projektu ustawy o zmianie ustawy o służbie cywilnej oraz niektórych innych ustaw z dnia 28 grudnia 2015r, (2015). Warszawa.
Stelina, J. (2006): Opinia prawna do poselskich projektów ustaw: o służbie cywilnej (druk 552), o państwowym zasobie kadrowym, obsadzaniu wysokich stanowisk państwowych oraz o zmianie niektórych ustaw (druk 553) oraz autopoprawki do ww. projektu (druk 553-A). *Biuro Analiz Sejmowych (commissioned opinion)*. Gdańsk.
Szewczyk, H. (2006a): Opinia prawna do projektu ustawy o służbie cywilnej (druk sejmowy 552 z dnia 29 marca 2006r.), projektu ustawy o państwowym zasobie kadrowym, obsadzaniu wysokich stanowisk państwowych oraz o zmianie niektórych ustaw (druk sejmowy 553 z dnia 29 marca 2006r.) oraz autopoprawki do projektu ustawy o państwowym zasobie kadrowym, obsadzaniu wysokich stanowisk państwowych oraz o zmianie niektórych ustaw (druk sejmowy 553-A z dnia 8 czerwca 2006r.). *Biuro Analiz Sejmowych (commissioned opinion)*. Katowice.
Szewczyk, H. (2008): Opinia prawna do rządowego projektu nowelizacji ustawy o zmianie ustawy o służbie cywilnej oraz o zmianie niektórych innych ustaw (druk sejmowy nr 595 z dnia 29 maja 2008 roku), poselskiego projektu nowelizacji ustawy o służbie cywilnej oraz o zmianie niektórych innych ustaw (druk sejmowy nr 125 z dnia 15 listopada 2007 roku), poselskiego projektu autopoprawki do projektu nowelizacji ustawy o zmianie ustawy o służbie cywilnej oraz o zmianie niektórych innych ustaw (druk sejmowy nr 125-A z dnia 21 stycznia 2008 roku). *Biuro Analiz Sejmowych (commissioned opinion)*. Warszawa.
Ura, E. (2006): Opinia na temat projektu ustawy o służbie cywilnej (druk 552) oraz projektu ustawy o państwowym zasobie kadrowym, obsadzaniu wysokich stanowisk państwowych oraz o zmianie niektórych ustaw (druk 553) oraz autopoprawki do projektu ustawy o państwowym zasobie kadrowym, obsadzaniu wysokich stanowisk państwowych oraz o zmianie niektórych ustaw (druk 553-A). *Biuro Analiz Sejmowych (commissioned opinion)*. Warszawa.
Uzasadnienie do projektu ustawy o państwowym zasobie kadrowym i wysokich stanowiskach państwowych, (2006). Warszawa.
Uzasadnienie projektu ustawy o zmianie ustawy o służbie cywilnej oraz niektórych innych ustaw, (2015). Warszawa.
Wniosek Rzecznika Praw Obywatelskich do Trybunału Konstytucyjnego z dnia 1 lutego 2016r. (III.7040.9.2016.ST/LN).

B. Press journalism

Andrzejewski, P. (2000): Polityczna mapa wpływów. *Wprost*, no. 10.
Paradowska, J. (2002): Korpus w rozkładzie. *Polityka*, 19 October, 42 (2372).
Radwan, A. (2009): 180 tys. zł kosztuje wykształcenie urzędnika. *Gazeta Prawna*, 4 August.
Urzędnik bez konkursu, (2006): Gazeta Prawna on 3 April, no. 66(1684).
Wyższe wynagrodzenia dla urzędników i likwidacja dodatku specjalnego, interview with Adam Leszkiewicz – Deputy Head of the Chancellery of the Prime Minister (2008). *Gazeta Prawna* of 15 September no. 180.

C. Normative acts

Ustawa z dnia 17 marca 1921r. Konstytucja Rzeczypospolitej Polskiej (Dz. U. z 1921, Nr 44, poz. 267).
Ustawa z 17 lutego 1922 roku o państwowej służbie cywilnej (Dz. U. z 1922, Nr 21, poz. 164 z późn. zm.).
Ustawa z dnia 17 lutego 1922 roku o organizacji władz dyscyplinarnych i postępowaniu dyscyplinarnem przeciwko funkcjonarjuszom państwowym (Dz. U. z 1922, Nr 21, poz. 165).
Rozporządzenie Rady Ministrów z dnia 23 lipca 1923 roku o komisjach kwalifikacyjnych (Dz. U. z 1923, Nr 82, poz. 638).
Rozporządzenie Prezydenta Rzeczypospolitej Polskiej z dnia 19 stycznia 1928 roku o organizacji i zakresie działania władz administracji ogólnej (Dz. U. z 1928, Nr 11, poz. 86).
Rozporządzenie Prezydenta Rzeczypospolitej Polskiej z dnia 16 marca 1928 roku o umowie o pracę pracowników umysłowych (Dz. U. Nr 35, poz. 323).
Rozporządzenie Prezydenta Rzeczypospolitej Polskiej z dnia 16 marca 1928 roku o umowie o pracę robotników (Dz. U. Nr 35, poz. 324).
Rozporządzenie Prezydenta RP z dnia 7 października 1932 roku o organizacji komisyj dyscyplinarnych i postępowaniu dyscyplinarnym przeciwko funkcjonariuszom państwowym (Dz. U. Nr 87, poz. 738).
Rozporządzenie Rady Ministrów z dnia 17 października 1932 roku o komisjach dyscyplinarnych i postępowaniu dyscyplinarnym przeciwko funkcjonariuszom państwowym (Dz. U. Nr 92, poz. 790).
Dekret PKWN z 27 grudnia 1944r. o tymczasowym unormowaniu stosunku służbowego i zaszeregowaniu funkcjonariuszów państwowych (Dz. U. Nr 16, poz. 89).
Dekret z dnia 14 maja 1946r. Rady Ministrów o tymczasowym unormowaniu stosunku służbowego funkcjonariuszów państwowych.
Instrukcja o technice postępowania przy przyjmowaniu do służby urzędników i pracowników kontraktowych Prezesa Rady Ministrów z dnia 28 grudnia 1946r.
Okólnik Prezesa Rady Ministrów Nr 33 z 10 października 1946r.
Dekret z dnia 25 października 1948r. o zmianie ustawy o państwowej służbie cywilnej (Dz. U. Nr 50, poz. 381).
Okólnik Prezesa Rady Ministrów z 31 stycznia 1949r. (Dz. Urz. Min. Adm. Publ. Nr 12, poz. 57).
Dekret z dnia 25 czerwca 1954r. o powszechnym zaopatrzeniu emerytalnym pracowników i ich rodzin (Dz. U. Nr 30, poz. 116).
Ustawa z dnia 15 lipca 1968 roku o pracownikach rad narodowych (Dz. U. Nr 25, poz. 164).

Ustawa z dnia 26 czerwca 1974 roku kodeks pracy (Dz. U. Nr 24, poz. 141 z późn. zm.).
Ustawa z dnia 26 czerwca 1974 roku przepisy wprowadzające kodeks pracy (Dz. U. Nr 24, poz. 142).
Rozporządzenie z dnia 20 grudnia 1974 roku w sprawie praw i obowiązków pracowników urzędów państwowych (Dz. U. Nr 49, poz. 300).
Ustawa z dnia 16 września 1982 roku o pracownikach urzędów państwowych (Dz. U. Nr 31, poz. 214 z późn. zm.).
Rozporządzenie Rady Ministrów z dnia 8 listopada 1982r. w sprawie określenia stanowisk urzędniczych oraz zasad nawiązywania z urzędnikami państwowymi stosunku pracy na podstawie mianowania (Dz. U. Nr 39, poz. 257 z późn. zm.).
Rozporządzenie Rady Ministrów z dnia 8 listopada 1982 roku w sprawie szczegółowych zasad nadawania odznaki honorowej „Zasłużony Pracownik Państwowy", trybu przedstawiania wniosków o nadanie odznaki, ustalenia wzoru odznaki oraz trybu jej wręczania i sposobu noszenia (Dz. U. z 1982r. Nr 39, poz. 262).
Uchwała nr 74 Rady Ministrów z 1990r. w sprawie utworzenia Krajowej Szkoły Administracji Publicznej (Monitor Polski Nr 21, poz. 167).
Ustawa z dnia 14 czerwca 1991r. o Krajowej Szkole Administracji Publicznej (Dz. U. Nr 63, poz. 266 z późn. zm.).
Ustawa z dnia 2 grudnia 1994r. o zmianie ustawy o pracownikach urzędów państwowych (Dz. U. z 1994, Nr 136, poz. 734).
Ustawa z dnia 5 lipca 1996 roku o służbie cywilnej (Dz. U. Nr 89, poz. 402 z późn. zm.).
Ustawa z dnia 8 sierpnia 1996r. o Radzie Ministrów (t. j. Dz. U. z 2003, Nr 24, poz. 199 z późn. zm.).
Rozporządzenie Prezesa Rady Ministrów z dnia 15 października 1996r. w sprawie liczby członków Rady Służby Cywilnej i ich wynagradzania (Dz. U. Nr 122, poz. 574).
Konstytucja RP z dnia 2 kwietnia 1997 roku (Dz. U. Nr 78, poz. 483 z późn. zm.)
Ustawa z dnia 18 grudnia 1998 roku o służbie cywilnej (Dz. U. Nr 49, poz. 483 z późn. zm.).
Rozporządzenie Rady Ministrów z dnia 29 października 1999r. w sprawie określenia stanowisk urzędniczych, wymaganych kwalifikacji zawodowych, stopni służbowych urzędników służby cywilnej, mnożników do ustalania wynagrodzenia oraz szczegółowych zasad ustalania i wypłacania innych świadczeń przysługujących członkom korpusu służby cywilnej (Dz. U. Nr 89, poz. 99 z późn. zm.).
Rozporządzenie Prezesa Rady Ministrów z dnia 28 września 1999r. w sprawie postępowania kwalifikacyjnego w służbie cywilnej (Dz. U. Nr 79, poz. 549).
Rozporządzenie Prezesa Rady Ministrów z dnia 3 listopada 1999r. w sprawie sposobu organizowania i szczegółowych zasad przeprowadzania konkursów na wyższe stanowiska w służbie cywilnej (Dz. U. Nr 91, poz. 1028).
Rozporządzenie Prezesa Rady Ministrów z dnia 22 marca 2000 roku w sprawie szczegółowych warunków organizowania i prowadzenia szkoleń w służbie cywilnej (Dz. U. Nr 22, poz. 280).
Ustawa z dnia 21 grudnia 2001r. o zmianie ustawy o organizacji i trybie pracy Rady Ministrów oraz o zakresie działania ministrów, ustawy o działach administracji rządowej oraz o zmianie niektórych ustaw (Dz. U. Nr 154, poz. 1800).
Zarządzenie Nr 114 Prezesa Rady Ministrów z dnia 11 października 2002r. w sprawie ustanowienia Kodeksu Etyki Służby Cywilnej (M. P. Nr 46, poz. 683).
Ustawa z dnia 10 marca 2006r. o zmianie ustawy o pracownikach samorządowych, ustawy o Najwyższej Izbie Kontroli oraz ustawy o służbie cywilnej (Dz. U. Nr 79, poz. 894).

Ustawa z dnia 24 sierpnia 2006 roku o służbie cywilnej (Dz. U. Nr 170, poz. 1218 z późn. zm.).
Ustawa z dnia 24 sierpnia 2006 roku o państwowym zasobie kadrowym i wysokich stanowiskach państwowych (Dz. U. Nr 170, poz. 1217 z późn. zm.).
Rozporządzenie Prezesa Rady Ministrów z dnia 30 października 2006r. w sprawie wykonywania przez Szefa Kancelarii Prezesa Rady Ministrów zadań z zakresu służby cywilnej (Dz. U. Nr 198, poz. 1456).
Rozporządzenie Prezesa Rady Ministrów z dnia 5 kwietnia 2007r. w sprawie szczegółowych zasad przeprowadzania ocen urzędników służby cywilnej (Dz. U. Nr 69, poz. 633).
Ustawa z 21 listopada 2008 roku o służbie cywilnej (Dz. U. Nr 227, poz. 1505 z późn. zm.).
Rozporządzenie Prezesa Rady Ministrów z dnia 9 kwietnia 2009r. w sprawie postępowania wyjaśniającego i dyscyplinarnego w służbie cywilnej (Dz. U. Nr 60, poz. 493).
Rozporządzenie Prezesa Rady Ministrów z dnia 9 kwietnia 2009r. w sprawie wynagradzania członków Rady Służby Cywilnej (Dz. U. z 2009, Nr 60, poz. 491).
Rozporządzenie Prezesa Rady Ministrów z dnia 15 czerwca 2009 roku w sprawie szczegółowych warunków i sposobu dokonywania pierwszej oceny w służbie cywilnej (Dz. U. Nr 94, poz. 772).
Rozporządzenie Prezesa Rady Ministrów z dnia 16 grudnia 2009r. w sprawie sposobu przeprowadzania postępowania kwalifikacyjnego w służbie cywilnej (Dz. U. Nr 218, poz. 1695).
Zarządzenie Prezesa Rady Ministrów z dnia 6 października 2011r. w sprawie wytycznych w zakresie przestrzegania zasad służby cywilnej oraz zasady etyki korpusu służby cywilnej (MP Nr 93, poz. 953).
Rozporządzenie Prezesa Rady Ministrów z dnia 19 grudnia 2014r. w sprawie uprawnień szczególnych przysługujących niektórym kategoriom członków korpusu służby cywilnej (Dz. U. 2014, poz. 30).
Ustawa z dnia 30 grudnia 2015r. o zmianie ustawy o służbie cywilnej oraz niektórych innych ustaw (Dz. U. z 2016, Nr 0, poz. 34).
Rozporządzenie Prezesa Rady Ministrów z dnia 24 czerwca 2015r. w sprawie szczegółowych warunków organizowania i prowadzenia szkoleń w służbie cywilnej (Dz. U. 2015, poz. 960).
Rozporządzenie Prezesa Rady Ministrów z dnia 23 lipca 2015r. w sprawie szczegółowych warunków i sposobu dokonywania pierwszej oceny w służbie cywilnej (Dz. U. 2015, poz. 1144).
Zarządzenie Nr 57 Prezesa Rady Ministrów z dnia 24 lipca 2015r. zmieniające zarządzenie w sprawie zasad dokonywania opisów i wartościowania stanowisk pracy w służbie cywilnej (M. P. Poz. 724).
Zarządzenie Nr 5 Szefa Służby Cywilnej z dnia 8 października 2015r. w sprawie warunków i trybu współdziałania Szefa Służby Cywilnej z dyrektorami generalnymi urzędów.
Uchwała Rady Służby Cywilnej nr 135 z dnia 18 grudnia 2015r.
Rozporządzenie Prezesa Rady Ministrów z dnia 4 kwietnia 2016r. w sprawie warunków przeprowadzania ocen okresowych urzędników służby cywilnej i pracowników służby cywilnej (Dz. U. poz. 470).
Ustawa z dnia 23 września 2016r. o zmianie niektórych ustaw w celu zwalczania chorób zakaźnych zwierząt (Dz. U. 2016, poz. 1605).
Ustawa z dnia 20 lipca 2017r. Prawo wodne (Dz. U. 2017, poz. 1566).
Ustawa z dnia 23 stycznia 2020 r. o zmianie ustawy o jakości handlowej artykułów rolno-spożywczych oraz niektórych innych ustaw (Dz. U. 2020, poz. 285).

D. Jurisprudence

Wyrok Trybunału Konstytucyjnego z dnia 28 kwietnia 1999 roku, Sygn. K. 3/99 (M.P. Nr 16, poz. 227).
Wyrok Trybunału Konstytucyjnego z dnia 13 marca 2000r., Sygn. K 1/99 (Dz.U. 2000, Nr 17, poz. 228).
Wyrok Trybunału Konstytucyjnego z dnia 10 kwietnia 2002 roku, Sygn. akt K 26/00 (Dz.U. Nr 56, poz. 517).
Wyrok Trybunału Konstytucyjnego z dnia 12 grudnia 2002 r. Sygn. akt K 9/02 (Dz.U. Nr 238, poz. 2025).
Wyrok Trybunału Konstytucyjnego z dnia 13 listopada 2003 roku, Sygn. akt K 51/02 (Dz.U. Nr 199, poz. 1952).
Postanowienie Trybunału Konstytucyjnego z dnia 27 listopada 2007 roku (sygn. akt K 14/06).
Postanowienie Trybunału Konstytucyjnego z dnia 28 listopada 2007 roku (sygn. akt K 41/06).
Wyrok Sądu Najwyższego z dnia 13 grudnia 2010r. (III KRS 17/10).
Wyrok Trybunału Konstytucyjnego z dnia 14 czerwca 2011r., Sygn. akt Kp 1/11. (M.P. Nr 57, poz. 577).
Wyrok Sądu Najwyższego z dnia 18 listopada 2014r., sygn. akt II PK 5/14.

E. Netography

The term "process"https://sjp.pwn.pl/sjp/proces;2508456.html (accessed: 2017/10/18)
Pełny zapis przebiegu posiedzenia Komisji Spraw Wewnętrznych i Administracji (2015) http://orka.sejm.gov.pl/zapisy8.nsf/0/B66C2526BFDFC766C1257F33005095EC/%24File/0011208.pdf (accessed: 2017/10/01)
Sprawozdanie Stenograficzne z 14 Posiedzenia Sejmu Rzeczypospolitej Polskiej w dniu 17 marca 2016 (drugi dzień obrad) http://orka2.sejm.gov.pl/StenoInter8.nsf/0/F096068642E4EF81C1257F790059CE10/$File/14_b_ksiazka_bis.pdf (accessed: 2019/09/20).

Index of tables and diagrams

A. Tables

B. Diagrams

Nordost-Archiv 32 (2023)

Herausgegeben vom Nordost-Institut (IKGN)

Gastherausgeber: Florian Coppenrath und Oxana Nagornaja

Medien und Menschen. Forschungen zu deutsch-russischen Verflechtungen im 20. Jahrhundert / Media and People. Research on German-Russian Entanglements in the 20th Century

NORDOST-ARCHIV – BAND 32
2024. 160 Seiten mit 6 s/w-Abbildungen

978-3-515-13616-7 KARTONIERT
978-3-515-13624-2 OPEN-ACCESS E-BOOK

Internationale Verflechtungen beginnen im Kleinen, sie sind immer auch Beziehungen zwischen Menschen, vermittelt und mitgestaltet durch Medien. Im Zeitalter konzentrierter Medialität bestimmen verbale, visuelle und auditive Medien auch die interkulturelle Kommunikation: die Selbst- und Fremdwahrnehmung, die Interaktion mit dem Anderen sowie die Erzählungen über die Vergangenheit. Dies gilt insbesondere für die zahlreichen Verflechtungsgeschichten im Kontext des „deutsch-russischen Jahrhunderts".
Die Beiträge dieses Bandes – allesamt Darstellungen historischer Forschung im Prozess – veranschaulichen solche Berührungspunkte zwischen Deutschland und Russland bzw. der Sowjetunion anhand einer Reihe von empirischen Beispielen. Sie greifen dafür auf aktuelle methodische Ansätze etwa der Biografie- und Medienforschung zurück und beleuchten unterschiedliche Aspekte der transnationalen Rezeption intellektueller Diskurse, der Produktion und Rezeption von Narrativen in diktatorischen Regimes und der interkulturellen Kontakte in einer Ära globaler Konfrontation.

MIT BEITRÄGEN VON
Nataliya Kopcha | Acelya Bakir | Sebastian Franzen | Sebastian Kindler | Bernd Christoph Ströhm | Nina Janz

Franz Steiner Verlag

Hier bestellen:
service@steiner-verlag.de